Lionel Carley

16 March 1976.

Percy Grainger

The
Inveterate Innovator

by Thomas C. Slattery

The Instrumentalist Co.
1418 Lake St., Evanston, Illinois 60204

To my friend Percy Grainger
John S. Sargent

. . . Biographers writing of eminent men, unearth every species of "skeleton in the closet" and rattle its bones in front of a lecherous public. Readers gloat over the follies, weaknesses, sexual complexes, perversities and what-not of deceased celebrities. Each member of the reading public becomes, as it were, the proverbial valet de chambre, to whom no man, however great, is a hero.

Cyril Scott

After all, the day is past when criticism of Kings, Queens and great artists savored of high treason. If biographers are to be anything they must have the impartial light of truth play'd upon them.

Percy Aldridge Grainger

❧ STEINWAY HALL ❧

Lower Seymour Street, W.

MR. PERCY

GRAINGER

(The young Australian Pianist

WILL GIVE HIS

FIRST

Pianoforte Recital

In LONDON

(Under the Direction of Miss ALICE E. JOSEPH)

ON

Tuesday, October 29th, 1901,

At THREE o'clock.

Stalls, Reserved, 7s. 6d.   Area, Unreserved, 3s.
Balcony, Unreserved, 1s.

Tickets to be obtained of Mr. PERCY GRAINGER, 11, Gordon Place, Kensington, W.; of Mr. MACKEY, Box Office, Steinway Hall; Mr. WHITEHEAD, Box Office, St. James's Hall; Usual Agents, and of

Miss ALICE E. JOSEPH,
Opera and Concert Agency,
7a, Hanover Street, Regent Street, W

J. MILES & CO., LTD., WARDOUR ST., W.   **[For Programme P.T.O.**

Table of Contents

Acknowledgments

I wish to express my thanks to Ella Grainger for her friendship and encouragement, as well as for the unlimited access to her husband's manuscripts and private papers.

I am also deeply grateful to the many librarians who answered requests for specific information, most particularly the Library of Congress, Mr. Edward N. Waters, Chief of the Music Division, and Mr. Carroll Wade; to them a special citation for repeated and expert advice and service. Mr. Stewart Manville, Archivist for the Grainger Library Society, has added much to this biography, especially in the arrangement of the index and all varieties of information which were needed from time to time. Through his skills, a lending library of Grainger's unpublished music will soon be a reality.

Information was furnished by many individuals, but Richard Franko Goldman, Burnett Cross, Cyril Scott, and Dom Anselm Hughes, O.S.B., were especially responsive and knowledgeable. Mr. Cross was most generous in allowing his drawings of Grainger's Free Music machine to be reproduced, as were Eric Hughes, A.F.K. Lawrence, Gerald Stonehill, and the British Institute of Recorded Sound for the excellent compilations of recordings which are carried herein. A portion of the research was financed by a Grant from The National Foundation for the Arts and Humanities in the summer of 1968.

And to C.L.D., the typist, co-researcher, editor, fellow traveler, cook, and real expert on Grainger, a promise of a personal annuity program which will be an attempt at repayment.

Thomas C. Slattery

October 1974

Foreword

The first time I saw Percy Grainger could not have been more perfectly programmed; it was Grainger all the way! The setting was the huge stage of Cleveland's Public Auditorium on which were assembled grand pianos in great profusion. Percy was conducting a select high school piano ensemble as part of the final concert of the 1932 meeting of the Music Supervisor's National Conference. It was about half an hour before concert time, and I was there early to fuss over the National High School kettledrums. Grainger was there early to fuss over his pianos. What a figure he cut as he strode from instrument to instrument, raising each lid, adjusting each piano bench. I could not take my eyes from him. It all registered — the beautiful, curly blond hair, the lithe body, the agile movement, the red silk-lined, black cape flowing from the shoulders, the infectious smile. Always sympathic — I found out later — to percussion players, he stopped at the edge of the stage and spoke, "It's fun to get here early, isn't it!"

Percy Aldridge Grainger was one of those fortunate artists who really got there early, and too many of us haven't really caught up with him yet. He got there early, thanks in large part to his talented, motivated, dedicated and dominant mother, whom he loved with uncommon devotion. His life was the direct result of her remarkable talents as the ultimate personal manager, the "Empress Impresario" of the twentieth century. All of this was possible only, of course, because of Percy's genius gifts, for which — in the department of genes — she was half responsible. His father, John, no dolt, was one of Australia's celebrated architects. But when Rose Grainger decided to shed him and take young Percy to Frankfurt, Germany, where a musical artist could be nurtured to her satisfaction, that was all there was to that.

From this point on, I must leave the story to Tom Slattery. I doubt that you can casually lay it aside, but even if you may be so inclined, let me please arrest you, for herein lies one of the remarkable, mostly untold tales of music in the first half of the twentieth century.

Frederick Fennell
Miami, Florida
January, 1973

Introduction

In the late 1950's, a number of cartons of original manuscripts, personal papers, and several hundred first editions arrived at the Grainger Museum in Melbourne, Australia. These cartons contained a portion of the life's work of Percy Aldridge Grainger, composer, pianist, and inventor. Written across the cartons was a statement from the composer which serves well as an epitaph for one of the most unusual and gifted musicians of recent times:

> These cases contain compositions that you not only have never heard, but probably have never heard of — the measure of my defeat![1]

Percy Grainger's distinguished music career began with a recital in Melbourne in 1892 and was concluded sixty-eight years later with an appearance at America's Dartmouth College. Perhaps no performer of his generation reached so wide an audience through personal appearances; yet, performance was only one facet of the life of this multi-talented man. Grainger was widely traveled, fluent in many languages, and interested in a vast array of subjects and disciplines. In addition to being a pianist of the first rank and a composer of unusual dimensions, he was an author, philologist, inventor, traveler, ethnomusicologist, and athlete.

Grainger can be credited with a great variety of accomplishments (many of which are generally unknown) which cut across every aspect of composition. In 1911 he composed what is possibly the earliest example of pure chance music. In addition, his experiments in Free Music and his attempts to construct a machine which could produce beatless and microtonal music predated similar work by later "avant-garde" composers. According to Richard Franko Goldman, the experimental work of Partch, Cage, Carter, Varese, and Stockhausen is clearly antedated by Grainger's work. He goes on to say that in comparing his use of new and original compositional techniques with Ives, "I should not hesitate to say that Grainger is quite simply the more musical."[2]

The area of band music was also affected by Grainger's pioneering efforts. Though primarily a pianist and composer, he became associated with bands after spending two years as a bandsman during the First World War. Grainger established his reputation as one of the finest twentieth century band composers with *Lincolnshire Posy*. His expanded use of percussion instruments and grouping of instruments into complete families in this and other works set a new standard in scoring for wind instruments.

Throughout his career, Grainger also composed light, tuneful pieces which kept his income comfortable and regular. These popular works along with his public performances extended his fame and made his name a household word among even the most unsophisticated listeners. It is interesting to note that he used the income derived from his "popular" activities to build a museum for his compositional experiments and to publish much of his less popular music.

The eccentric behavior for which he became legend is amusing and interesting, but — as the result of his effort to be natural and pursue his interests without compromise — it can be related to the diversity of style in his compositional output. In fact, in attempting to label either his personality or his music, both of which ranged from the conventional to the "experimental," one can only say that in an age when most composers were neo-classical, neo-romantic, or neo-baroque, Grainger was merely neo.

Concerning Grainger's private life, there emerges the picture of a highly creative man whose early domination by his mother was to drastically affect his personality — forcing the natural extrovert into a shy and secretive person who would keep extensive records of his personal thoughts, ideas, and unconventional behavior. His masochistic nature found vent both in his music and in his habits; he recorded everything with exacting detail. His life story shows the drive and frustration of a man who was more concerned with his place in history as an innovator than with the personal amenities associated with a successful career.

In order to begin to understand this complex and controversial individual, it is necessary to examine his parents' lives and his relationships with them. Here begins the thread which becomes entangled in his personality, his habits, his performing, and his composition. Perhaps no artist in recent times has had a mother who more carefully and rigidly supervised the development of the personality and prejudices of her child. His statements were her statements and her desires — his.

Percy Aldridge Grainger was an enigma to his generation, a delightful puzzle to his public, and a riddle to all who tried to understand him.

The Australian

Rose and Family

Percy Aldridge Grainger was an Australian, not only by familial heritage, but by choice. His maternal grandparents, George Aldridge and Sarah Jane Grant, were born in England and emigrated to Adelaide in 1847 via clipper ship. After settling in Adelaide, they became the proprietors of various rooming houses that comfortably supported their expanding family. The question that their marriage may have been illegally contracted was resolved in 1856 when, after learning that George's first wife was no longer alive, they repeated the ceremony.

By mid-century Australia was a land with a colonial history of only sixty years and, like the United States, had to develop from a talent pool of outcasts, adventurers, fortune hunters, and naive immigrants. It was a time when the country was more concerned with expansion than with art. It would have been incomprehensible to George and Sarah Aldridge to consider that, sixty years hence, their grandchild would be a successful international pianist and composer whose clandestine originality would take an additional sixty years to become known.

Percy's grandfather, impulsive and quick-tempered, purchased books in lots and often read them aloud into the night. He was short and rather inclined to be stout — a rugged man who personally threw the ruffians from the bar of his hotel. Among other diversions, he drank. In matters of business, George Aldridge was a success. His hotel was prosperous and the most celebrated artists were frequently featured in concerts at his establishments. Some of the earliest memories of Percy's mother were of these performers appearing at "White's" and, later, at "The Prince Alfred Hotel."

George and his family moved frequently and each time they improved their fortunes. On Angas Street, close to the law courts, they owned a large home and paddock which contained pets of all kinds, including dogs, rabbits, pigeons, silkworms, and a tortoise. An adjacent poultry yard provided the turkeys, geese, and ducks that graced the table of the large and growing family. The father often sang the popular songs of the day, such as "Tom Bowling," "My Pretty Jane," and "Hearts of Oak," always augmenting his repertoire with the latest American tunes and jokes gathered from the international array of customers that frequented his hotel.

In 1861, in "White's Rooms," on King William Street, Percy's strong-willed mother, Rose Aldridge, was born. The eighth of nine children, she was a skinny tomboy, who drank "cod liver oil to get fatter." Not until thirty years later were its effects evident. She was attracted to musical sounds quite early and as a child often ran after street bands, trying to imitate their sounds on a Jew's harp or on a little musical instrument made of wood and elastic bands. She had given up combs and tissue paper as the means of her music-making, for it had "tickled her lips horribly." With five older brothers, Rose was in the constant companionship of boys, usually shunning her two older sisters. She soon became proficient at marbles, football, knuckle-bones, climbing trees, and driving the billy-goat cart. When dressed in proper little-girl attire, she would often change in the family out-building to her tweed shirt, jacket and cap, and dash to the nearest park to out-shinny the boys to the top of the highest gum tree. Her early tomboy behavior was also exhibited by her partic-ipation in the local fox hunts; she would follow the hounds in her buggy by whatever available path, always taking the corners on two wheels.

Like her father, Rose was an avid reader and devoured masses of literature. Her favorites were the *Fairy Tales* of Hans Christian Anderson, stories from Greek mythology, *The Arabian Nights*, and poetry. The world of fantasy found in her reading contrasted sharply with her physical competition with six brothers.

An excellent student, Rose had few close companions, but she was "loved by the head teacher [and] petted and spoiled by men examiners who gave [her] extra prizes."[3] With a school chum as her instructor, Rose began to study the piano. Her early training was concerned with the light operatic pieces so popular in the non-metropolitan areas of the times. After a successful day at the races in Sydney, her brother purchased for her a set of the Beethoven *Sonatas* and the Brahms *Hungarian Dances*. This was her first exposure to the more substantial piano literature, and she soon developed into a competent amateur pianist. After a while, her interest in music (and literature) devel-oped into an appreciation of the other arts and a firm belief in the nineteenth century romantic concept of the artist.

Rose's maturing beauty and personality made her popular among the young men of Adelaide; she never lacked for escorts. In 1880, she married John H. Grainger, an architect and civil engineer who had been educated in England. Care-free and flippant, the young bride remarked to her aunt: "If I'm happy with him for a fortnight, that's enough."[4] Her estimate was conservative, for the marriage lasted ten difficult years.

Among John Grainger's accomplishments was the dubious honor of having been born on a train bound for London. He had received his early training in the Monastery School at Evator, France and later at the Westminster School in England. His apprenticeship in civil engineering included work on the construction of London's King's Cross Rail Station. Firmly grounded in a much-needed profession, John left England in 1876 to seek his fortune "down under."

After he arrived in Australia, he became assistant architect and engineer in the South Australian Government and, in addition, opened a small private practice in Adelaide. Aside from one trip to see his aging father, nothing further is documented of John Grainger's relationship with his parents.

John's artistic leanings complemented those of his wife. He spent his adolescent and early adult years in the home of an uncle who was an ardent opera buff, and, in his uncle's stall, he had heard all the first-rate singers and prima donnas of the day. Shortly after settling in Adelaide he organized the city's first string quartet. One of the original members of this quartet, Frank Winterbottom*, later returned to England and distinguished himself as Bandmaster to the Chatham Marines. Although John himself did not play a musical instrument, he sang whenever the occasion presented itself. He was also keen on painting and poetry. In fact, during evening visits when he "read poetry by the hours to the Aldridge girls," he made his earliest acquaintance with Rose. In addition to his love of poetry, John had more than a passing affection for girls.

The fortunes of John Grainger and his wife fluctuated widely depending upon the demand for his services as an

---

*Born in London in 1861, Frank Winterbottom became one of the foremost arrangers for military band of his generation. He held appointments as professor of music at Dulwich College and as conductor of several orchestral societies in addition to his military appointment in 1890.

architect. That he was an able and respected craftsman there is no doubt. By 1897 he had become the principal architect in Western Australia, and some of his most remarkable work was yet to be done. Among his many projects were the Princess Bridge and the Masonic Building in Melbourne, the Swing Bridge in Sale, Gippsland, and the Law Courts in Perth, as well as other public buildings in Australia and New Zealand. In the first years of their marriage, John received over L2350, in prize money alone, for his architectural designs.

The Living Spit of "Bubbles"

In the 1880's Melbourne was a thriving city of more than 175,000. Founded less than fifty years before, it still had the trappings of a sprawling provincial English city. It's older sister-city of Sydney had been founded as a penal colony but nothing as colorful as that could be noted in Melbourne's history. Being six to seven weeks from Europe by steamship, it was out of touch with most of the mother country's day to day developments. In the 1880's, Australia as a whole, and Melbourne in particular, was rich in American influences as exhibited by the ballads of Brett Hart and the songs of Stephen Foster. It was Melbourne's European bloodline meeting American and Oriental influences that created the unique atmosphere in which Percy Grainger would spend his childhood.

Near Melbourne in the North Brighton home designed by his father and staffed with three servants, George Percy Grainger was born. This child, arriving July 8, 1882, was one of exceptional beauty, distinguished by his curly blond-red hair and fair features. In a few years his father would comment: "Percy 'the only boy' is very fair, with long curling golden hair, blue eyes, and legs fit to carry the tower of Babel. If he does not turn out to be a genius, in the words of old Hobbs, 'I be jiggered.' "[5] Many years later, Percy attributed another comment to his father concerning his birth: "It's nothing to make such a fuss about. You needn't think it's the first time I've been a father!"[6]

The influences that Rose had experienced in her formative years were to set the pattern for her son's education. When Percy was five years old, his mother began to read aloud to him parts of the *Icelandic Sagas* and the *Anglo-Saxon Chronicle*. Thomas Sisley, an English elocution teacher who was friendly with the Graingers, was possibly the source of their interest in literature of the north. These stories of the Vikings and their conquests left a lasting impression on Percy and set for him high literary standards. The habit of daily reading recitals continued throughout his mother's life. Together they read Greek mythology, Homer, Shakespeare, Balzac, Goethe, Kipling, Shaw, Swinburne, and Tolstoy. Percy's early interest in languages probably began with these readings. Mother and son became deeply attached.

About this same time Percy began to study piano with his mother. For five years she sat with him daily during his two-hour practice. Piano instruction was second in his interests, for the young boy was fascinated by the sea. On one occasion, Percy neglected his prescribed practice in order to make a model of one of the boats he had seen in the bay. Rose was furious and burned the boat which had consumed his interest. Although sullen with the loss, the boy informed his mother at bedtime:"Tomorrow I shall make a better one!" The tenacious quality which typified his later years was already apparent.

Percy's formal schooling lasted but a few weeks. In writing of the reason for this short tenure, he said that his classmates "tortured hens." This upset him and resulted in his mother withdrawing him from school. Percy goes on to say, "I didn't want to play with other boys. I said something to mother like this: 'Must I play that game [cricket]? I get so cold, waiting for the ball to come my way, and when it does, I miss it.' "[7] It seems likely that the Fauntleroy clothing and white gloves he was forced to wear ("to protect his hands") were contributing factors to any real or imaginary problems he had with his peers. When he was about ten, he fought a boy for stealing flowers from his mother's garden. As if he had long anticipated the conflict and was proud of his victory, he dashed into his mother's music room, shouting "I've done it! I've done it!"

The marriage between Percy's parents was not successful, for the handsome John was easily distracted from his family. In 1926, John's sister-in-law told Percy about an incident involving a neighbor girl: "I hear, after, that your father went round there a great deal," and, "When your mother would come over here on one of her flying fits, George [Rose's father] would use his influence to bring them together again."[8] In spite of the family situation, John Grainger was very fond of Percy. He was amused by the Fauntleroy dress and was frequently heard describing his son as being the living spit of Bubbles, a character similarly dressed who appeared in local advertising for Pear's Soap.

There is no question that Rose completely dictated the thinking of the sensitive and precocious boy and that all his creative energies were guided through and according to her design. His early interest in drawing and painting, as well as his fondness for literature and music, were nurtured by the dominating mother, whose failing marriage directed her attentions without distraction to the development of Percy's many talents. Had she fancied his becoming a surgeon or an artist, he certainly would have succeeded. Writing in 1939, Grainger's American concert manager recalled a conversation with Rose Grainger: "His mother told me once that both she and his father knew that he could become a great painter or a sculptor, but his mother wanted him to be a musician."[9]

In reflecting on their mother-son attachment, Rose would later write: "The greatest feeling in my life — intense love & devotion to my beautiful boy — whose physical beauty & whose genius was, & is, a great joy to me. He is, to me, like some glorious work of art — good to live with, & look upon. I feel his genius is sacred to me & to the world."[10] This adoration was certainly not one-sided, for Percy's life-purpose began and ended with his mother. Describing his early feelings for her, he later wrote:

> As a child the thought of this came to me: that mother was really God. She was the only creature I had seen who seemed as if she had created everything, was responsible for everything. So I suspected that she was really God and that she had the Bible written and the church services going just to fool me.[11]

The Grainger home in Melbourne was generously graced with reproductions of Rubens, Titian, and Greek statues. The young Percy delighted in sketching them and Rose referred to them when they could be related to the literature she was reading aloud to her son. Percy soon accepted his mother's concept of beauty which was greatly influenced by her aversion to unnaturalness, and he began to "view grown women with horror — as being dirty with beauty grease, foul in their powder and rouge."[12]

The determined love of mother for son seems to have been the reason for the harsh training the youngster experienced in his home. Discipline was severe; it was dispensed with a riding whip, a method Rose's father had used to control his six sons. On occasion, Rose was known to have "feather-dusted" her husband as well. Percy must have accepted this for he was to write: "Clearly no mother is worth having who is not cruel and who does not misuse her mother power . . . The bullied child gasps, howls, smarts and gives thanks."[13] To be able to stand extremes of pain appealed to Percy even as a young boy. One of his favorite games was "Spears and Shields," which dictated each combatant to take as many blows as possible without flinching. Master Percy was soon the neighborhood champion.

The Australian culture Percy knew as a child was permeated by American influences — musical touring groups, black-faced minstrels, and ballads of the New World. Only occasionally did the more substantial artists venture to this distant frontier. One of Percy's earliest recollections was of his mother singing him to sleep with Stephen Foster's *Camptown Races*. Rose also saw and heard many artists from England, among them the conductor, Frederick Cowen, who appeared at the Melbourne Centennial Exhibition in 1888, and shortly thereafter, Charles Hallé, the pianist. It is probable that her young son was also present. The elements of the East also had their effects on the young boy; he later vividly recalled a visit to a Japanese Bazaar when he was but six years old. The roots of his *Arrival Platform Humlet*, 24 years later, could certainly be traced to this and other early encounters with local Eastern influences.

Percy's sixth year is memorable for another experience which he claimed as the basis of his Free Music experiments. Rose would often take her son out on Melbourne's Albert Park Lagoon, since Percy's fascination with boats and the motion of water stimulated his desire to capture musically the sound of nature and their irregular rhythms. The dedication to this goal continued throughout his professional career.

The fortunes of the Grainger family had reversed by 1889 when they moved to a hotel in Heidelberg, a northern suburb of Melbourne. Writing to his father in 1890, John Grainger complained: "I lost all in over-speculating in mines," but he added optimistically, ". . .am making a good deal of money now. Have designed a church for L100,

won a competition for L25, and will soon go into partnership in Melbourne."[14]

The partnership to which John Grainger referred was
with the contractor, David Mitchell, father of Nellie Melba.
One of their most successful projects was the multi-laned
Princess Bridge in Melbourne. This unusually wide bridge,
though ridiculed in the days of horse-drawn vehicles, exists
today as one of the main arteries over the Yarra River in
Melbourne. The friendship which was later to develop
between Melba and Percy had its roots in the business
affairs of their parents.

Financial conditions combined with the social liaisons of
John Grainger at last brought the marriage to an impasse.
The caustic and ironic nature of the usually gregarious
father was intensified by his drinking and smoking —
habits which Rose openly disliked. By the time Percy was
seven years old, John Grainger was no longer living at
229 New Street. Officially the family excused his absence
as poor health and stated that he had returned to England.
Although no public mention was thereafter made of John
Grainger by his family, it is known that in later years
Percy did meet him on several occasions. At least one of
these meetings was with Rose, when the trio enjoyed a
London concert of Harry Lauder.

The collapse of Victoria's banks in 1890, which left
thousands starving, caused Rose and Percy to open their
doors to boarders. Additional income was provided by
Rose's piano students and, from time to time, her appearance in concert in Melbourne. As John Grainger described
Rose: "She is only about a five foot girl, which annoys
her frightfully, because she wants to be big...she is the
best amateur piano player in the city."[15]

While still under the tutelage of his mother, Percy
became friends with Dr. Hamilton Russell, a newly arrived
surgeon and amateur pianist, described by John as a
"poseur." With Dr. Russell, Percy heard Sir Charles Hallé

and other concert pianists who performed frequently in the Melbourne area. Dr. Russell even brought Sir Charles and Lady Hallé to visit Percy when he was ill. The ease with which the performing artists of Melbourne came in contact with Rose and Percy gives an indication as to the esteem in which Rose was held, both as a teacher and as the mother of an unusual talent. In 1894, Russell introduced Percy to Ernest Hutcheson. "My memory of the beauty, perfection, and smoothness of his Bach playing has never dimmed." Percy later remarked. That same year Percy's first authenticated attempts at composition appeared as several short piano pieces, presented to Rose as "A Birthday Gift."

At the age of ten, Percy became the pupil of Louis Pabst, a distinguished professor of piano who had founded an Academy of Music in Melbourne in 1887. After two years of study, Pabst recommended to the family that this *Wunderkind* be taken to Europe for further study. Through the persuasion of Professor William Adolphus Laver, a friend and lecturer in the Music Department of Melbourne University, Rose and Percy selected Frankfurt. Laver himself had studied under Frederic Lamond at the Hoch Conservatorium and was in continual correspondence with the music community there. Clara Schumann had been head of the piano department, and although the Graingers were surely aware of her recent retirement, they had hoped that Percy could become her pupil.

Rose, forever ambitious for Percy's career, began immediate plans to realize Pabst's suggestion. Percy played a series of public recitals which provided him with critical acclaim and, along with Rose's income from teaching, supplied them with sufficient means for travel to Frankfurt. One review of a very early Melbourne recital described his abundant musical talent:

> Master Percy Grainger is one of the most remarkable instances of juvenile precocity that

> has ever come under our notice, inasmuch as
> his piano-forte playing exhibits the possession
> not only of adequately trained fingers but what
> is of far more importance, the intuitive artistic
> perception, truly phenomenal in one so young,
> and plainly pointing to a greatly distinguished
> future.[16]

Rose appeared to the Australian public for the final time at
a breaking-up concert in 1895 at the school where she often
taught. Percy's farewell concert was held at the Melbourne
Town Hall on Tuesday, May 14, 1895. The program was
under the direction of Marshall Hall, with all proceeds
"for the benefit of Master Percy Grainger." On May 25,
1895, with L50 collected at his benefit, Master Percy and
his mother boarded the freighter *S.S. Gera* and sailed
for Europe.

The Frankfurt Group

Mother and son arrived in Frankfurt early in the fall
of 1895. A great sense of liberation greeted them there,
because they were self-sufficient for the first time in their
lives. But the fact that money was not as available as it
had been in Australia caused them some minor inconven-
iences. The absence of servants, for instance, meant that
Rose must prepare meals. With no experience in household
chores, Rose proved to be a poor cook; consequently the
food was often burned. Percy recalled that on at least one
occasion she had "turned toffee into enamel." Resorting
to commercial establishments for his meals, Percy soon
obtained a reputation for consuming unusual amounts of
Berliner pancakes at a single sitting. Her culinary talents
notwithstanding, Rose became a keen business woman,

a trait which contributed greatly to her son's later success. "Nevertheless, it was I [Percy], not mother, who first hatched the thought that we must save money. I will never forget how surprised my mother looked when I pronounced the word 'save.' I don't suppose mother had ever heard it mentioned before — in her family or by my father."[17]

In addition to their new found independence, the Graingers had much wider opportunities to attend theatrical and musical events. They were especially fond of Wagner, and Ludwig Wüllner was their favorite artist (his blending of the vocal and dramatic aspects in concert recitals appealed to Rose and, therefore, to Percy).

The Graingers' usual method of transportation was the bicycle, mother and son spending their free moments riding and hiking in the forests surrounding Frankfurt, along the Rhine, and to neighboring points of interest. A series of drawings and pencil sketches (now in the Library of Congress) discloses this largely unknown aspect of Grainger's activity. These drawings of landscapes, castles, and river scenes show a remarkable talent for detail and an economy of line.

Rose continued to exert almost total control over her young son. Shortly after arriving in Frankfurt she began to feel that Percy was losing his "angel-look," a common occurrence among thirteen-year-old boys. To test him, she purchased a child's game called "The Farm," which they played together. When Percy began to show an exaggerated interest in it, she took it away, remarking "I can see you're quite childish enough. That's all I wanted to know."[18] Losing her son's dependence was a constant threat. His submission was her only security in the unfamiliar surroundings of this foreign country.

Soon after arriving in Frankfurt, the Graingers discovered that Frau Schumann had indeed retired and was teaching only a few pupils privately. Even though Frau Schumann was no longer formally associated with Dr. Hoch'schen

Conservatoriums, the piano department was partially directed by her students and the school was considered by most to be one of the finest training centers in Europe.

The conservatory was founded in 1877 under the direction of Joseph Raff from the proceeds of a legacy left by a prominent Frankfurter. Its distinguished faculty included James Kwast, piano; Iwan Knorr, composition; Hugo Becker, cellist; Frau Schoeder-Hanfstaengle, prima donna; Hugo Heermann, violinist; as well as the absent-minded Engelbert Humperdinck, instructor of orchestration. Instruction on each of the orchestral instruments was available from members of the leading Frankfurt orchestras. Italian, the basic foreign language taught at the conservatory, was offered along with the usual subjects of solfeggio, composition, theory, counterpoint, and history. Literature and poetry were also included in the strong basics comprising the curriculum.

Over 250 students attended the school each year, with girls outnumbering boys almost two to one. The students represented a wide range of backgrounds and nationalities, the majority coming from the Frankfurt area and adjacent German states. Great Britain was the nation supplying the next largest segment of students; and America contributed about fifteen musicians yearly. In addition to Grainger, three other Australians were in attendance in 1895. The reputation of the Conservatory and its instructors held great attraction for students from all the English-speaking countries.

Each week a recital was held featuring students performing pieces which they were studying in their private lessons. On the Conservatory's October 30th "Vortragsabend" in 1895, Grainger performed the first movement of the Mozart *Sonata* in G Major, K. 283 — his first public performance outside Australia. He was then thirteen years old. The next few years found him performing most of the standard piano literature, often appearing with his fellow student, Walter Braunfels, as second pianist in concertos and two-piano pieces.

Piano study with Kwast was the only portion of Percy's academic training in which he excelled. Percy's friend and fellow student, Cyril Scott, later wrote: "I always remember this bearded little man [Kwast] as wearing a light buff and colored suit of which the trousers had so materially shrunk that he was obliged to let them down to the fullest capacity. This gave him a fullness in the seat and a shortness in the leg which suggested an elephant's posterior."[19]

Apart from Professors Uzielli and Becker, all the teachers at the Conservatory seemed to have a lamentable taste in dress. Perhaps the worst offender was Herr Direktor Bernard Scholz: "Over his light bile-coloured trousers and waistcoat he would wear a long black frock coat that flapped about as he shuffled along and which appeared to have no lining."[20]

In his second year, Percy enrolled in the composition class of Iwan Knorr. From the beginning of their relationship, Knorr doubted Grainger's compositional ability. It would appear that the reception the young and sensitive Grainger received in Frankfurt was directly responsible for the non-academic attitude evidenced throughout his life. One of these stormy composition classes was described by Grainger:

> The task was to write Theme & Vars for string quartet. One of my vars was "der pfeiffender Reiter". My mother and I had been bycicling [sic] in the woods south of Frankfurt. I heard a rider whistling as he rode thru the wood, it fascinated me and I wrote a variation on it. When Knorr saw it he applied his sarcasm. "This is important [sic]. You must hear it played" which I thought very kind of him. He told the whole staff they must come and hear it — that they would laugh themselves to death. And they did. They simply squirmed with laughter.[21]

Recalling the "feeble way composition was taught at the Frankfurt Conservatory," Grainger later wrote to a friend: "Meeting that Russian last night recalled to me my (not nice) composition teacher in Frankfurt, Knorr, who was also a sort of a Russian. Kindliness to the young and the very old is grand thing."[22]

These student years brought Percy into contact with a number of young and vibrant musicians who had traveled from England for study at the Conservatory. Three of these students, Cyril Scott, Balfour Gardiner, and Roger Quilter, equally bent on compositional careers, joined Grainger to form the Frankfurt Group. This hearty band, destined to become life-long friends, used as a common bond their British temperament, their German training, and their expressed hatred of Beethoven. The tastes of the members were diverse, as Grainger explained: "The English boys liked Tchai, Bizet, Wagner. But my taste ran to Bach, Brahms, Wagner. The one thing we were all united on: We all hated *Beethoven*."[23]

This newly christened fraternity formed the elite core of the pianists at the Conservatory; all studied piano with Kwast and composition with Knorr. Cyril Scott first enrolled in 1891. Then only twelve years old, he stayed but a few months, returning in 1895 for more extensive study. Balfour Gardiner arrived in 1894 and Roger Quilter two years later. By 1896, all were in residence.

Upon his return to Frankfurt, Scott had brought with him selected books and pictorial art of Maurice Maeterlinck, Stefan George, Ernest Dowson, Walt Whitman, and Aubrey Beardsley. With Scott as connoisseur, the Frankfurt Group rapidly became familiar with the London avant garde tastes of the day.

Percy first met Scott at the home of Karl Klimsch, an amateur painter and composer who retired after founding a well-known Frankfurt lithographic business. Recalling his first meeting with Percy, Scott remarked: "The first thing that struck me was the peculiarity of his clothes. I had never seen a boy dressed in such a fashion before, and presumed that his appearance was characteristic of Australians."[24]

It is quite possible that Klimsch introduced Grainger to English folk song, for it was known that the subject held an interest for him. Although Percy would later give much credit to Klimsch for encouraging his writing, he severely criticized his playing. "Karl Klimsch had an upsetting, meaningless expressiveness (gashes of loudness and softness which seemed to have little bearing on the musical phrase). A widespread habit of the generation."[25]

This renegade group of Englishmen was to find Klimsch a sympathetic supporter of their compositional efforts, and Grainger and his friends would try out many of their writings in his home. Once, learning that Scott had written a string quartet, Klimsch made the necessary arrangements for a reading of the work at his home. After the performance, Herr Klimsch pointed out what he felt to be ineffective or faulty, and produced a quartet of Beethoven's, stating: "Now you will hear how a quartet *ought to be*."[26] Scott asked if he might listen from the next room and was later discovered there by his host, fast asleep. Collectively, as well as individually, the members of the Frankfurt Group avoided Beethoven.

Balfour Gardiner was the cornerstone of the group. His background included training at Oxford and an abundant income which afforded him the leisure to pursue friends and keep their relationships in constant repair. It enabled him to develop interests aside from the obligations of making a livelihood. He was to remain single and would not have to adjust his schedule to accommodate spouse or family. He had studied with the organist at Eltham and had been educated at Charterhouse. He spent one and one-half years in Frankfurt before entering Oxford, then returned to Frankfurt in 1894.

Roger Quilter, the last to arrive, was the same age as Gardiner. Together they supplied the conservative elements of the group. Quilter was well-bred, popular, and highly regarded for his mimicry and entertaining spirit. There were underlying similarities in the temperaments of the members of the group, but above all, they were individuals. It was not an organization of conformists.

Percy's individuality was perhaps the most pronounced. He was very athletic, but his diet ran to extremes and his clothes were usually ill-fitted. He was often seen in an Eton collar which complimented his pale cheeks. Though generally popular with his peers, he was quite outspoken — many times to the point of being thought impudent; his reasoning may have appeared sound yet his conclusions were often regarded as ridiculous. His seeming delight in shocking others with his unusual viewpoints did not pass unnoticed. A foreigner, he played the part well. Two additional factors distinguished him from the other students — a shock of unmanageable curly hair and his mother.

Grainger's initial disappointment in Germany came from observations of boys his own age. Having been trained almost completely on German music and having read of the superiority of the German people, he "was longing to see German *kriegspiel* played by boys in the streets. But a more sissified lot of soft-paps than the boys I saw in Frankfurt I would never want to meet." This contradiction to his idea of the German people existed in the conservatory as well and may have been the basis for his problems with Knorr and the rethinking of his own lineage, for he later remarked: "as for musical talent at the Conservatorium among the young Germans and other foreigners — it was just nonexistent." Almost without exception it was the English students whom he most admired. "Cyril Scott was a delicious Mozart player (as was Ethel Liggins, later Leginska) and Balfour Gardiner a fine rich-toned player of Schumann and such music . . . And the English Leonard Borwick has been the *only student* of the Conservatorium to play at the Museum's Gesellschaft Symphony Concerts while still a pupil. So I found no reason to believe the German dictum that the English were without musical talent."[27]

The presence of some English students was certainly evident when Brahms appeared with the Frankfurt Chamber Music String Players in a performance of his G minor piano quartet.* The Saalbau was filled with an abnormal amount of flowers that evening, and at the performance the composer was presented with several additional floral wreaths in acknowledgement of his visit. Whether or not Grainger was one of the English students who wrote some ribald verses about "Pots and palms in honour of Brahms," is not confirmed — only suspected.

Grainger's early penchant for doing everything the most difficult way was observed by Scott: "If he could do a thing in discomfort, he would do it rather than in comfort."[28] While still in his teens, a definite tendency toward algolagnia was apparent. Scott described how the young pianist would often go into the country, "take off his clothes, and stand in the snow."[20] Extreme temperatures seemed agreeable. While still a student he would frequently "lay with the windows open, on top of the grand piano, stark-naked, until almost frozen to the bone."[30]

The essence of creativity was, to Percy, plunging into those projects that held his interest. Although physically well disciplined, he felt that artistic expression should not be structured, and that total attempts at expression were a genius's prerogative — even a responsibility. No moral convention or social norm had precedent and al-

*On that particular visit to Frankfurt, Brahms was accompanied by the clarinetist, Muhlfeld. He brought the renowned performer to the home of Clara Schumann to play his two new and, as yet, unpublished Sonatas for Clarinet. This may be the first recorded performance of the Brahms Clarinet Sonatas!

though he was to keep these practices from his general
public, his close friends and associates accepted them as
being something not at all unusual and in the case of Percy,
a neceesary expression. The years that followed saw him
less and less inhibited with respect to drives and practices which had found their origin in his unusual family
beginnings and the philosophies of a mother who saw in
her son genius, success, and compensation for her own
social and artistic frustrations.

The imaginative Grainger caught the fancy of the
English students and his idea of "mechanical devices which
would obviate the necessity for bar-lines altogether"[31] met
with awed reception. He explained: "In this way the orchestral player would simply play from a strip of music
passing across a given space at a given time, somewhat
after the fashion of a pianola roll."[32] Prophetic thoughts
indeed for a fifteen year old boy in the late 19th century.

Each year Percy dedicated several of his compositions to
"beloved mother," as either birthday gifts or "Yulegifts,"
thereby setting a custom he was to continue throughout
her life. Each occasion seemed to be as important to him
as the other.

Composition occupied a great share of Grainger's time in
Frankfurt and originality came before everything else.
After one and a half years of arguments, he discontinued
study with Knorr. Scott explains their impasse:

> . . .yet with Iwan Knorr he could not be said to
> "get on," and apart from a certain grounding in
> harmony and counterpoint, he never availed
> himself of that master's valuable criticism in
> purely compositional matters. From the first,
> Grainger elected to go his own way, and to be
> guided by intuitions rather than the suggestions
> of a teacher, and I think he never really under-
> stood Knorr, nor did Knorr really understand
> him.[33]

It is interesting to note that Knorr had been influenced in

his own compositions by folk elements, and that Brahms had recommended him for the Frankfurt position on the merit of a set of variations for orchestra based on a Ukrainian folk song. Grainger perhaps was not aware of his teacher's interest in folk songs, yet it is ironic that less than ten years later, this renegade pupil should become famous for a like interest. Cyril Scott observed:

> Knorr never took him very seriously — on the one hand his themes were too Anglo-Saxon and nonclassical for him, and on the other, his harmonies too daring and revolutionary for those times.[34]

Musically, Scott influenced Grainger more than any other member of the group by acquainting him with the music of Tchaikovsky, Grieg, and Debussy. Scott, appalled by the apparent old-fashionedness of Grainger's student attempts to compose, inquired of the Australian: "Don't you like modern harmonies?" "What do you mean by modern harmonies?" answered the younger man. Scott replied by playing the opening of Grieg's *Ballade* and the beginning of an *Air and Variations* by Tchaikovsky. Percy was stunned. Recalling the incident he commented, "I was bewitched and became a modernist overnight."[35]

Intervals and their characteristic sounds seemed to fascinate the youthful Grainger, and to examine each combination fed his appetite for unusual experimentation. On one occasion, he persuaded Gardiner and Scott to sing parallel fifths in the countryside, while he ran to the next field to listen. The compositional ideas which were to occupy Grainger throughout his life date from these early years. In a letter to John Tasker Howard many years later, he explained:

> Ever since I was about ten or eleven years old (in Australia) I have heard in my imagination what I call "free music" — music that is not tied down to the slavery of scales, intervals, rhythm, harmony, but in which the tones dart,

glide, pitch, and changes of tone-strength can
occur with the smooth gradualness we see in
nature.[36]

All of Grainger's early instrumental compositions are
unpublished, and in many instances, unfinished, though
he returned to them intermittently in later years. His
instrumental works from before the turn of the century
include *Youthful Suite* and *Kleine Variationen* for orchestra,
a *Concerto* for piano (described by Scott as being very much
in the style of Handel), and the *Set of Variations on a
German Tune* for string quartet. A *Piece for Orchestra*
and two short piano selections are dated 1898. During the
years 1898 and 1899, Grainger wrote a great many compositions for solo voice with piano accompaniment and for
chorus with various instrumental accompaniments. The
texts were from the writings of Longfellow, A. Conan
Doyle, and Rudyard Kipling. Grainger's original acquaintance with Kipling had been through his father. "My father
(in Australia) wrote to a friend: 'The boy (me) is getting
too Teutonic. I must send him some Kipling to tickle up
the British lion in him.' And it did."[37] This fondness for
Kipling continued beyond Percy's youth and resulted in
over thirty-six settings of Kipling's verses, twenty-two
of which were published between 1912 and 1948.

A prolific experimenter, Grainger began around 1899 to
evolve irregular rhythms as a "counterpoint of the spoken
rhythms of 'poetical prose'." He filled whole sketch books
at that time with transcriptions of the speech-rhythms of
passages from the Old Testament into musical notation.
"Roger Quilter would read biblical and other prose aloud
to me and I would write down what I thought the rhythms
were."[39] These unusual rhythms first appeared in his 1899-
1900 sketches for the *Love Verses from "The Song of
Solomon,"* scored in 1931 for soloists and chorus, chamber
orchestra, or keyboard. The Bach procedures he outlines
in his letter to Harold Bauer were fastidiously followed.

Possessing an international outlook mature for his years, Grainger resented the Conservatory's emphasis on German music. For example, he did not dislike Beethoven, per se, but he and his friends felt that Beethoven was too often performed at the expense of other composers. He believed a distinct lack in the general music education of the Conservatory was the knowledge of folk and art music of the East. The viewpoint of a student was not readily considered in a 19th-century German Conservatory — but Grainger persisted. When asked to compete for the Mendelssohn Prize, an award for ability in composition and keyboard, Grainger inquired if he might be allowed to study Chinese music in China if he won. "No," Kwast replied, "The Mendelssohn Prize is not awarded to idiots."[41] Grainger did not compete.

In the Fall of 1899, he once again attempted the composition classes of Knorr, but their relationship had not improved. Scott described Knorr as being "a really broad-minded man and far from an academic 'stickler.' Actually he [Knorr] was noted for his large-mindedness as a teacher and he encouraged originality — provided it was not tinctured with vulgarities!"[41] Scott, however, felt that Knorr "had deeply offended him [Grainger] by not taking either him or his compositions seriously."[42] Grainger admitted: "Knorr was very sarcastic and was supposed to be very clever," and, "at the beginning I liked him very much." The final break came when Knorr criticized Grainger's experiments with whole-tone writing: "I don't know what all this superchromaticism is good for." Percy deeply resented his clever terminology, but did show his instructor one additional set of songs based on Kipling texts. Knorr's sarcasm was ill-received when he commented: "The music is crazy and the poems are crazy too."[43] It was humiliating enough for the proud Australian to be criticized in his own creative attempts, but he objected when a German called

Kipling "crazy." Although his mother had paid for further classes with the money she was earning as a tutor, Percy refused to return to Knorr. Scott's appeal to Rose to urge her son to continue his study was futile, and no further contact was made between the rebel and the Teuton.

The effect of Kipling's poetry on the young Australian cannot be discounted. As he set the Kipling poems to music, he began to take a chauvinistic attitude in his use of titles and directions. It was as a student that he first discarded conventional terms such as sonata, cantata, and symphony, for being too German, Austrian, or Italian. For the expression markings of *crescendo* and *staccato* he substituted the words "louden lots" and "shorten." Grainger's Anglo-Saxon approach to all things had begun.

This aggressively British attitude which permeated his writing became a negative quality in the acceptance of Grainger's music. After a number of his works were published in London a few years later, a reviewer would remark:

> . . . His directions are written in English (of a sort) with, however, the better known Italian expressions printed in small type below like the finger posts in the neighborhood of Dublin, where small names in English lurk shamefacedly below legends which only some members of the Gaelic league can read. Here we have "louden lots bit by bit" modestly explained by poco a poco crescendo molto . . . But Mr. Grainger is more successful with his music than with the English language. . . . We can laugh with him over his stage directions and they will not disturb one's enjoyment of the music.[44]

Percy's agility on his two-wheeler was extraordinary. Encountering Knorr one day, he performed a few of his more dexterous tricks of balance and gliding to get the professor's attention and approval. Knorr replied in his usual sarcastic manner: "It is a pity you are not equally skillful at counterpoint." Feeling that counterpoint was one of the assets of his writing, Grainger later remarked: "Strange that my composition teacher saw not sprouting countermelodies in me." During one of his cycling exhibitions, Percy lost the tip of his index finger when it became entangled in his bicycle chain. This did not detract from his technical ability as a pianist, though at the time the fledgling composer had hoped that the accident would put an end to his performing and allow more time to be devoted to writing.

Rose and Percy spent one summer in Kronberg where Percy continued his piano study with vacationing Herr Kwast. During their stay at the picturesque village, Percy fell in love with Minnie Kwast, the professor's daughter. After a delightful summer together, Minnie received an urgent letter from the composer and conductor Hans Pfitzner who had been her neurotic beau in Frankfurt It stated that he should kill himself if she did not come immediately and marry him. The Australian, unwilling to become responsible for such an act, helped his sweetheart pack and accompanied her to the station. Although he seldom spoke of her again, he carried a broken comb she had hurriedly discarded as a souvenir. "I wouldn't lose that comb for anything," he told Scott. "Minnie Kwast has often combed her hair with it." Nearly ten years later, Percy wrote of his childhood love: "I can remember lying awake one night at Kronberg (when 15 or 16 just when I fell in love with _____) crying over having become so ordinary in contrast to my earlier self."[45]

The Boer War, then a major political question in Europe, had resulted in anti-British sentiment in Germany and the Graingers were often the brunt of remarks concerning England's unpopular colonial policy. "I hope as many of your people as possible get killed in Africa," one of Rose's students remarked to her. Whenever the English had a reverse in South Africa, Grainger would turn up his trousers to show his independence, not one fold, but even two!

Between Christmas of 1899 and the summer of 1900, Percy and Rose visited San Remo, Nice, Paris, Amsterdam, London, and Glasgow. The trip was financed by Karl Klimsch to help Rose recover from a physical breakdown. Although still legally married, Rose considered for a short time a proposal from Klimsch, but the thought of her son becoming German ended the consideration. She seemed equally suspicious of the English; because of an English neighbor, she had moved from the Pension Shoen, remarking: "The English are always trouble-makers." During this trip Grainger gave no public performances, although he had begun appearing locally in Frankfurt as well as teaching and accompanying to help support himself and his mother, who was unable to continue her tutoring.

In February of 1900, Cyril Scott's *First Symphony* was scheduled to be performed in Darmstadt. It was a major occasion for the Frankfurt Group inasmuch as this was the first performance of an extended work by any of its members. The Graingers arranged their tour to allow them to be present for the concert. The performance was arranged by Scott's mentor, Stefan George; Willem de Hann would conduct. The orchestral parts, which were to be ready in advance, had been neglected by an irresponsible copyist, so Grainger and Scott spent the night before the rehearsal copying the necessary music. Scott's attempts to conduct part of the rehearsal on the following day ended in disaster, and he soon turned the direction of the rehearsal back to Herr Hann. Gardiner, Quilter, and even Knorr journeyed to Darmstadt for the performance which was received with mixed reactions. Standing in the back of the stalls during the premier, Scott and Grainger overheard a patron remark: "Des solle de Englander de Bure einmal vorspiele; dann laufe sie bis zum Equarte erauf." (If the English would play that to the Boers, they would run up to the Equator.")[46]

Following the Scott performance, Rose and Percy resumed their holiday from Darmstadt to San Remo. At this time, Grainger began a series of Train Music Sketches, inspired by the jerky, arrhythmic motion of the Italian train. These sketches, dated February 10, 1900, are some of the first examples of Grainger's irregular barring, the opening twenty-three measures written in twenty-three different meter signatures. The scoring in February of 1901 calls for an orchestra of unusually large proportions.[47]

In April, mother and son visited the Paris International Exposition. Representing Western Australia at the Exposition was its chief architect, John H. Grainger, but it is not known whether Rose was present when Percy met his father. In later years, the son proudly acknowledged that his father had been the recipient of a bronze medal from the "Société des Architects Française," as well as several gold and silver medals for his work at the Exposition.

The Paris Exposition of 1900 brought Percy once again in contact with music of the East. He was especially impressed by the gamelon orchestra and, as a result, he became very interested in the instruments of percussion.

The exposition was also where Percy first came in contact with Egyptian double reeds. The extreme nasal sound of these instruments as well as that of the harsh-toned Italian *piffero* and the Scottish bagpipes, which he also encountered on this tour, appealed to his ear. *Hill Song No. 1* (1901) resulted, scored for 2 piccolos, 6 oboes, 6 English horns, 6 bassoons, and 1 contrabassoon. (In 1969, nearly seventy years later, this piece was first performed in its original form at Northwestern University.)

The athletic exuberance of the young pianist knew no restrictions. Traveling by ship on one leg of the trip, Grainger was discovered in the furnace room shoveling coal. His hands were blistered and raw, but the young man seemed unconcerned. "They'll heal in time," he replied.

In addition to the capable faculty of the Hoch Conservatory, there was another notable advantage in music study in Frankfurt in the 1890's. The Municipal Opera House, designed by Lucae and completed in 1880, was one of the finest in Germany. Here the most gifted conductors and musicians appeared, setting a standard in performance which had its effects throughout all of Europe. In addition, the Frankfurt opera was noted for the extreme obesity of its singers. They possessed the fattest Brunnhildes and Isoldes in the Rhineland, and their love scenes were more humorous than erotic. This state of affairs caused Cyril Scott and Grainger to lend their hand to the following couplet:

> Altho' it is not difficult to see
> Why doctors have invented that disease called "housemaid's knee,"
> Yet what has always filled me with surprise
> Is that there's no disease called "singer's size."[48]

Percy's affection for the Tchaikovsky B-flat minor concerto possibly dates from his hearing Ossip Gabrilowitsch's performance at the Opera House shortly before the turn of the century. Remarking many years later about the incident, Grainger stated: "He then seemed to be a very sparkling player — much more so than in his American years."

But of all the visiting pianists, it was Eugéne D'Albert who most impressed the young Australian. He was enthralled by D'Albert's "slap-dash" English style and informed him: "I like your style, so wicked and free." Commenting on his performance, Grainger later wrote: "When I saw D'Albert swash around over the piano, with the wrong notes flying to the right and left and the whole thing a welter of recklessness, I said to myself: 'That's the way I must play.' I am afraid I learnt his propensity for wrong notes all too thoroughly!" When Frederick Lamond appeared two years later, Grainger was less impressed with this teacher of Professor Laver, his friend in Australia, but did arrange to play for him. Grainger was "very struck with his [Lamond's] typically British sweetness, kindliness, and tenderness of manner, when I [was such] a miserably raw pianist."[49]

Although Grainger had matured considerably as a pianist while in Frankfurt, he remained embittered toward the teaching and the narrow span of literature he had come in contact with at the Conservatory. He was later to remark:

> ...that *liberal* musical education which the Germans had never given me (because they — embroiled in anti-Wagner or anti-Brahms strife — never knew it existed), but which my English fellow-students in Frankfort had started me on, was continued in all my contacts with orchestra, choirs, musicians, etc. I quickly got to know all that world of Tschaikovsky, Gabrieli, Fauré, Debussy, Ravel, Skryabin, Balakirev, Albéniz, Puccini, that had been a closed book to me in Frankfurt.[50]

Notes

[1] Interview with Burnett Cross, July 15, 1967.

[2] Richard Franko Goldman, "Percy Grainger's 'Free Music,'" *Juilliard Review*, II (Fall, 1955), p. 38.

[3] Percy A. Grainger, *Photos of Rose Grainger and 3 short accounts of her life by herself, in her own hand-writing* (Munich: privately published, 1923), p. 10.

[4] Grainger, "Bird's-Eye View of the Together Life of Rose Grainger and Percy Grainger" (18-page typescript, dated 1947).

[5] Letter from John Grainger to his father, January 14, 1890.

[6] Grainger, "The Aldridge-Grainger-Ström Saga" (233-page typescript located in the Library of Congress, dated 1934).

[7] Grainger, "The Life of My Mother and Her Son" (75-page typescript located in the Library of Congress, dated 1922-1930).

[8] *Ibid.*

[9] Antonia Sawyer, *Songs at Twilight* (New York: Devon-Adair Co., 1939), pp. 128-129.

[10] Grainger, "Photos of Rose Grainger and 3 short accounts of her life, in her own hand-writing," p. 11.

[11] Grainger, "The Life of My Mother and Her Son."

[12]Grainger, "Bird's-Eye View of the Together Life of Rose Grainger and Percy Grainger," p. 8.

[13]Grainger, "Thunks" (unpublished typescript dated March 25, 1937).

[14]Letter from John Grainger to his father, dated January 14, 1890.

[15]*Ibid.*

[16]*The Argus* (Melbourne), October 10, 1894.

[17]Grainger, "Bird's-Eye View of the Together Life of Rose Grainger and Percy Grainger."

[18]*Ibid.*

[19]Cyril Scott, "Percy Grainger and the Frankfurt Group" (unpublished typescript, October, 1936).

[20]*Ibid.*

[21]Letter to Sir Thomas Armstrong from Percy Grainger, White Plains, New York, dated Oct. 17, 1958.

[22]Letter to Miss Karen Holten from Percy Grainger, London, England, dated April 6, 1907.

[23]Letter to Sir Thomas Armstrong from Grainger.

[24]Scott, "Percy Grainger and the Frankfurt Group."

[25]Percy Grainger, "Bird's-Eye View . . ."

[26]Letter to Armstrong from Grainger.

[27]Grainger, "English Speaking Leadership in Tone-Art" (8-page typescript, Oct. 21, 1943).

[28]Scott, "Percy Grainger and the Frankfurt Group."

[29]*Ibid.*

[30]*Ibid.*

[31]*Ibid.*

[32]*Ibid.*

[33]Cyril Scott, "Percy Grainger: The Music and the Man," *The Musical Quarterly*, II (1916), 425.

[34]Scott, "Percy Grainger and the Frankfurt Group."

[35]Letter to Armstrong from Grainger.

[36]John Tasker Howard, *Our American Composers* (3rd ed.; New York: Thomas Y. Crowell Co., 1946), p. 416.

[37]Letter to Armstrong from Grainger.

[38]Letter to Harold Bauer from Grainger, White Plains, New York, dated Aug. 26, 1947.

[39]Letter to Sir Thomas from Percy Grainger, White Plains, New York, dated Oct. 21, 1958.

[40]*The Evening Post* (New York), Sept. 11, 1915.

[41]Letter to author from Cyril Scott, Eastbourne, England, Aug. 5, 1965.

[42]*Ibid.*

[43]Letter to Armstrong from Grainger, Oct. 17, 1958.

[44]*The Times* (London), Jan. 23, 1912.

[45]Letter to Holten from Grainger, Nov. 27, 1907.

[46]Grainger to Armstrong, Oct. 17, 1958.

[47]The scoring for "Train Music Sketches" includes 2 piccolos, 6 flutes, 8 oboes, 4 English horns, 8 clarinets, 2 bass-clarinets, 6 bassoons, 2 contrabassoons, 4 French horns, 8 trumpets, 3 trombones, 36 violins, 28 violas, 24 celli, 12 string basses.

[48]Scott, "Percy Grainger and the Frankfurt Group."

[49]Grainger, "P.A. Grainger: English Pianist & Harold Bauer" (unpublished typescript, sketch for article, dated Feb. 19, 1945. Jacksonville, Fla.)

[50]*Ibid.*

The English Years

"Apollo"

Grainger's concert career began in 1901. The striking appearance of this sharp-featured young man with his shock of unruly auburn curls caught the public fancy. From the first he was a success. His professional name, Percy Aldridge Grainger, began to appear on programs shortly after his concert career began. In an effort to pay homage to his mother, he dropped his christened first name, George, and incorporated his mother's maiden name as his middle name.

Although he had appeared earlier at private parties and salons, Grainger's first solo concert appearance was at London's Steinway Hall on October 29, 1901. An especially warm reception from the press started his English success.

> Mr. Percy Grainger, whose first recital took place at the Steinway Hall on Tuesday afternoon, is a young Australian pianist of great talent. His performance of *Liszt's arrangement of Bach's Organ Prelude and Fugue in A minor* as his opening number revealed qualities entitling him to rank high among our young artists on the keyboard instrument; seldom do we hear,

except in much older artists, such a fine sense
of *legato* or gradual *crescendo* tone. He draws
the music from the keys, and secures the most
pleasing effect even from the greatest *fortissimo*
passages. He also appreciates the melodic significance of, for instance, the *Intermezzo, No. 6,
Op. 116 of Brahms*. No less satisfactory was the
Capriccio, No. 2, Op. 76, of the same master
. . . . Among the distinguished-looking audience
present was Mme. Melba.[1]

A major portion of the concert circuit in London at that
time included appearances in the homes of music patrons.
Although public performances were frequent, it was the
salon engagements that determined the actual success of
performers. Ability to be accepted in polite society was
as necessary as keyboard technique. Grainger was a master of both. The distinguished patrons soon to demand
his services were drawn from the best families; Queen
Alexandra, for instance, often heard him perform at meetings of the Oxford Ladies' Music Society.

During the next few years, he introduced the music of
Debussy, Scott, Ravel, and Albéniz to the English public.
But his London career really began with a performance of
the Tchaikovsky B♭ minor Concerto at St. James Hall.
The following summer, Grainger was booked to perform
with Hans Richter and the Hallé Orchestra in Manchester.

Until this time, Percy's career had consisted mainly of
solo recitals rather than appearances with orchestras. He
was, therefore, lacking in the amenities that characterize
a seasoned performer, and he did not realize that it was
customary for the soloist to provide the orchestra parts.
So when he appeared at his first rehearsal for Richter without the proper music, Richter graciously intervened and
found a set of parts in the orchestra's library. All was well
until the second movement. Grainger described the event:
"In the middle I suddenly heard a scherzo I'd never heard
before. This was an old edition. The scherzo had been cut

out of the edition I had." Again, Richter was kind: "Just listen until we come to the next part you know and then we will cut out the parts you don't know." "But it was a shock," Percy explained, "when, in the tone-fest, Richter took a theme (against which I had hard octaves to play) almost double as fast as in the rehearsal. I was able to keep going by playing lightly & slovenly. But it nearly threw me off the rails. From such shocks a squeemish, scary make-up like mine never heals. Such things turned me on public playing for life. It was nobody's fault. But I was simply not made for such a rough life."[2]

As a pianist, however, Grainger had few equals in sheer technique, contrapuntal mastery, and stamina. His eccentric behavior excepted, here was a great pianist. A London music reviewer described these qualities:

> . . . Mr. Grainger, with his crisp, clear touch and his knowledge of folk-music, was altogether admirable; and in the prelude and fugue in C-sharp minor, from the first book of the "48," he enabled one to follow each part just as though it were before one on the printed page.[3]

In his early training under Pabst and Kwast, Percy became especially adept in the use of the sostenuto pedal. This technique gave him exceptional facility in the most awkward passages and allowed him to achieve unusual colors and tonal combinations. His American manager, Antonio Sawyer, would later remark: "At a young age he loved color and would cut a piece of silk or cloth he fancied out of anything he came in contact with."[4] Cyril Scott recalled that when Grainger performed a Mozart concerto with an orchestra during his student days, he "play'd it with such taste and charm — or so it seemed to me at the time."[5]

Rose's efforts to fashion Percy into a distinguished performer who would be accepted into the proper circles resulted in their conflict. Percy was never fond of these "society creatures" and bitterly complained: "She had brought me up to enjoy superior things & people, & here I was hilariously happy in getting close to common things & people." Rose also exhibited a strong "dislike of joculence about mating & flirting & love-making." She seemed to have a neurotic wish to provide me with sweethearts (followed at any moment by the wish to get rid of the same sweetheart)."[6] Herman Sandby, a Frankfurt school chum, disapproved of Rose's dominating nature, and "was hurt in his soul, when he came to London, to find that I 'had no manly freedom'."[7]

In London, Grainger spent much time in the company of his student friends from Frankfurt. They, along with the painters, John Singer Sargent, Glyn Philpot, and Harold Speed and the authors, William Butler Yeats, John Galsworthy, and Arnold Bennett, were to be found at the most fashionable London parties. At Percy's flat over a tobacconist's shop in King's Road, Chelsea, many of the newly written compositions of the Frankfurt group were first performed. A distinguished member and second violinist for these informal gatherings was Eugene Goosens.

Grainger soon began to associate with the performing artists of the city. When he had arrived in London, his only acquaintance outside the Frankfurt Group had been Nellie Melba, who had immediately become his "sponsor and herald." Percy's first London engagement had come through Melba and a camaraderie between the two Australians lasted many years.

Rose Grainger was pleased knowing that her son's career was assured. Newspapers doted on him, and among the many complimentary phrases which they used to describe him, "Apollo" was her favorite. They could never have known (nor would they ever have believed) that during her pregnancy, Rose had placed a reproduction of the Roman god of "music and manly beauty" where she could view it while she rested, contemplating her unborn son.

Percy was soon dubbed "the running pianist" because of his habit of running through the London streets between appointments. As he viewed it, the exuberance served two purposes; he arrived at his destination quickly and cheaply and he was exercising enroute. Always in superb physical condition, the young performer never walked when he could run; often he negotiated stairways two and three steps at a time. His mind was as quick as his reflexes and he dominated his audience in conversation, in concert halls and on the street. Only to his mother was he submissive.

Returning to London one day after a successful performance with Max Heymann and the Bath Orchestra, Percy was exceptionally elated. His mother was furious with him for being so happy when she had not accompanied him. As Percy explained: "For the first time I'd escaped her apron strings." But these short excursions away from his mother were infrequent and Percy was generally content in allowing Rose to remain the dominant member of the partnership.

In 1902, several events occurred which were of special significance to Grainger. He heard the British pianist Harold Bauer perform the Cesar Franck piano quintet at St. James Hall. This was his initial exposure to Franck's music and the beginning of a long friendship with Bauer. Later that fall, Grainger was engaged to tour most of the provincial centers of England with Adelina Patti, Sir Charles Santely (baritone), Alice Liebman (violinist), and John Harrison (tenor). It was most certainly because of his friendship with Melba that the young and relatively unknown pianist became a part of Patti's distinguished touring company. At each concert Percy would perform a Bach organ transcription, an item of Scott's or Albéniz's, and a sonata movement with Miss Liebman. In Edinburgh Grainger met and heard Blanche Marchesi, the daughter of the teacher of Melba and of Ada Crossley (with whom he was to tour the following year). The entire troup attended the performance of *Tannhauser* in which she starred.

Although Grainger generally disliked solo singers, he got

on well with Patti. She regarded the 19-year-old pianist as
her son and spoke glowingly of his performing abilities.
There was, however, a distinct animosity between Grainger
and Santely who openly professed his disdain for Kipling.
At the conclusion of the tour, Percy received an autographed photo of Patti which he prized highly. But later he
would complain about her artificiality, for when she would
grow tired of the applause and encores, she was known to
don her travel costume and return to the stage with valise
in hand, indicating that she really must be off now to the
train.

That same year, he met Ada Crossley, the Australian contralto, then at the height of her career. It was proposed
that he be engaged as an assisting artist to participate the
following year in some three hundred concerts with her in
Australia, New Zealand, and South Africa. Grainger, thirst-
ing for all things Australian, immediately accepted. Several
weeks before the troupe left England, Grainger was introduced to Ferruccio Busoni, who extended an offer of free
lessons. The interest earlier aroused among the students in
Frankfurt over Busoni's playing probably attracted Grainger as well. According to one of Percy's classmates, "Busoni
was much admired and brought new lights to bear on the
use of pedalling."[8] Grainger's own concern with the possibilities of the sostenuto pedal may have originated at that
time. "I'll have to leave for Australia in three weeks," replied Grainger. "Never mind, then come for two weeks,"[9]
said Busoni. It was agreed that these few lessons were to be
spent only in the study of Bach. This interest in Bach was
already evident in Grainger's student days when he asked
Knorr about the possibility of using Bach, rather than
Tchaikovsky, as a model of orchestration. "Bach is not
orchestration," he was informed. However, it sounded
perfect to Percy's ears and he continued to use it.

Although Grainger remained on good terms with Busoni,
their lessons did not go well. Wishing to spend more time

composing, Percy continually neglected his practice. Then Busoni would invite his students in to hear Grainger play octave runs, a feat he never quite mastered. Grainger, Busoni, and the students would laugh at his ragged efforts "until tears ran down their cheeks." But, when Grainger would play a short piece of Bach or Mozart as an encore, the students would burst into applause. They affectionately referred to him as the "Kreisler of the piano," a term Busoni openly disliked. Busoni's inability to understand the musically undisciplined youth frustrated further study and soon Grainger, with his copies of Bernarr Macfadden's *Physical Culture Magazine*, was off to Australia.

Although there is no evidence that Grainger studied composition with Busoni, it is known that he presented some of his work to his teacher. Speaking of *Hill Song No. 1*, Grainger wrote in 1907, "Busoni thought it by far my most strong, original and worthful style."[10]

The extreme egotism which drove the young Australian existed more in his compositional life than in his performing career. On stage he was generous though flamboyant, courteous yet aloof, but, above all, a talented performer who could deeply move his audiences. As a composer his greatest interest was in experimentation. The basic purpose of the quest was to achieve "Free Music," music made up of "beatless lilts, gliding interval-less tones and non-harmonic voice-leadings," the type of music he had envisioned since he was ten or eleven years old.

Grainger was deeply concerned with the idea of composing music which would be free of the tonal restrictions imposed by conventional instruments. This concept, which was to burst forth in his electronic music experiments many years later, may have had some influence on Busoni and his paper, *An Esthetic of New Music* published in Trieste in 1907. Busoni's theory of dividing the octave into more than twelve segments was merely an approximation of Grainger's theory of gliding tones. Although there is no documentation that the two men discussed these theories, it seems unlikely that such parallel ideas would go undetected.

After the unsuccessful lessons with Busoni, Percy joined Crossley's troupe. This "concert party" consisted of a soprano, a tenor, a bass, a violinist, a pianist, and an accompanist; each contributed a portion of the program. Grainger's repertoire had expanded to include several Busoni transcriptions of Bach *Organ Preludes*. Possibly because of Crossley's Australian background, Grainger exhibited more enthusiasm for her than for Patti. He spoke glowingly of her voice and interpretive style, but most of all he felt her to be "kindly, helpful, appreciative, and a democratic Australian." It was Ada who made him practice his stage entrance for at first he presented a very awkward sight. Dr. Francis Muecke, Ada's future husband, also met with Percy's approval. "He was also a typical Australian whom I found it easy to get along with."

The Australian tour had noticeable affects upon Grainger's compositional style. Prior to this return to Australia, pieces of a most complex nature, such as *Marching Song of Democracy, English Dance,* and *Hill Song No. 1,* were occupying his time. The rhythms were irregular and the harmonic structures dissonant. Feeling that so complicated a style would mean nothing to the Australian public, he conceived a simpler and more direct approach. *Molly on the Shore, Australian Up-Country Song, Shepherd's Hey,* and *Mock Morris* resulted a few years later from this new approach. An exception to his complex rhythms but nevertheless experimental, was his 1902 choral setting of *The Irish Tune from County Derry*. This work called for nonsense syllables, a technique soon to be employed by Debussy, Delius, and Vaughan Williams. One year earlier he had notated the Scottish folktune, *Ye Banks and Braes O'Bonnie Doon,* in a version for men's chorus and whistlers.

Because of the pioneer qualities of Australia, Grainger viewed its people as experimenters and developers, rather than adapters and refiners as he viewed Europeans. "In my early years as a modernist, I took it for granted that I, *as an Australian,* would be ahead of my European tone-followers in original inventivity and experimentalism."[11] This attitude was graphically displayed when the French portraitist Jacques-Emile Blanche brought him some of Debussy's music. In typical Grainger fashion, he replied: "That is only one of the trees in my forest!" Further explaining that: "So much bigger than any European did I feel myself to be. For if I took it for granted that an Englishman was a super-European, I equally took it for granted that an Australian was a super-Englishman."[12]

Returning from the Crossley tour in 1904, Grainger borrowed a different reed instrument each week from Boosey & Company of London. The immediate result of this study was the *Lads of Wamphray,* Grainger's first large work written directly for wind band; the famous *Hill Song No. 2,* scored for 21 wind instruments, followed two years later. Balance was extremely important to him, and he was very much against the use of a large orchestra as an accompaniment to a solo voice. He felt it was indeed a find then, when he became acquainted with the reed organ. He had already ruled out the piano as an accompanying instrument, "so when I heard Metzger, the London trade-handler for the Mustel reed organ, play his Mustel reed organ with a small group of strings and winds at the Savage Club, London, about 1904, I knew that the reed organ would save the day for me and my 'large-room-music'."

The unusual array of infrequently used instruments found in many of Grainger's early pieces is explainable by his attempts to balance the background for solo voices. He later explained that he felt that "it has been my duty to bring sung tonery, and its background, back to the size of man's voice. Therefore, I have used (e.g. trombones) as little as I could and used weak-toned-tools (reed organ, guitar, marimba) as much as I could."[13] That same year several of his compositions for orchestra and chorus were performed at a Competition Festival at Hunstanton and King's Lynn with the orchestra made up of several players from the Coldstream Guards Band. J. MacKenzie Rogan, the conductor of the Coldstream Band, was in attendance and remarked afterward to Grainger, "You seem to like woodwinds." When Percy admitted that he preferred them to the strings, he was invited to attend some of the band's rehearsals and an offer was made to try out any of Grainger's compositions for military band or wind groups.

Percy was soon off to Denmark, where he participated in a number of concerts with cellist Herman Sandby and soprano Alhild deLuce. Through Sandby, Grainger met Karen Holten, the daughter of a Copenhagen physician. Karen proved to be the perfect friend for the shy and introverted Grainger. Their common interests were literature, an adventurous spirit, and music; Karen was a pianist. An intimate correspondence between the two began with Grainger's return to London. Through his letters, Percy tried to fashion Karen into the "perfect example of Nordic independence." He counseled her to learn to ride, to be a proficient sailor, and even learn to shoot. For a while he thought of having her try to become a first-rate reader of music. "If one can accompany really well, there is always a real good living to be earned in London, but one must know one's job . . . read ½ hour daily . . . it is so good for one's technique, too."[14] Almost every trait he wished to instill in Karen could have been found in Rose Grainger.

Rose took an unusual attitude toward Percy's Danish friend. She encouraged their friendship and even arranged to be absent when Karen would visit London or when they planned to meet in Denmark. The Graingers' flat did not afford the privacy Percy desired, and a change of quarters was made.

Explaining to Karen, he wrote:

We are going to move. We don't find Chelsea

healthy and I can't stand the studio, and *chiefly:*
jag kan ikke taale maudfolk; not to live with.
Fletcherina perfect dear, but still I'm happier
without men to live with. So when you come
there will be no English influence to stand between us. Tak for Købeuh anø klip.[15]

In 1905, J. MacKenzie Rogan and the Band of his Maj-
esty's Coldstream Guards tried out *Lads of Wamphray* for
the composer. Writing that same day to Karen, Grainger
described his reaction:

This morning the "Coldstreams" played thru my
Wamphray March. They are a wonderful band;
They read it straight thru & did the hardest
things amazingly well. Lots of it sounded splendid and some didn't. My feeling is that it is
successful taking it all round (& except certain
impossible bits) but that it is *fearfully badly
scored.* I fear I have few gifts that way. I feel
that even tho parts that sound well could easily
sound as well if I weren't such an ass. I am
going to rework a heap of it and cut a lot out.
It is much too long, thank God; for my fault
has always been overshortness, (like in my
"figure") It made me happy to hear it though
the democraticness of army discipline makes
me more miserable than I can say. I feel, somehow, that I'm better among women-folk than
among these curious proud strong smelling
creatures — men. They weren't thinking of
me when they made this world either, so it
comes right in the end. But the way the March
went was nothing to make me sad, little Karen.
They are going to give it a longer rehearsal
in Dec or Jan; when I've altered what I hate
particularly in it. Goodnight.[16]

Kings and Queens of Song

The folk song movement which existed in England at this
time did not escape Grainger's attention. Early in 1905,

Percy was fired by a lecture delivered by Lucy E. Broadwood and illustrated with songs she had collected locally.
A few weeks later, at a Competition Festival in Lincolnshire organized by Gervase Elwes, Lady Winifrede Elwes,
and her brother-in-law, Everard Fielding, Percy notated
his first folk song.

At Grainger's insistence, the succeeding music competition at Brigg added an additional category: Class XII,
Folk Songs — Open to All. The purpose was to encourage
singers and non-singers to bring forward any unpublished
songs which they knew. The prize was not for the performance — which might be whistled, sung, or presented in any
way — but for the tune itself.[17] A wealth of material appeared and the new collector excitedly wrote Gervase Elwes:

> The results are so rousing that I am going to
> see I get a week off sometime in the summer and
> do a sort of bike tour through Lincolnshire
> gathering tunes . . . I risk asking you all this
> because one can ask folksong lovers to do any-
> thing, and I dare say Linc'll prove rich. Anyway,
> you must feel proud at the jolly results your
> forethought of this year rounded up.[18]

Grainger's systematic collection began shortly afterwards
in the workhouse at Brigg. With the assistance of Lady
Elwes, he met with many of the residents who were able
practitioners of this disappearing art. In September,
while a guest of Lady Elwes, Grainger worked the countryside. He was quite uninhibited in approaching singers
to parade their wares. He might walk up to a man plough-
ing in the fields, ask if he knew any songs, and then wait
until the man could recall one. He would jot the tune down
on bits of paper while Geoffrey and Rolf, sons of Gervase
Elwes, would catch the words. It was not unusual for him
to bring an old man or two to join them at lunch. Lady
Elwes never minded.

While Percy was recuperating from a sprained ankle
suffered in negotiating the stairs two at a time, his friends

collected the local singers and brought them to his bedroom to sing. On one occasion, Lady Elwes came home to
find a circle of ten singers sitting around his bed, waiting
their turn as he took down their tunes. Writing to Lady
Elwes a few weeks after his departure, Grainger remarked:
"The lovely tunes you helped me to gather in; to think how
few lands in Europe could boast such a crop — good old
supposed-to-be-unmusical England!"[19]

From the first, Grainger was not satisfied with the usual
method of transcribing the songs. This method required the
singer to repeat the song, or a section of the song, until
the collector was satisfied that he had achieved the correct
notation. This laborious and inaccurate method appealed
neither to the singers, who resented being asked to render
identical versions fitted into preconceived meters, nor
to the meticulous Australian, who insisted on detailing
accurate rhythm, local dialect, microtonal intervals, and
differences in the various singers' renditions. H.G. Wells
once accompanied Grainger on a folk-song hunt in Glouces-
tershire. He observed the detail Grainger followed in his
work, and when he found him noting even the conversations
among the rural singers, he remarked: "You are trying to
do a more difficult thing than record folk songs, you are
trying to record life."[20]

After laboriously working the district of Brigg-Barrow-
Barton-Scunthorpe during the summer of 1905, Grainger
began to seek a better method of collecting. It was at this
time that he came into contact with Madame Lineva's notations of Russian folk-art songs, which had been collected
with the aid of a phonograph. That fall, Grainger arranged
a luncheon with the English mathematician Sir Arthur
Balfour and discussed the possibility of using a machine
to record folk songs scientifically, that is, by the number
of vibrations. The result of this conversation was an Edison-
Bell wax cylinder phonograph. The following year (1906)
the young collector used the phonograph in his collecting,

its first known use in folk-song collecting in England.

Following his fruitful summer, Grainger was asked to speak before the Folk-Song Society concerning the use of his phonograph and the discoveries he had made. The members of the group were eager to hear the new recording machine. "They are going to propose me for the committee of the Folk-Song Society, which is an honor that gladdens me lots," he wrote to Karen Holten. Two days later, he commented: "My folk-song business went alright. I wasn't nervous speaking (curiously)."[21]

The *Journal of the Folk-Song Society* devoted its issue No. 12, 1908, to a portion of the songs Grainger had collected in and around London. These songs were prefaced with an extensive essay by Grainger, "Collecting with the Phonograph," in which he outlined his methods and findings. All were new; many were controversial. Not only was it then novel to use a phonograph to record the folk singers, but Grainger's notational practice was revolutionary as well. Rather than force a newly acquired tune to fit into conventional meter or to arbitrarily assign a pitch to the nearest semi-tone, Grainger wrote exactly what the singer sang. This practice was not warmly received by some veteran English folklorists.

> The bars of 5/8 [Rufford Park Poachers] time are probably due to an exaggerated accent being put on the third note of a bar of 2/4 time. The bars of 3/4 time are clearly uniform in design with these, and the whole tune points to a perfectly regular original in 2/4 time.[22]

Although basically approving of Grainger's insight and detail in notating folk songs, Lucy E. Broadwood did criticize him for taking into account the various melodic changes a singer might make in rendering the different verses to a song. She felt that the general experience of collectors showed that the singer rarely altered the mode throughout the song. Grainger disagreed and suggested that although "most people want their folksongs middle-class," his singers sang their songs in "one loosely-knit modal folk-song scale," rather than in a distinct Mixolydian, Dorian, or Aeolian mode. In general, Grainger did not approve of the harmonizing of folk tunes by collectors, or even by the younger singers themselves.

> I must admit that I am prejudiced against folk- ish harmonic support for the tunes — such in- struments as guitar, accordion, etc., in the hands of the folk musicians themselves, for I always find that harmonies thus arrived at are common- place intervals in the tunes they sing. The old folk-singers were not limited to the harmonic poverty of instruments.[23]

One great advantage of the phonograph over the original method was that the singers did not have to stop contin- ually to allow the transcriber to catch up. This continuity stabilized the rhythms and allowed for an exactness which theretofore had not been possible, or even desired. In tran- scribing from the cylinder, Grainger would ingeniously slow the speed of the machine which enabled him to notate unusual intervals, ornaments, and intricate runs. Rhyth- mically, he was still frustrated: "As regards rhythms, for instance, I have had to put up with the *nearest writable* form of what I actually heard."

In addition to the rural folk songs of England and else- where, Grainger became interested in sea chanties. They differed greatly from their rural cousins in their function as an accompaniment to the sailor's work, in their length, and in their general lack of plot. After recording them, Grainger found that their rhythmic irregularities did not show a uniform pattern as had the Lincolnshire tunes he had previously collected. At a party at Frank Schuster's after a folk gathering hike, he was introduced to Adrian Boult, who was later to distinguish himself as a conductor. Boult had a passing affection for the folk song and its singers, and he knew H.E. Piggot, one of Grainger's sources for sea chanties.

Grainger's best source for the chanties was a retired sailor named Rosher, who was at that time working as a house painter. On one occasion, Percy gathered over twenty tunes from him, but Rosher had trouble remembering the words. In the fall, Grainger had the ex-sailor come by his apartment regularly on Tuesday and Wednesday evenings, helped him recall the words, and even captured several new tunes. They were quite different from anything Grainger had anticipated; simpler, shorter, "more meager in invention, tho quite as good in their own grim terse way." Many of British origin were built on a pentatonic scale with two short refrains to each tune. "These can be very weird, grand, bold sounding, with the curious barren-like feeling that the sea gives to them." In addition to the British tunes, there were American chanties — "dreamy and poetic & Huck Finn-like." Grainger described them as having high and low sweeping lines, "dancy," and often rhymed. "The words are, on the whole, *appallingly indecent, & quite impossible* to me. At any rate, they unwithstandably call up a *living picture* of a *whole type of life,* which is (to my mind) one of the loveliest powers of art."[24]

Rosher was an interesting and persistent fellow. He kept in contact with Grainger and later turned his hand to poetry, dedicating his "The Poet Boon" to William Butler Yeats on the Irishman's reception of the Nobel Prize in 1916. Growing blind and short of funds, he appealed to Grainger in 1923 to try to place some of his poems in American journals:

> If you can find a shop for it in some good American magazine it might do me some good financially & otherwise. The English as a whole are far too sordid to appreciate either poets or verse. They have perhaps heard of Shakespeare, Byron, and Kipling. The names of race-horses and halfbacks are more familiar to the mass of the unspeakable herd of Philistines.[25]

It was not only the songs of the folk singers which

impressed Grainger, but the singers themselves and their performances. In comparing them to concert singers, Grainger flatly stated:

> No concert singer I have ever heard approached these rural warblers in variety of tone-quality, range of dynamics, rhythmic resourcefulness and individuality of style. For while our concert singers (dull-dogs that they are — with their monotonous mooing and bellowing between *mf* and *ff*, and with never a *pp* to their name!) can show nothing better as slavish obedience to the tyrannical behests of composers, our folksingers were lords in their own domain — were at once performers and creators.

In essays such as "Collecting with the Phonograph," Grainger dealt not only with the music and the dialect, but also included biographical sketches of his singers. His theory that art was a total expression of the artist is clearly reflected in his approach to folk-song collecting.

Tunes were considered a type of personal property and singers guarded them jealously. It was not uncommon for a singer to devise clandestine methods in order to acquire a rival's tune. When one old woman refused to sing a tune for Grainger, he hid under her bed and noted the tune without her knowledge. Each singer had his own particular variant of a song, and no two singers would perform a given tune in the same manner. After hearing a version of a tune recorded by a rival musician, a singer observed: "I don't know if it's being fine or not — I only know it's wrong!"

In many of the rural families in England at that time, the singing of the old tunes was discouraged as exhibiting social backwardness or illiteracy. Few families would permit their elders to sing for the collectors. Because of this, Grainger found it profitable to spend his time among the residents of the local work-house, a shelter for indigents.

In Lincolnshire, where he made his first cylinder recording, Grainger met Joseph Taylor. Taylor was one of his best sources and an exception to the usual type of folk singer. He had been a choir singer for over forty-five years, and his relatives (musicians themselves) were not at all ashamed of the singing of an eighty-year-old man. Among the memorable tunes Grainger collected from Taylor were: *Brigg Fair, The Sprig of Thyme, Died for Love, Green Bushes,* and *The Pretty Maid Milking Her Cow.* The complex "Rufford Park Poachers," which later appeared as movement five of *Lincolnshire Posy,* was Taylor's property as well. Four separate variations of the tune were recorded on August 4, 1906, and all of them appear in the military band version completed by Grainger in 1937.

All of the singers, many of whom were over seventy, were proud of their songs, but Grainger often had to surmount obstacles in his quest for an unusual melody. In the summer of 1905, the matron of the work-house at Brigg asked Grainger to stop because of his subject's weak heart. Returning the next year with his phonograph, he was determined to get the tune, "dead or alive." As Grainger explained: "He might as well die singing it as die not singing it."[26] Under such circumstances, the famous "Dublin Bay" was committed to wax.

The singers were not upset by having to sing into the horn of Grainger's new machine. Rather, they took to it readily and delighted at hearing their own voices. Speaking of the phonograph, one commented: "He's learnt that quicker nor I," and another, "It do follow up we wonderful!" But Joseph Taylor complained: "It's läke singin' with a muzzle on." When, about this time, Grainger was approached by His Master's Voice to make recordings of his piano performance, he stipulated that commercial pressings of the singing of Joseph Taylor be issued as well, and that they be kept available. Grainger personally escorted Taylor, then in his eighties, to the London studios of the record company.

Folk song collecting was one of Grainger's greatest

personal accomplishments and his enthusiasm for collecting carried over into everything he did. In the fall of 1907, he spent a day with the woman who had been his governess in Melbourne between his fourth and twelfth birthdays. "I enthused both her and her uncle to help me in folk song collecting."[27] However, it is quite unlikely that the two ever took to the field. By 1908 Grainger had interviewed countless English and Scottish singers and transcribed some five hundred of their songs.

The Running Pianist

In 1906 Edvard Grieg was invited to conduct a series of concerts of his music in London. As guests of Sir Edgar and Lady Speyer, he was asked whom he would most like to meet and his reply, "Grainger," came as a shock to his sophisticated hosts. Although Grainger had acquired a reputation as a remarkable pianist, his circle of friends, combined with his eccentric off-stage behavior, set him apart from the Speyers' social circle. Nevertheless, the Norwegian's wishes were respected and the exuberant Australian was summoned.

Grainger was familiar with Grieg's music, having been presented a copy of the Norwegian's folk songs (*Op. 66*) a few years earlier by Herman Sandby. It is evident that Grieg was familiar with Grainger's compositions, for Grainger had received an autographed portrait from the Norwegian as an acknowledgment of the gift of several choral pieces presented to him by Sandby. At their initial meeting, Percy performed Grieg's *Opus 66* and the difficult *Slaater, Op. 72*. Grieg was astonished at the young pianist's ability and reacted by writing to the European press about his impressions of Grainger:

I wrote Norwegian Peasant Dances that none

of my own countrymen could play. Here comes this young Australian, and is the first to play them as they ought to be played. He has the true folksong poetry in him, and yet it is quite a way from Australia to Norway! Percy Grainger is a genius, such as we Scandinavians must love.[28]

Privately, Grieg reaffirmed his assessment of Grainger with his diary entry on October 3: "When he played . . . my teeth were set on edge. Why in all the world does Percy Grainger, an Australian, play these things perfectly in rhythm and modulation while a Norwegian cannot grasp either? It's quite the wrong way 'round."[29]

Immediately the two men became friends, and before departing from London, Grieg invited Grainger to "Trold-haugen," his home near Bergen, for the following summer. In addition, Grainger was asked to perform Grieg's *Piano Concerto* at Leeds in the fall of 1907, with a tour of the European capitals immediately following. Grieg would conduct.

The 1906-07 concert season was not a profitable one for Grainger. Except for an English tour with Ada Crossley, for which he was poorly paid, the few engagements that came his way meant long hours and each became more laborious than the previous one. Although Grieg's support would accelerate the demand for his services, it would be almost a full year before these effects would be financially profitable to Grainger. That fall, he wrote to his friend Karen:

Those bloody British kept me working up to nearly 3 o'clock last night, playing and playing. I felt so frightened and tired, and they seemed so loathsomely fresh and gluttenous, and as if they'd been sleeping all the day. How I hate the English at moments; the society folk are such grabbers. One needs one's fullest strength to cope with them. They were very sweet of

course, but I felt near to the knife, I can tell
you!"[30]

In the spring of 1907, he confided in Karen once again:
"Money matters are worrying me deeply just now. I have
hardly any concert engagements for this summer and not
many pupils. I fear the society folks are sick of me and if
it were not for Ada's tour I'd be what we Australians call
'up a gum'!"[31] Even in his relationships with fellow musicians his frayed nerves were apparent. After meeting the
Russian conductor, Safanov, he complained: "He ran down
Debussy to me for a good solid hour."[32] But the young,
aggressive Grainger tackled society anew in an attempt to
"re- & newly-popularize myself. I want to make goodest
efforts, and feel quite glad at and tolerable fit for the
game."[33]

Money was becoming important to Grainger — not the
money itself, but rather the defense it would give him
against the injustices he felt from the moneyed class of
London. Across the face of a program he had given for a
rather select London audience, he wrote:

> When I'm rich (if?) I'm going to once put in a
> season in London like a mere society creature,
> and go to all the homes and listen to the other
> beggars sweating. And then, I love to meet and
> know titled rich people. I feast on the smell of
> money and power, and feel such a ripping snob —
> I am a shocking snob.[34]

The professional salon circuit in London in which Grainger found himself ensnared, often demanded more of the
performer than mere musical performance. One "Mrs. L."
whom Cyril Scott described as having been an elderly,
emotional woman with somewhat projecting teeth, was
unhappily married to a gambler and inebriant. She would
"console herself in the charm of this golden-haired & talented Adonis [Grainger]. She had been kind to him and one
day she demanded that he should be kind to her — and
while her husband was snoring in the next bedroom at

that." Later, when "Grainger told me [Scott] that he had gratified this highly unattractive woman, I was dumbfounded and wonder'd how on earth he had contrived to do so."[35]

The performance with Grieg at the coming Leeds Festival concerned Grainger daily, and in April he received the preliminary acknowledgment: "Just heard from the Leeds Festival people so that's going to come off, I think: dear old darling Grieg."[36]

The lack of engagements was nothing more than a financial inconvenience to Grainger. Public appearances were merely a source of income and although he enjoyed playing the concerts when he once started, he preferred to spend his time composing. In seclusion he found his greatest happiness.

> . . . Such a stirring and rich week. The last 5 days (Wed., Thurs., Fri.) I've been putting in from 8 to 12 hours composing daily on an old work of mine (started in 1901) called "Hillsong." It was this work that Busoni thought by far my most strong, original and worthful style, but then he is not a sentimentalist, like me, & feels rather thru his head, so I don't know how far he's to be trusted. But I think it's 1 of the very richest in "herzblut" of all my stuff. The original version of it (lengthy & vastly full of minute work) was not a possible thing at all, as it was a helter skelter jumble of two quite unblendable styles, each of these 2 styles is now (sooner or later) to be worked up into a separate Hillsong; 1, *slow*, for strings (& maybe a few voices as well.) This is the one I wrote of sketching for in my last letter, & 2, *fast & wild*, for woodwind & maybe a trifle brass.
>
> This fast Hillsong, that I am now at, is one of my toughest form-problems, & the instrumentation for reeds only is dead surely the hardest thing I've tried yet & working at it strains me more than anything. Each night I've wanted to write you of my happiness working, but each

night I felt too fogged for it to be any use, &
how much more I'm deserving than I'm getting.[37]

It may have been through Busoni that Grainger became
familiar with the music of Frederick Delius; Busoni and
Delius had studied composition together in Leipzig in 1886
and afterward had maintained a strong friendship. In 1907
Grainger met Frederick Delius in London. Delius' amenuen-
sis felt that "These two, though so different, seemed to
have a strong attraction for each other and a very real
admiration for each other's musical gifts."[38] This friendship proved to be a source of inspiration to both men and
lasted until Delius' death in 1934. Their literary and musical tastes were nearly identical, as Grainger explained:

> Our outlook on life was very similar, our artistic
> tastes met at many points. Both of us consid-
> ered the Icelandic sagas the pinnacle of narrative
> prose. Both of us knew the Scandinavian lan-
> guages and admired the culture of Scandinavia
> as the flower of Europeanism. Both of us wor-
> shipped Walt Whitman, Wagner, Grieg, and Jens
> Peter Jacobsen. Both of us detested the music
> of the Haydn-Mozart-Beethoven period.[39]

The subject of folk songs greatly interested both men,
and Grainger played his 1905 wax cylinder recording of
Joseph Taylor singing *Brigg Fair* for Delius. He then presented a setting he had made for tenor solo and humming
chorus and gave Delius permission to use the tune if he
should so choose. Grainger knew that Delius was not the
type of man to collect folk tunes in the field and would
not appreciate a tune unless it was harmonized. The result
was *Brigg Fair, An English Rhapsody*, written later that
year and dedicated to Grainger. The premier, conducted by
Sir Thomas Beecham at Queen's Hall in 1908 was attended
by both Percy and Joseph Taylor, then a guest at Percy's
flat. That evening the two men and Rose Grainger were
accompanied by Everad Fielding, Lady Winefried Carey,
and Gervase Elwes' brother. During the performance, Tay-

lor, struck by the familiarity of his tune and ignoring the
formal surroundings, delighted the audience by singing
along with the orchestra. The piece was enthusiastically
received by both its collector and its previous owner.

Grainger's tendency to emphasize his personal role as an
innovator in musical affairs was often carried to illogical
lengths. Criticizing Delius for not wishing to collect his
own folk tunes, Grainger wrote, "it had not occurred to
him [Delius] to write *Song of the Hills* until he had heard
my two *Hill Songs*."[40] Yet Grainger gives no credit to
Delius for his tone poem, *Over the Hills and Far Away*,
which antedates, by twenty-three years, Grainger's *Children's March, Over the Hills and Far Away*.

The friendship that existed between Delius and Grainger
was mutually beneficial, especially for Delius, as Percy
began to insist that if he was to appear as soloist, conductors must program Delius' music. Even Mengelberg and the
Concertgebouw Orchestra would acquiesce in order to secure the services of the popular pianist. It was to be Grainger who would convince Delius to flee France to avoid the
approaching war, wanting Delius to join him in America,
but Delius would choose England.

Grainger was looking forward to his next meeting with
Grieg and the study of the concerto. He was impressed that
the highly-regarded Norwegian would be interested in
him. Writing to Karen, he explained his pleasure: "How
splendid it is when important folk like old Grieg are thoroughly untyrannical and never force their opinion down
one's throat."

In July of 1907, Rose Grainger traveled to Norway to
visit friends while Percy proceeded to Bergen, stopping
for a few days in Copenhagen to visit Karen. Grieg's asthma
was troublesome during the whole of Grainger's visit, but
it did not deter the Norwegian from physical exercise. Since
Grieg could not walk and speak simultaneously, it was
necessary for him to stop during the hike in order to make

a remark. On August 3, he and Grainger hiked to a mountain top near Bergen. After reaching the top, Grieg stopped to praise the glorious view: "Here we need a peasant fiddle to play a dance for us." Turning to descend, Grieg prophetically declared, "I shall never get up here again."[41]

The deepening friendship between these two musicians was due to their many common interests and achievements; the absence of an imposing masculine figure in Grainger's life may have contributed as well. Percy's interest in the North, aroused and nurtured by his mother's readings, was by now a creed of superiority which dominated his future. Grainger's study of the Scandinavian languages had been initiated to allow him to read its medieval literature in the original and Grieg's nationalistic bent did not go unnoticed by the Australian. Perhaps most important, Grainger found a sympathetic voice in Grieg. Here was a man whose stature was greater than either Busoni or Knorr, yet a man who found significant merit in Percy's creative efforts. "Let me put it this way," Percy concluded, "If I say that Grieg's music is cloudberries with cream, then my own music is apple pie."

Grainger, with his limitless energies, managed to complete *Soldier, Soldier*, although the rehearsal of the piano concerto occupied the greater share of the two musicians' time. The Grainger edition of the Grieg Concerto, which Schirmer released in 1920, shows the result of these two weeks work. Grainger meticulously marked alterations and suggestions by placing them into three categories: (1) those written into his own score by Grieg in 1907, (2) those suggested by himself and approved by Grieg, and (3) those of a technical nature not submitted to Grieg.

The Norwegian composer, as a rule, showed little sympathy toward performers. In his diary of April 4, 1907, he made a sweeping indictment:

> These soloists! They should be exterminated!
> One should induce them to kill each other off.

Egotists one and all. Themselves first, with
Art a bad second.[42]

But Grainger was the exception. Grieg's diary contains
many complimentary entries about the Australian who
possessed this unusual command of piano technique.

Julius Röntgen, the Dutch composer, was visiting Grieg
at the same time as Percy, and the presence of these two
greatly cheered the ailing Norwegian. Describing these
days, Grieg wrote:

On the morning of the 25th Percy Grainger arrived and I had the great joy of bringing these
two splendid men together — for I knew they
would understand one another. Few musicians
possess the wide artistic vision that Julius has.
In spite of all the exoticness of Grainger's talent,
Röntgen at once sensed its significance, and he
listened to Grainger's music with enthusiasm
— to his masterly and deeply original folk song
settings.

For my own part, I must say this: That I
had to become 64 years old before I could hear
Norwegian piano music rendered with such
genius and understanding. In playing my Peasant Dances and Norwegian Folksongs as he
does, Grainger is blazing a new trail for himself, for me, and for Norway. And then his de-
liciously natural, profound, serious and yet
childlike, personality. To have won such a young
friend — what joy! In it I could forget the in-
firmities of my body, were they not emphasized
all to clearly by the contrast between his condition and mine. He is *crescendo*. I am *diminuendo*.
And to view this fact objectively is difficult.[43]

During his stay at Troldhagen, Grainger demonstrated
to his host many of the folk songs he had collected with
his wax cylinder phonograph. The Norwegian was impressed with the method and expressed regretfully that
no one had done a similar service for Norway. Although
Grieg utilized folk songs in the same way as many of his
contemporaries, his approach was quite different than

Grainger's. Discussing his *Ballade, Op. 24*, the composer admitted that the source of the tune was a rowdy drinking song with words to match, although the mood of the composition did not reflect this origin. Explaining, Grieg remarked: "This is the difference between you and me, in our approach to folksong. You approach it as a scientist, while I still approach it wholly as a romanticist."[44] Grieg believed that through folksongs England might achieve a distinct national style and Grainger was leading the way. In one of his last letters, Grieg wrote:

> Thanks for your post-card! But above all else thanks for the days you gave us! I had wanted so much to get to know you more nearly, both as an artist and as a man, as I had the feeling that we would understand each other. And so it turned out. You have become a dear young friend to me, who has made more rich for me the evening of my life. I have always found that they are mistaken who would divide the artist from the man; on the contrary, the two are indissolubly wedded one to the other. In the man can be found the parallels of all the artist's traits. (Yes even the most minute.) Even your stubborn "unnecessary fifths" (!) I could recognize again in my dear Percy Grainger! Not that I cherish the least doubt that they will sound well in your choral treatment.
>
> I have again immersed myself in your folksong settings and I see more and more clearly how "genial" they are. In them you have thrown a clear light upon how the English folk-song (to my mind so different to the Scotch and Irish) is worthy of the privilege of being lifted up into the "niveau" of Art; thereby to create an independent English Music. The folk-songs will doubtless be able to form the basis for a national style, as they have done in other lands, those of the greatest musical culture not excepted. I am impressed by the earnestness and energy with which the English "Folk-Song

Society" carries out its object. May it ever enjoy fresh increase of strength and enthusiasm to pursue its goal! And may you, in the midst of all your other rich activities (the most important for you and your art) be able to afford time and strength for the inclusion of your personality in the endeavor!

And herewith a hearty greeting, also to your Mother.[45]

Grieg died a few weeks later and Grainger was to have the distinction of being one of his last guests. Reflecting on these weeks with Grieg, Percy wrote in his diary:

It was lucky for me that Grieg did not live to hear me play his concerto before an audience. It was a boon indeed that my fame-rich friend did not have to withdraw his high praise words about me.[46]

Percy believed that he was unable to perform the octaves at the end of the first movement quite as fast as Busoni; he was certain that Grieg would have preferred the latter.

Various authors give Grieg credit for instilling in Grainger his love of folk songs, but the responsibility for the original interest must, in part at least, be attributed to Herman Sandby. In 1928, Grainger dedicated to Sandby a setting of the Danish folk song, *The Nightingale*. He recognized that Sandby had taught him "already in 1900, to know and love the Danish folk song."[47] In 1905, prior to meeting Grieg, Percy had become a member of the English Folk Song Society. Four songs he collected in Lincolnshire were published in the *Journal* of the Society that year. His early interest in Danish folk music is evidenced also by his meeting in 1905 with Hjalmar Thuren, a specialist in folk songs from the Faroe Islands. Percy inquired about printed sources for original Danish folk songs, and was told of the publications of Evald Tang Kristensen, a Danish folklorist. Thuren arranged a meeting of Grainger and Kristensen. In 1922, 1925, and 1927, with the aid of Percy's wax cylinder phonograph, they collected nearly two hundred

folk songs from the Jutland peninsula. Grainger's respect
for non-western culture and primitive art forms, already
evident on these early tours, was the result of his identi-
fication with the old Teutonic tribes and their roots in the
land; folk song collecting was merely a search for these
roots.

In 1909 Delius consented to join with Sir Edward Elgar in forming a league of British Music, if Grainger's
music would be included at the first festival. It was in
such a setting that Grainger's *Irish Tune from County
Derry* and *Brigg Fair* were first performed in Liverpool.
Except for some small choruses sung at rural competition
festivals, this was the first time that Grainger heard a
formal performance of his own work.

The *Irish Tune* was generally well-received, but Sir
Charles Stanford was not convinced of its Gaelic treat-
ment. "It's Grieg, my lad, not Irish," remarked Stanford.
When Carl Fischer later offered L200 for it, Percy wrote
Stanford inquiring if he should accept and Sir Charles
responded that there was no reason to refuse the offer.
Grainger lamented that Stanford's letter was "like a man
writing to one who had deeply disappointed him."[48]

Although several of Grainger's major works had been
written by this time, he claimed that their public performance had been delayed intentionally. He explained:

> This condition of being unperformed was of
> my own choosing. Both my parents were in-
> valids [see below] and my first interest in life
> was to be able to provide for them and their
> comfort, which I feared would be upset if my
> compositions (with their irregular rhythms,
> endless chains of unresolved dischords, and
> monotonous form-lengths — things then un-
> heard of) were performed and aroused great
> opposition.[49]

Grainger frequently repeated the statement that his
parents were invalids, and, indeed, both John and Rose

suffered from syphilis. But while Percy did support Rose, he would have had no obligation to support his father until the last year of his life when paralysis forced him to retire from his career as an architect. In addition to this, Rose herself (as early as 1902) attempted to persuade Percy to seek public approval of his music.

> As you are experimenting with new ideas in music, you yourself must prove to the world that they are practical. If you don't prove it yourself, nobody else will. Bach and Wagner are about the most famous of composers, and they both financed concerts of their own music, and showed the world how their music should be conducted.[50]

The severe criticism he had received from his Frankfurt composition professor may have been the real reason Grainger was reluctant to offer many of his writings to the public. Later, he wrote: "I don't want to offend European ideas yet because I'm so poor."[51]

Residence in London was confining for Grainger and he became restless. He often spoke of his homeland with nostalgia. "Now it's summer," he wrote to Karen, "And the rich-rotten are dressing voluptuously and the beer-swillers are sweating ruddily, readily. How I love the warmth! London reminds me today of Sydney and its small, dark, gay-tired, somewhat Irish folk."[52]

Grainger's formative years in Australia had left an indelible mark on him — resulting not only in nostalgic memories but in some deep-seated personality-traits as well. Since Rose was always determined to mold him into a famous pianist, his childhood had been severe. As a result of the frequent beatings given to him, Percy began to delight in inflicting pain, and receiving it seemed to reassure him of his manliness. One early manifestation of this tendency resulted in his "savagely kicking the Bruce's cat around the room."[53] But more volatile forms of release were found as he grew older, and his regular girl friends seemed tolerant of most of his wishes.

In 1908-09 Grainger returned to Australia with the Crossley troupe. His penchant for hiking came to the attention of the Australian press when he walked the forty-six miles between Yarram and Sile in eleven and one-half hours. He had negotiated shorter walks during his first Crossley tour, but had escaped the publicity.

At stops in New Zealand and the South Sea Islands, he pursued his interest in folk music. He added examples of Rarotongan and Maori music to his collection, photographed and sketched the natives, and gathered samples of their art and communal culture. When, however, he began to collect whips and similar types of objects, it became clear that his fascination with the Maori tribes was not wholly musical or cultural. In 1909, he wrote Karen about some of the souvenirs from this second Crossley tour and described these items as "stinging gloriously . . . wherever there is intensity, glad madness, wild energy, swooning joys, ecstatic agonies, there is God." He was later to confide, "I love to think of women being hurt."[54]

Whether transcribing English folk songs or Maori music, he was enthusiastically received and most reluctantly dismissed. And he thought it was not at all unusual to sit an entire evening in a native hut, recording traditional music, and then dine with the white governor the following day.

Grainger later described the Maori people as "the most artistic race I've met," and spent time photographing and sketching the natives and collecting beadwork and necklaces. Not unlike his folk song collecting in England, Grainger attempted to record all aspects of the people, music being only a small portion of his interest. This extended as well to their burial customs, for he admitted that the "whole being of folk art is closely akin to all manner of racial and artistic burials."[55]

Rose accompanied her son as far as Melbourne where

she stayed with relatives. Almost daily she wrote to him, administering guide lines for his dress, conduct, and general health. "On no account lend any money...I am like in prison when you're away...Telegraph me at once if you are ill in that hateful place [West Australia]... Oh, how I hate men that drink — they are worse than any animal — loathsome creatures!"[56]

Percy saw his father again that year (1909), but the details of their meeting are not recorded. Rose wrote from Melbourne speaking graciously of her husband: "Tell father how happy I am about him and his continued good health & success."[57] The intermittent meetings of Percy and his father continued to be cordial and there appeared to be a warmth of respect between them. However, it was more of a relationship of colleagues than that of father and son. Percy later stated that "my associations with my father were never revolting or terrible," as some had suggested. "He was always pleasant and kindly. That he drank himself into disaster, gave syphilis to my mother, we always regarded as bad luck on his part and never held it against him."[58] Rose's offer of a divorce brought no response from John. She was ready to admit that it was she who had deserted. "If you have found someone you like and would like to marry," she wrote, "I will never stand in your way. You can have a divorce anytime you like. You can get it for desertion and I will never contest it."[59]

That same year, Melba engaged John Grainger to design her retirement cottage near Melbourne. He was not chosen because he had known her father or because Percy had been her friend — only because she believed him to be the best man for the job. His vision of a large, one-story house with wide verandas built on an already existing structure, became the design of the Coombe Cottage.

Percy's attachment to his homeland was detailed in his many letters to Karen describing its cities, deserts, and animal life. Examining the independence of the people, he noted that:

> The Captain of the ship (in dock) was requested
> by a passenger to speak to several young la-
> dies, reprimanding them for bathing nude along-
> side the ship. In response to his long verbal
> lashing, one girl "stood up like Venus rising
> from the water," and called to the Captain: "If
> you see anything here God didn't make, throw
> your cap at it!"[60]

Although Percy was psychologically revived by his tour
of Australia, he did not feel that he was earning as much
as he should and wrote Karen regarding a forthcoming
Danish trip: "Alas, it seems I shall earn next to nothing
this year so let's shake *all we possibly can* out of Denmark."[61] And his mother advised: "You must accept no
more tours — perform from now on alone."[62]

After returning to England, Grainger's career as a performer began to take shape. Public acclaim for the young
artist grew and his company was sought by the famous,
the would-be famous, and friends. When Rose allotted his
time in twenty-minute intervals, many of his friends refused to visit him complaining that his schedule was too
like a dentist's office. An invitation to dinner at Bellini's
with Paderewski was delayed two weeks. "Paderewski
asked me to dine out tonight," Percy wrote, "But I can't.
I have something else on."[63] Percy did not approve of the
pianist and later scolded Scott for their friendship, admon-
ishing, "I begged you not to curry favor with molting eagles
such as Paderewski."[64] Other famous admirers included
George Bernard Shaw, Richard Strauss, and the Duchess
of Sutherlands (who placed Grainger next to Rodin whenever he came to dinner). He was a keen judge of his audience and knew the art of programming. At a performance
at Buckingham Palace, he once offered a set of Danish
folk songs as an encore. The dowager, Queen Alexandra,
was delighted with the reference to her homeland and "sent
around a gold and diamond tie-pin" on the following day.

By the end of 1909, Grainger's career as a pianist was firmly established. After the difficult climb, he had reached a point where he could dictate his programs and his tours. He confided in Karen again: "I have never before lived thru such coming glory — the whole year has schemed to draw now to perfection."[65]

One of Grainger's closest friends, though an outsider to the Frankfurt Group, was the portraitist, John Singer Sargent. Some of the early introductions in London which matured into remunerative engagements were results of Sargent's connections. In 1910, the artist did a charcoal drawing of Percy which later became his most popular likeness. Sargent's aggressive and anti-social nature encouraged Grainger to be boldly controversial. This encouragement was hardly necessary. "Shake them like rats," offered Sargent, and Percy's personality exploded on the Victorian concert public. "He knocked them all into cocked hats."

Percy was always considerate and seemed especially concerned with the less fortunate. In one instance, he even retrieved the hat of a garbage collector, who replied in amazement: "Thank you Gouv'ner, but it's just my little sun bonnet." Grainger's acquaintances were all fond of him, but each had their individual ways of describing his uninhibited nature. Ethyl Smyth felt that he "was by 'Messiah' out of cake-walk,"[66] but Lady Speyer was known to have remarked, "Every town has its village idiot, Percy, and you're London's!"[67]

Grainger seldom received an uncomplimentary review, but he was constantly critical of his own performances. On one occasion, when he was engaged by Lady Charles Berenford, Melba and Edouard Reisler were present. Grainger was very dissatisfied with his performance and he wrote: "It does make me so sick to do real bad. But Reisler is a dear, although I played shockingly, he was so sweet and kind, like all great folk are."[68]

Grainger's strong democratic approach to life gave him distinct political viewpoints, but (in spite of his uninhibited nature) he usually kept his ideas from the public. On one occasion, however, he became publicly involved in a political question. In July of 1910, he circulated a petition among the leading musicians of London expressing approval of a bill for Women's Sufferage. It is quite likely that Ethyl Smyth, the active sufferagette and composer-friend of Percy's, was responsible for his involvement.

Well to the Fore

The premier of Percy's *English Dance* occurred in 1911 in a performance at the Palladium under Beecham. This work was the largest example, to date, of Grainger's idea of non-repetition of themes, or as Cyril Scott had labeled it, "the great flow." Beecham was not sympathetic to the composer or his music and in the future their meetings were never cordial.

There were two major concert series in the spring of the following year that brought the Grainger name, as a composer, dramatically before the London public. Now, his already substantial fame as a performer would extend to the field of composition. A series of four concerts was presented in April and May of 1912 under the title, "The Balfour Gardiner Choral and Orchestral Concerts." These programs drew the interest of both musicians and patrons:

> To keep abreast of modern music Elgar looked
> in at one of Balfour Gardiner's rehearsals, the
> newest works then being undertaken coming
> from Delius, Bax, Grainger, and John Ireland.[69]

The days of the Balfour Gardiner concerts were happy ones for the Frankfurt Group. Gardiner had a town house in Kennsington, where the group would meet to go over the scores, plan the programs, and discuss developing styles of composition. Grainger would play his own pieces while Bax, with his "unrivaled power of score-reading" would usually play the compositions of the other members. The Frankfurt Group, its forces marshalled and inspired by Cyril Scott, was financially supported by Balfour Gardiner. Although Gardiner was producing the concert series, Grainger was quick to offer the advice of a seasoned performer. He insisted that Balfour distribute enough free tickets to fill the hall and, if necessary, "even turn some late-comers away."

Only contemporary British works were performed; in most instances, the composer conducted. Some of the distinguished composers included Cyril Scott, Sir Hamilton Harty, Norman O'Neill, Balfour Gardiner, John Ireland, Arnold Bax, Ralph Vaughan Williams, Frederick Delius, and Percy Grainger. Although not participating formally, Gustav Holst was often in attendance.

It was the performance of Grainger's *Father and Daughter* during this series (later repeated at the London Chorale Society) that brought to Cecil Forsyth's attention Grainger's unique scoring for guitars. Forsyth devoted a chapter in his orchestration manual to Grainger's use of these specialized instruments. Unfortunately, he did not examine the entire body of the manuscripts which Grainger had completed by this time, for the search would have revealed the compositional innovations for which Percy later became known.

On May 21, a few weeks after the successful first series, E.L. Robinson, Grainger's London manager, arranged a concert of Percy's music in London's Aeolian Hall. The array and quality of the assisting singers and musicians, borrowed in part from the recent Gardiner concerts, were impressive. They included: Frederick Austin, baritone; Gervase Elwes, tenor; Charles Draper, clarinetist; Eugene

Goosens ably assisted the string quartet on second violin. Composers Roger Quilter and Balfour Gardiner lent their support as well. The program consisted primarily of several *British Folk Music Settings* that Grainger had scored with small chamber music accompaniment. Included also were *Died for Love, Six Dukes went a-fishin', Molly on the Shore, My Robin is to the Greenwood Gone, Walking Tune,* and *Scotch Strathspey and Reel.* Rose Grainger contributed her services on guitar.

The London *Times* generally applauded the evening, but disagreed with Grainger in his attempts to distinguish between his own music and that which came from traditional sources. "But the whole instrumental part of the concert had the disadvantage of a joke which its author finds inexhaustible. One had to be in very high spirits to keep on enjoying it."[70] A few weeks earlier the same paper had spoken glowingly of *Mock Morris* when it was performed on the Gardiner series. Describing it as "extraordinarily exhilarating," the critic went on to add that "there is not one bar, one note, or one mark of expression which could be sacrificed without loss to the vigour of the piece."

The scheduling of the first all-Grainger concert was well planned, as it followed the initial success of the Gardiner concerts, but the extent of its success was not envisioned. Grainger would no longer remain just a pianist.

That same month, John Grainger arrived in London while on a leave of absence from his post in Western Australia. Although his arrival coincided with his son's concerts, no one knows whether or not he attended them. But he did accompany Rose and Percy to a music hall to see the Scottish comedian-singer, Harry Lauder, perform.

Gardiner's second series, presented in February and March of the following year, brought these unique concerts to an end. Rather than be involved in an unpleasant dispute over wages with some of the orchestra players, Gardiner cancelled the series. There is no question that

Grainger's compositions stirred the greatest interest. One of those in attendance later wrote to Grainger: "I was present at the Balfour Gardiner Concerts when your works knocked us all sideways! What a reception they got!"

It was on this second series that Grainger conducted the first performance of his *Colonial Song*, scored for soprano, tenor, harp, and orchestra. A curious addition to this program was the "first performance" of *Hill Song,* scored for 15 woodwinds, 8 brass, and 5 percussion. As there is no known manuscript of any *Hill Song* in this particular setting, it is most certain that this was a try out of *No. 2* with the saxophone parts being written for brass. *Hill Song No. 1,* written in 1901, was scored almost exclusively for double reeds; *Hill Song No. 2* (1907) was scored for 20 woodwinds, 4 brass, and cymbal. Grainger, however, later gave credit to Basil Cameron for the 1929 premier of *Hill Song No. 2.* That this 1913 performance was of a third *Hill Song* is quite unlikely, since Grainger meticulously saved manuscripts and detailed when and where pieces were written and rewritten.

Throughout their years in England, Rose Grainger was never far from her son. Her health, periodically shaken by the syphilitic condition contracted earlier from her husband, caused her much inconvenience. As might be expected, this disease had been a central issue in the break-up of her marriage. Although its severity would not become apparent until her later years, its recurring effects incapacitated her from time to time — even as early as the years in Frankfurt. Rose's energies, however, were still comparable to her son's.

Rose had become a shrewd manipulator of Percy's career. His will was completely subservient to hers. Together, in the flat they shared at 31 King's Cross Road, even their limited diets were identical. Eggs, milk, bread, butter, and jam were the main diet items with raw fruits, nuts, meat, chicken, cold tongue, and porridge rice taken to break the routine. Rose was partial to George Washington coffee, but Percy abstained. His diet became more restrictive, his physique remained lean, and his exercise was vigorous.

Rose was careful to expose her son to people who could help his career. She may have been referring to Brahm's favorite clarinetist when she wrote in 1907: "Make friends with dear old Muhlfeld — Return his very kind greetings to me."[71] It seems likely that they may have met in Frankfurt during Percy's student days. Rose attended all the fashionable concerts and lectures, but by choice remained without close personal friends. One of her favorite memories was a lecture by George Bernard Shaw, ushered in by a Bach prelude and fugue; and she had been "crazy with delight" at Max Beerbohm's *A Christmas Garland.* "I shall never feel at home here," she spoke of London, "All is sham."[72] Although she began to collect English furniture and woodcarvings, her dominant interest continued to be reading and she, like her father, read omnivorously.

Rose had become disenchanted with Roger Quilter, of whom she had been so fond, for he had promised to publish some of Percy's music when he came into money. Later, "he only offered excuses." She referred to him as a "half-friend" but he and Percy remained close.

In 1908 she had met Fauré at Sargent's salon when the artist brought him from Paris to perform for an audience of dowagers. She had, of course, met Grieg and attended his London concerts. She even performed the guitar accompaniment in several performances of Percy's *Scotch Strathspey and Reel.*

Both she and Percy frequented the music halls; they were especially fond of Harry Lauder. And when she accompanied Percy on continental tours, which she often did, it was not unusual for her to join her son in visiting a bawdy show or two. Her behavior was not at all unusual when you consider that she had been an Australian tomboy.

Rose had little control over Percy's choice of female

companions, yet she did manage to frustrate any attempt to ensnare her son in marriage. As Cyril Scott described him, Percy was "a lion of the lion-huntresses." Women flocked to his concerts, but Percy somehow remained aloof.

His confidante during these years was Karen Holten. They maintained regular correspondence relating daily activities. Many of his most private thoughts were reserved for her. When he was scheduled to meet Fauré he spoke of his apprehension to Karen rather than his mother. "Play Tschaikovsky at Queens Hall in the afternoon and meet Fauré in the evening — pray for me on both occasions." "I wonder if you realize how often men have striven in music to reproduce the sexual climaxes," he wrote. "The whole Tristan Prelude is an attempt at this and is, I think, photographically accurate — you listen once to it from that standpoint."[73] Karen seemed to have an understanding of the musician which did not exist in either his mother or his Frankfurt friends. Reflecting on his unusual arrangement with Karen, he later wrote: "My Danish sweetheart was strong and kind and with her I was happy for 8 years — except that I hardly ever saw her."[74]

In the steady flow of letters between them, marriage was not an item overlooked — at least not by Karen. Percy's response was frank and pragmatic: "My brain doesn't see wisdom in marriage for me." And later, more explicit, he added, "It would never enter my head to do so [marry] because I don't believe in such things."[75]

In 1913 Percy briefly departed from these declarations to become betrothed to Margo Harrison, an English girl. She was the daughter of a successful London businessman and had been a pupil of Percy's since 1911. He did not attempt to hide his intentions from Karen, and wrote her on the very day of the engagement: "It is gloomy enough, but I am engaged to Margot Harrison." In reflecting on these developments Grainger admitted that "after breaking with Karen, I stood at the window of the second floor, thinking of whether I should take my life or not."[76]

The engagement with Harrison soon came to an end, for Percy seemed unable to convince himself that marriage was to be considered. He gave two reasons: "The root of the matter is obviously the relation of me and my mother ...One thing's certain, if mother and I were parted often or much, we'd mope, that's all." The second reason he gave exposes a serious aspect of his self-concept: "No woman would want her child to look like me — my body, yes, but not my inner self."[77] Grainger knew that his fascination with physical pain was not a normal drive, but he believed that his role as an artist granted him license to follow his individual expressions. It was common knowledge among his friends, many of whom had unusual deviations themselves, that his feminine companions were expected to submit to his demands. He was known to have practiced with his souvenir whips on one girl in Hyde Park after lightly binding her to a tree.

A packet of letters, dating from July of that year, hint at the insecurity of the proposed union with Margot. One letter from Margot's mother admonished Percy for having sent "such a rude letter" to her daughter, but she continued: "Everything will be all right as soon as you are married. May I suggest you get married as soon as possible?" Subsequent letters from his fiancee exhibited alternating happiness and depression. On July 28, Grainger received the final correspondence from the Harrison family — a telegram from the father: "Grainger: Coming up this afternoon. Must see you on important business. Harrison."[78]

Following the break in his engagement, Rose had her son read aloud works of the Irish author, Stephens. These works were better balm than the Bible, "that awful depressing book," she remarked. Percy immediately began work on *The Bride's Tragedy*, a double chorus set to the words of Swinburn. "I felt it was describing my case — the young man who loses his sweetheart because his mother delays him."[79] Although there is no documentation of Rose Grainger's influence, there can be little doubt that she was involved in the final decision.

Between 1910 and 1914, Grainger annually averaged over 150 concerts in journeys to Denmark, Norway, Holland, Germany, Russia, and Finland. He performed with the famed Concertgebouw in Amsterdam under Mengelberg, with the Gurzenich in Cologne, and with the St. Petersburg Orchestra under Siloti. Ada Crossley, with whom Grainger had made two earlier Australian tours, occasionally appeared on his programs, but her offerings were limited to Grainger's compositions.

Rose accompanied her son, collecting embroidery, woodcarvings, and relics. In Russia they attended current stage productions of Oscar Wilde, Tolstoy, and Ibsen, and were struck by the oriental lavishment of the Hermitage Palace in their visit to Petrograd. In Kristiania they observed *slaater* playing by peasant fiddlers and heard the writer Hermann Bang read from his novels and stories. They were present when Sibelius conducted his orchestral compositions in Finland, were amused by a humorous film in Copenhagen, and applauded a production of Strindberg's *Totentanz* in Berlin. When time permitted they studied the Icelandic, Danish, and Maori languages. Rose felt better than she had for years; the climate of the North appealed to her and it was more beautiful than she had remembered.

Actual sums meant little to Grainger although he expressed interest in making money. Rose guarded the finances and Percy was only to continue earning. "Mother trained me to think about the ability to earn," he remarked, "not about the money itself."[80] Many years later, his wife would conclude that "I have married a veritable money-machine." Often he was paid in cash but would immediately post the sum to his mother if she were not with him. Packing his duffel bag for a return to Holland, Percy once discovered a large quantity of money left from a previous trip. Rose had trained him well.

It was customary for Grainger to perform encores after a successful program. In Holland, after an especially well-received appearance in February of 1911, he returned to the piano for the second encore when the curtain suddenly began to descend; the stage manager had not been informed of the additional selections. As the curtain reached the floor of the stage, the energetic pianist looked laughingly at the audience from beneath it, cautioning them not to leave for he had several more pieces to perform.

In 1912 Grainger visited the Ethnological Museum at Leyden, Holland. There his interest was renewed in the exotic music of the East, which had begun when he first heard a Japanese troupe in the Melbourne Bazaar. The Javanese percussion instruments were of special interest to him, and unusual percussion effects began to find their way into his orchestral scores. D.C. Parker, as early as 1915, predicted that "One of his great desires is to arouse an interest in the possibilities of percussion instruments."[81] And Eugene Goossens observed that Percy had acquired a variety of exotic percussion instruments during his Australian tours.

Experimental composition occupied more of his time, and during this Dutch tour he began what has proved to be one of the earliest pieces of music based on strict aleatoric principles. Inspired by the improvisational Rarotongan folk songs he had encountered in the South Seas, Grainger scored *Random Round* for a few voices, guitars, and mandoline, "to which could be added marimbaphone, strings, and wind instruments." It was composed in sections designated A, B, etc., each of which was divided into 10-20 variants labeled A1, A2, etc.; "each bar of each variant being composed in such a manner that it would form some sort of a harmonic whole when performed together with any bar of any or all of the other variants of the same selection."[82]

With a background ostinato provided by the guitars, the singers and/or instrumentalists could join in whenever or wherever they pleased with any variant of Section A. Until a Javanese gong was sounded, the performers could dwell on any bar they found agreeable and proceed at any speed that seemed appropriate. The gong would indicate that all the players should proceed to section B, select one of the variants, and repeat as before.

The success of the piece would depend on each player's "natural sense for contrasts, form, and dynamics . . . and their judgment in entering and leaving the general ensemble at suitable moments."[83] He admitted no facetiousness confessing only that "My hookworm is tonal fun." In 1914 at his flat in Chelsea, Grainger tried out this new piece with members of his close circle of friends. They expressed interest in its unusual properties but Percy was not satisfied. He admitted, however, that "The results obtained were very instructive to me personally . . . after a little practice together the whole thing took form, color and clarity, and sounded harmonious enough, though a frequent swash of passing discords was noticeable also." Even though Grainger was to include a description of the new piece in an article published in the *Musical Quarterly* a few years later, the credit for such innovation went generally unrecognized.

The assassination of Archduke Ferdinand in June of 1914 brought the major powers of Europe almost immediately to conflict, and Grainger, fearing for his mother's safety, made plans to flee England. Although his success at the Gardiner concerts in 1913 was without reservation, the lack of enthusiasm for *Colonial Song* from Gardiner and the critics response made Grainger feel "not at home" in England. He felt an indifference toward his "Australian side" but an acceptance from his English public for his folk song work and "English side" in general. He had been interested in America since his early years in Australia and recently had been approached about a concert tour there; Herman Sandby had been principal cellist with the Philadelphia Orchestra since 1912, and it is most certain that Sandby's enthusiasm for America was known to Grainger.

In one of his last London appearances during the summer of 1914, he was hired to perform at a party given by Princesse de Folingnois. Included on the program was Debussy's *Prelude to the Afternoon of a Faun* and Grainger's own *Colonial Song*, both in piano arrangements by the Australian. Sir Thomas Beecham, a guest of honor that day, commented to Grainger about his new composition: "My dear Grainger, you have achieved the almost impossible; you have written the worst orchestral piece of modern time."[84]

In September of 1914, enroute to New York City, Percy, Rose, and *The Colonial Song* arrived in Boston aboard the freighter *Laconia*.

Notes

[1]*The London Musical Courier*, Nov. 2, 1901.
[2]Percy A. Grainger, "Deemths" (unpublished typescript, no date).
[3]*The Times* (London), June 15, 1907, p. 10.
[4]Antonia Sawyer, *Songs at Twilight* (New York: Devon-Adair Co., 1939), pp. 128-129.
[5]Cyril Scott, "Percy Grainger and the Frankfurt Group" (unpublished typescript, October, 1936).
[6]Percy Grainger, "Bird's-Eye View of the Together Life of Rose Grainger and Percy Grainger" (18-page typescript, date 1947).
[7]*Ibid.*
[8]Edith Heymann, "Musical Memories" (unpublished typescript, no date).
[9]Grainger, "Round Letter to Kin and Friends," Feb. 15-17, 1942.
[10]Letter to Holten from Grainger, June 4, 1907.
[11]Grainger, "English-Speaking Leadership in Tone-Art" (unpublished typescript, Sept. 20, 1944), p. 4.
[12]*Ibid.*

[13]Letter to Bauer from Grainger, Dec. 10, 1939.
[14]Letter to Holten from Grainger, Dec. 8, 1906.
[15]*Ibid.*
[16]Letter to Holten from Grainger, Nov. 6, 1906.
[17]The winner of this first contest was Joseph Taylor — with the singing of "Brigg Fair." Both Taylor and his folk tune were to contribute much to Grainger's success in the folk song business.
[18]Lady Winifred and Richard Elwes, *Gervase Elwes* (London: Grayson & Grayson, 1935).
[19]*Ibid.*
[20]*Ibid.*
[21]Letter to Holten from Grainger, Dec. 8, 1906.
[22]*Journal of the Folk Song Society*, III/12 (1908-09), editor's footnote.
[23]Letter to Holton from Grainger, July 6, 1907.
[24]*Ibid.*
[25]Letter from Mr. Rosher to Grainger, December 31, 1923.
[26]Grainger, "Program Notes," to *Lincolnshire Posy* (New York: Geo. Schirmer, 1940), p. 3.
[27]Letter to Holten from Grainger, Nov. 26, 1907.
[28]Grieg, Edvard. Quoted in publicity release compiled by Percy Grainger shortly after Grieg's death.
[29]Edvard Grieg, Diary entry, Oct. 3, 1907.
[30]Letter to Holten from Grainger, June 10, 1907.
[31]*Ibid.*, April 28, 1907.
[32]*Ibid.*, May 8, 1907.
[33]*Ibid.*, May 12, 1907.
[34]Note written in Grainger's hand. The program on which this note was written is included in the collection of letters from Grainger to Karen Holten, dated June 5, 1907, and is located in the Library of Congress Grainger Collection.
[35]Scott, "Percy Grainger and the Frankfurt Group."
[36]Letter to Holton from Grainger, April 8, 1907.
[37]*Ibid.* June 4, 1907.
[38]Peter Warlock (Philip Heseltine), *Frederick Delius*, (reprinted with additions, annotations, and comments by Hubert Foss; New York: Oxford University Press, 1952), p. 155.
[39]*Ibid.*, p. 178.
[40]*Ibid.*, p. 172.
[41]*Australian Phonograph Monthly*, I/12 (June 20, 1926).
[42]Grieg, Diary entry dated April 4, 1907.
[43]*Ibid.*, July, 1907.
[44]*The Etude* (July, 1943), 472.
[45]Henry Theophilus Finck, *Grieg and His Music* (London: John Lane, The Bodley Head, 1909). pp. 284-85.
[46]Grainger, "Deemths."
[47]Grainger, *The Nightingale* (New York: G. Schirmer, 1928).
[48]Letter to Grainger from Charles Stanford, no date.
[49]Warlock, p. 177.
[50]Grainger, "Bird's-Eye View . . ."
[51]Letter to Holten from Grainger, June 30, 1909.
[52]*Ibid.*, April 30, 1908.
[53]Grainger, "The Aldridge-Grainger-Ström Saga" (233-page typescript located in the Library of Congress, dated 1934).

[54]Letter to Holten from Grainger, 1909.

[55]*Ibid.*, January 16, 1909.

[56]Letter to Percy Grainger from Rose Grainger, March 31, 1909.

[57]*Ibid.*, November, 1908.

[58]Percy Grainger to Ellen Bull, Oct. 23, 1941.

[59]Rose Grainger to John Grainger, 1909.

[60]Percy Grainger to Holten, February, 1909.

[61]*Ibid.*, Sept. 19, 1909.

[62]Rose Grainger to Percy Grainger, November, 1908.

[63]Grainger to Holton, Nov. 6, 1909.

[64]Percy Grainger to Cyril Scott, Sept. 20, 1941, p. 3.

[65]Grainger to Holten, August 6, 1909.

[66]Christopher St. John, *Ethel Smyth* (New York: Longmans, Green & Co., 1959).

[67]Charles Merrill Mount, *John Singer Sargent, A Biography* (New York: W.W. Norton & Co., 1955).

[68]Grainger to Holton, Nov. 23, 1906.

[69]Percy Young, *Elgar, O.M.* (London: Collins, 1955), p. 162.

[70]The *Times* (London), May 22, 1912.

[71]Rose Grainger to Percy Grainger, Feb. 5, 1907.

[72]Grainger, "Bird's-Eye View . . ." (1902).

[73]Grainger to Holton, Jan. 30, 1907.

[74]Grainger, "Round Letter to Kin and Friends" Feb. 15-17, 1942.

[75]Grainger to Holton, Feb. 3, 1909.

[76]*Ibid.*, April 7, 1913.

[77]Percy Grainger to Margot Harrison, July, 1913.

[78]Telegram to Percy Grainger from Mr. Harrison, London, England, dated July 28, 1913.

[79]Grainger, "Bird's-Eye View . . ."

[80]*Ibid.*

[81]D.C. Parker, "The Art of Percy Grainger," *The Monthly Musical Record*, XLV/537 (1915), 152-53.

[82]Grainger, "The Impress of Personality in Unwritten Music," *The Musical Quarterly*, I (1915), 416.

[83]*Ibid.*

[84]Grainger, "Deemths II" (October 10, 1949).

America — The World's Great Arena for the Arts

Debut

In the period preceding America's entry into the war, New York City stood in dramatic contrast to her European counterparts. New skyscrapers of 50 and 60 stories broke through the horizontal mass "like extravagant pins in a cushion already overplanted." Elbowing masses pressed into subways attempting to escape the din of elevated trains and surface traffic which seemed to multiply like jungle fauna. To control the maze of vehicles, mechanical devices with inhibiting signals began to appear. The "heavy low, musical roar" of the city which had appealed to Whitman 50 years before had now given way to unceasing noise, constant movement, and perpetual change. The chronic state of pulling down and building up altered the landscape daily, and the city seemed to constantly belch a hungry roar of effort. Optimistic workers with peasant blood and immigrant hope clogged the streetcars, and the air was a-hum with Yiddish, Italian, and Greek, broken only by splashes of German, Russian, or Polish. English could have been considered a foreign tongue. The original WASP stock was becoming a less visible factor. The influx of immigrants was creating the most multilingual center of the day.

With a population that had already outdistanced London's by 1910, it would soon be an accepted cliché that New York was built by the Italians, run by the Irish, and owned by the Jews. It was only a matter of time until it would replace the British capital as the financial center of the world. These nervous years of neutrality that greeted the Graingers spawned bomb threats, strikes, and Manhattan slums, yet a prosperity which ignored these problems seemed to be everywhere.

The city was no stranger to musicians, for it was often the port of entry for many of the continent's finest performers who regularly journeyed to America. Those who could not surmount the professional circle of the area used it as a base for tours into the frontier — some traveling as far west as Buffalo. All returned. Soon H.L. Mencken would write that the city would possess more orchestral conductors than Berlin and note that "the town has more theaters and far better ones than London. It is . . .loaded with art to the gunwales and steadily piling more on deck."

Grainger's reputation as a successful pianist and composer had preceded him. His popularity would continue in England and the following year his compositions would be more frequently performed in England than those of any other composer of the British Empire.

In the autumn of 1914, the 32-year old pianist and his mother presented themselves to Rudolph Schirmer, president of the firm which was to publish Grainger's music. The need for a manager was obvious so Schirmer provided a letter of introduction to Antonia Sawyer, a soprano recently retired from the stage, who was then building a small reputation for herself as a concert manager.

The following morning, mother and son arrived at Mrs. Sawyer's office in Aeolian Hall and it was agreed that

Percy would perform for his prospective manager at the Steinway firm the next day. Following the successful audition, Mrs. Sawyer arranged for him to perform the orchestral piano part of his *Shepherd's Hey* with Walter Damrosch and the New York Symphony Orchestra scheduled for the coming Sunday. Although not appearing as a soloist, this initial exposure brought enthusiastic response from the audience and his American career looked promising.

Mrs. Sawyer was a capable manager and planned carefully for his coming debut. She arranged for other artists to program his compositions and the Grainger name began to appear on concert programs throughout the area. Damrosch performed several of his *British Folk Music Settings* in November, and Daniel Gregory Mason devoted a substantial portion of the Symphony's program notes to them and their pianist-composer. (It should be noted that the Grainger name had already been introduced to the American public by Kurt Schindler the year before with performances by the McDowell Chorus of *Father and Daughter*, *Irish Tune from County Derry*, and *I'm Seventeen Come Sunday*).

On February 11, 1915, Grainger made his debut at a matinee performance in Aeolian Hall. The house was sold out, boxes $15.00 top. A distinguished audience was present and society was out in force. Every major artist in New York was there, including Enrico Caruso, who refused to make himself known to the audience explaining "This is Grainger's recital!"[1] Recalling the triumph, his manager remarked: "Percy's success was instantaneous. The press of New York City acclaimed him and his American career was made."[2]

Grainger's program contained works by Bach, Brahms, Grieg, Chopin, Ravel, and Albéniz, together with his own *Colonial Song* and *Mock Morris*. Henry T. Finck, music critic for the *Evening Post* and later a close friend of Grainger, described the event:

> And what a Bach! The pianist made the contra-
> puntal network as clear to the ear of even the
> uninitiated as a piece of Venetian lace is to every-
> body's eyes. No less astonishing were the opulence
> and variety of his tone — his instrument seemed
> both piano and organ — and he showed at once,
> as he did in several other pieces following this,
> that he can build up a climax as gradually and
> overwhelmingly on the piano as Anton Seidl
> did with his Wagnerian orchestra. The audience
> was stunned, bewildered, delighted.[3]

The next month Grainger appeared with the New York
Philharmonic in a performance of the Grieg Concerto.
Performances with the New York Symphony Orchestra
followed, as did regular appearances with the orchestras
of Washington, Philadelphia, Minneapolis, San Francisco
and Chicago. His date book soon contained the names of
the prominent musical figures with whom he met from
time to time — with the names of Melba, Busoni, Sousa,
Stravinsky, and Schönberg appearing most frequently.
From the beginning he was in the first rank of concert performers. Even the array of personalities did not detract him
from his goals and he continued to champion Delius' music,
happily reporting some success:

> That is jolly: Philadelphia Orchestra doing
> Dance Rhapsody, Damrosch (New York Sym-
> phony) giving your *Stimmungsbilder* and the
> New York Philharmonic and I doing the Con-
> certo. Now I'll write to Stock and enthuse him
> . . . .If he could be roped in too, that would be a
> decent beginning.[4]

The next two years were extremely busy for the Australian. He continued to be in demand as a soloist and his compositions became widely popular; *Shepherd's Hey* and *Molly on the Shore* appeared often on the symphony programs
of Oberhoffer in Minneapolis, Hertz in San Francisco, Stokowski in Philadelphia, and Damrosch in New York. John

Philip Sousa programmed *Handel in the Strand* and *Shepherd's Hey,* the latter described in his Hippodrome program as "a modern conceit on an ancient air." Music festivals in the Northeast sought Grainger's services and vied to present his music. The Grainger name became a household word.

Mrs. Sawyer shrewdly teamed her pianist with the popular Dutch contralto, Julia Culp, and together they performed with amazing success. Grainger's first Boston recital was held in Jordon Hall, March 6, 1915, and he appeared there several times during the next two seasons with such assisting artists as Julia Culp, Florence Hinkle, and Mme. Melba — the only time the two Australians ever appeared together professionally.

Antonia Sawyer soon became the envy of her New York colleagues. Two popular New York booking offices offered her a partnership, but when Grainger and Culp objected, she declined. Even Thomas Edison spent a day with Mrs. Sawyer trying to convince her that either Culp or Grainger should become associated with his recording company; but Culp continued with Victor and Grainger remained with Columbia. Edison later berated one of his men for not having secured them before they were so firmly established. Mrs. Sawyer got along famously with Edison, though he was quite deaf, and in her later years she loved to recall their meeting.

Almost from the first, Grainger began to contribute articles to the more scholarly American music journals, and numerous interviews appeared in the popular magazines of the day. His "The Impress of Personality on Unwritten Music," which appeared in the *Musical Quarterly* that year (1915) was received as the definitive case for his method of folk song notation. A description of his improvisational piece, *Random Round*, in the same article, drew no attention. Oscar Sonneck, editor of the *Musical Quarterly,* became a champion of Grainger although they would have strong

differences of opinion in the years to come. They had similar
educational backgrounds, and the details of Percy's academic
problems in Frankfurt were known to him. "I, too, was a
pupil of Kwast and Knorr," wrote Sonneck, "It appears
that you and he did not get on very well."[5] But quick to
defend his composition teacher, Grainger, in typical gra-
ciousness, replied, "[I] was deeply sorry to learn of Knorr's
death. I liked him very much and quite realized that I was
a bad pupil. Anyhow I dislike the idea of training in composition under all circumstances."[6] In fact, Grainger gave
credit to only one person for helping him with his composition, and that was Karl Klimsch, the patron of the
Frankfurt group.

The sinking of the *Lusitania* in May of 1915 brought
sinister rumblings of war to the country. While European
cities felt the bite of conflict, America in general and New
York in particular, was prospering. The war seemed far
away and Grainger's career continued to grow. In October
Percy learned of the illness of his father. John Grainger's
final communique from his American family arrived a few
days before his death: "Loving wishes. Quick recovery.
Rose and Percy Grainger."[7]

Grainger's first extensive tour outside the New York
area began in 1916. It included the premier of John Alden
Carpenter's *Concertino* with Frederick Stock and the Chicago
Symphony and took him as far as the west coast. In spite
of his concert activity Grainger continued to write. Earlier
that year his recently completed orchestral suite *In a Nutshell* was premiered under Arthur Meese (on June 8) at
the Norfolk Connecticut Festival, with Grainger assisting
at the piano. It was an unusual work, bringing together
many of the technical ideas that had been occupying him.
Scored for orchestra and piano, it included parts for the
(then) novel Deagan percussion instruments, which demanded eight additional percussion players. Although the
premiere was well-received, it was controversial. Late that

year the Minneapolis critics gave it a scathing denunciation
and described it as "one of the two curiosities of the decade,"
the second being "the appearance of Carlo Liten, Belgian
tragedian, in a reading of his poems." Grainger was merci-
lessly ribbed when he assembled the strange percussion
instruments for the Minneapolis rehearsal. "Steel and
wooden marimbaphones, a namimba, a stand of Swiss bells,
a celesta, a glockenspiel, and a xylophone, all clustered
about the conductor's dais like a herd of queer looking
monsters." The public reaction to this array of instruments
was mixed. Charles Flandreau, critic for the St. Paul newspapers, was admittedly unnerved, "when a small army of
attendants carted on stage a kitchen range, a soda water
fountain, twenty-six stove pipes, three dozen brand new
coffee pots, an ice-box, and a small but perfectly appointed
operating table." Despite the odd hardware, he found the
piece to be "a work of extraordinary interest and fascination."[8] The Minneapolis papers dismissed the premier of
In a Nutshell — and its creator — with exceptional candor:
"If you don't care for the shell, go and enjoy the nut."[9]

In December of that year (1916), Grainger completed
The Warriors, his largest orchestral work to date and the
product of nearly three years' work. December continued to
plague him; Christmas was spent snow-bound on a train
near Medicine Bow, Wyoming.

The Warriors was premiered at the Norfolk Festival
in the spring of 1917, and it brought warm though not
ecstatic response from the critics. It was an unusual orchestral
piece from an unusual composer. Nothing he had written
previously had prepared the audience for the near-gargantuan
proportions of the orchestra. In addition to complete wind
and brass families, and the usual complement of strings,
Grainger's score required two harps and three pianos. The
most spectacular aspect of the score, however, was the percussion. Four to six players utilized kettle drums, xylo-

phone, marimba, bass-xylophone, glockenspiel, staff bells, and tubular bells, in addition to three performers playing the usual battery of instruments. Three conductors, though not necessary, were preferred. The critics were generous, but cautious, referring to Grainger as a "Pagan Peter Pan." There is no question as to the "din" that evening, but the most perceptive review came from the conservative *Christian Science Monitor*:

> Adding a complete harmony of percussion instruments to the string, woodwind and brass groups that comprise the historic orchestra of Beethoven and Berlioz, and the supposedly modern orchestra of Strauss and Debussy as well, and reorganizing the plan of symphony scoring from a contrast of three general sonorities into a contrast of four, Percy Grainger won the praise of high artistic invention here Thursday night with his new music, "The Warriors." Mr. Grainger in his latest contribution elaborates into a thorough-going system some of the notations which he advanced a year ago in his suite for piano and orchestra, "In a Nutshell." He incorporates the piano, however, not as a solo instrument, but as a percussion chord sounder, with bells and other beaten things, adding to the orchestra a fourth tone clan. This new clan he individualizes as effectually as composers in the 150 years before him individualized first the clan in which violin, viola and cello, then that in which flute, oboe, clarinet and bassoon, and lastly that in which trumpet, trombone and tuba consort with one another. In brief, he has made the orchestra a quartet instead of a trio of harmonic groups. Because of this achievement, "The Warriors" makes a stronger claim to international regard than does any of the other three works which were presented at this season's festival; and it is perhaps the work that is destined to give the Norfolk concerts the greatest renown of anything brought out in nine years of novelty producing.[10]

Army Togs

The New York business community found 1916 to be an excellent year. The Stock Exchange had its largest volume in fifteen years and, in supplying Europe's insatiable needs, exports had doubled. On April 6, 1917 the United States entered the war. Distress and gloom gripped the City, and a limbo of decision-making precipitated the roaring war times.

Grainger sought the advice of Captain Arthur A. Clappé, conductor of one of the local Army bands, concerning his "joining up." The pressure of his career, the unsettled concert atmosphere, and his father's recent death seemed to make the decision easier. On Clappé's suggestion, he applied for the 15th Army Band under Rocco Resta, a highly respected musician. Clappé pointed out the main advantage of being with Resta's unit; it was apparently exempt from hazardous front-line duties — a fate awaiting many of the other local units. On July 12, 1917, possessing the "Bluebells of Scotland" as his total saxophone repertoire, George Percy Grainger presented himself for audition and was accepted. Not until the first rehearsal, when asked to play a simple passage, was his lack of saxophone proficiency exposed. "I'll play it for you on the piano," he countered, and he remained with the band. He was assigned to Resta at Brooklyn's Fort Hamilton as a Musician, Second Class and carried on the role as an oboe and saxophone player. Relieved of the constant strain of public recitals, Grainger remarked: "For the first time in years, I was at peace."[11]

His enlistment in the Army prompted a message from a Mrs. Hunter, an old friend in London: "Your friends are proud of you again,"[12] she cabled, referring to the unfriendly stand they had taken when Percy left England rather than "join up" there. But Percy remarked: "I am

not keen on friends who wish to get me killed in wars —
friends who rejoice to hear I have donned Army togs."[13]

Rose Grainger was not far from her recruit. She was
given access to the Post and frequently visited her son,
yet she seemed upset that he thrived so well in the Army.
"It was a disloyalty on my part toward her immunity effort,"
Percy explained.[14]

Grainger's life of peaceful seclusion ended when a photographer recognized the famous pianist and he was again
called upon to perform. Soon he was appearing in New York
for Liberty Loan drives and Red Cross benefits. *Country
Gardens*, an improvisation on an old Morris dance collected
by Cecil Sharp, originated with these appearances. Grainger
later assigned a portion of his royalties to finance a publication of Sharp's *English Folk Songs of the Southern
Appalachian Mountains*. Sharp had originally refused to
take any profits from *Country Gardens* for himself, but
in the year of his death, he was persuaded by Maud Karples
to accept the continuing offer to help finance his last project.
This composition, *Country Gardens*, came to be the first
of many light works which would give Grainger the financial
security he desired.

Percy was inherently shy and inseparable from his mother,
and he repeatedly stated his disapproval at being forced
to perform in order to secure an income. Although the
philanthropist, E.J. DeCoppet, offered him a liberal annuity
should he wish to give up playing and teaching to devote
himself entirely to composition, Percy refused. Yet he
complained of public appearances being distasteful to him
and conducted his recitals in the most informal manner.
His personality often appeared as contradictory as his music.

> As I stand in the wings waiting to go on, I'm
> doing one of two things — wondering if it wouldn't
> be easier to shoot myself than to walk to the
> piano, or phrasing a speech of apology in case
> they start to hiss.[15]

He insisted that he had joined the Army to escape the concert limelight, but, as his Army appearances became more frequent, his manager manipulated his publicity to every advantage. His hair was shorn, of course, but only where his hat did not conceal it; Grainger remained Grainger, Apollo-featured and golden haired. His health was always strong for he constantly exercised, hiked, and subjected himself to physical strain to further improve it. He ran, swam, carried his luggage to the chagrin of the redcaps, and ascended stairs two or more at a time — polite company unexcepted. He had sprained his ankle once when descending a staircase in his usual manner, but miraculously his body survived the tremendous demands he placed on it. It was ironic that while a mature man in the Army, he should contract the childhood disease of measles, and the wide coverage given to his illness in the press brought a deluge of mail from his fans.

His first concert with Resta's Band, following the brief illness, was held at the Colony Club Auditorium on Park Avenue, with the proceeds going for the Red Cross Workroom of the Colony Club. The afternoon was dominated by the recruit who performed his *Gumsucker's March* and *Colonial Song*. Also included on the program were his *One More Day, My John*, the "Lullaby" from *Tribute to Foster*, and Stanford's *Leprechaun's Dance* and *McGuire's Kick*.

During the 1917-18 concert season, Mrs. Sawyer freely borrowed her star from the Government and advertised that 85% of his fees would be contributed directly to the Red Cross. In one three-month period, Grainger earned over $7000 for the Red Cross and was booked ahead for $13,000 more when the Army jealously demanded his return. By the end of his Army career, the Australian had conquered yet another country.

That spring Grainger received his United States citizenship, an accomplishment of which he was singularly proud. It would be nearly two years before his mother would receive hers. On the very day he became an American citizen, Grainger wrote a setting of *Rule Brittania* and recalled that he had refused Melba's request to write an Australian anthem.

It was in this first year with the Army that Grainger's earliest recordings for Columbia were released. He had recorded three discs in 1908 and two in 1912 for His Master's Voice, but these recordings had been a novelty and he had not taken them seriously. His first release for Columbia was the Liszt *Second Hungarian Rhapsody*. In their publicity announcements that year, Columbia advertised that "no such piano tone has ever been equalled in recorded music."

Later the same year, Dr. Arthur Meese directed a first performance of his *Marching Song of Democracy*. The concert, described as one which would be remembered in "the annals of the Worcester Festivals as one of the most brilliant in History," saw Grainger in his khaki uniform presented with two large floral wreaths. Perhaps he recalled the verses he had been accused of writing about Brahms as he returned to the stage to accept the continuing applause. The *Marching Song of Democracy*, inspired by Whitman verses, had been completed the previous year in a scoring for chorus, orchestra, and organ. Its wordless text and strong rhythmic pulses heavily overshadowed Henry Hadley's setting of Van Dyke's *Ode to Music*, premiered on the same program. Enthusiastic press releases followed but Krehbiel of the New York *Tribune* was later to embarrass him when he used Shakespeare's phrase to describe it as "sound and fury, signifying nothing."

In his second year in the Army, Grainger was transferred to the Army Band Training School at Governor's Island as assistant instructor. With his greater freedom, he began staying with his mother at their New York apartment, leaving daily at 5:00 A.M. to fulfill his military obligations. Francis Resta, younger brother of Grainger's first Army leader and the future West Point Band leader, was then a

student at the School. The two became good friends. Arthur
A. Clappé was directing the School, and Percy often appeared
with the student band under Clappé's direction.

Grainger delighted in conducting the Post Band and
trying out his arrangements. He was popular with the men,
but they often complained that he overworked them. He
spent his days involving himself with instruments and
writing, and he could often be found in the "band shack,"
banging away on their collection of mallet percussion.
Rose, too, became involved with the percussion instruments
that her son loved and, on one occasion, even filled in on
resnophone with the 15th Army Band of the Coast Artillery
Corps when Percy conducted. Writing to Balfour Gardiner
that year, Percy explained his pleasure in his new surroundings: "It is so lovely to hear instruments booming away
around one all day long & so instructive compositionally.
All my life I've longed for just such an experience."[16]

One of the greatest benefits of his Army career was this
close association Grainger had with the band. His interest
in woodwinds was renewed and in Clappé he had found
a sympathetic superior. He referred to Clappé's book, *The
Wind Band and Its Instruments*, as doing for the band
what Berlioz' treatise on instruments had done for the
orchestra. They were in agreement that the ideal band was
no larger than sixty-five men. It is not surprising, then, to
find that in the years 1917 and 1918, a large share of his
writings was concerned with wind instruments. This interest in reed instruments dates from his early youth:

> I was in love with the double-reeds (oboe, English
> horn, etc.) as the wildest & fiercest of musical
> tone-types. In 1900 I had heard a very harsh-
> toned rustic oboe (piffero) in Italy, some extremely
> nasal Egyptian double reeds at the Paris Exhi-
> bition and bagpipes in the Scottish Highlands.[17]

His earliest writing for the band medium had been *Lads
of Wamphray* and the exquisite *Hill Song No. 2* for twenty-
two winds. The *Children's March* was his next excursion

into scoring for band. "Especially written to use all the forces of the Coast Artillery Corps Band in which I was serving in 1918."[18] It is generally regarded as the earliest known composition for piano and band. It was that same year that *Colonial Song* was rescored for the band. Listed in his files, and No. 1 of a series entitled 'Sentimentals," *Colonial Song* was originally a piano piece given to his mother in 1911 as a "Yule-Gift." Grainger felt that it was "an attempt to write a melody as typical of the Australian countryside as Stephen Foster's exquisite songs are typical of rural America."[19]

His skill at transcribing for winds is evident in his 1917 settings of the famous *Irish Tune from County Derry* and his *Gumsucker's March*. Richard Franko Goldman believes that these pieces, plus Grainger's settings of *Shepherd's Hey* and *Molly on the Shore*, which date from the previous year, comprise the first interesting body of band literature after the Holst *Suites* of 1909-1911. Grainger's unpublished arrangement of Debussy's *Bruyères*, scored for ten winds and harmonium, also belongs to these Army days.

The influence of Holland's Ethnomusicological Museum and Grainger's interest in percussion instruments could now be readily seen in his compositions. *Shepherd's Hey,* in its scoring for band, boasted of an indispensible part for xylophone with sections where the player was instructed to "roll the hammer about on any notes." Percy constantly experimented with new percussion effects and even visited George A. Braun, a local inventor, to see a machine he had developed which could create a vibrato on the glockenspiel. Nothing was too bizarre to consider, but Grainger's immense personal charm made the most unusual confrontations seem rather commonplace.

At the end of the war, Grainger was not immediately discharged. His wartime activities had extended his fame and, while still in the Army, he was offered the conductorship of the St. Louis Symphony Orchestra upon his separa-

tion. In addition, the city of St. Louis would consider a
municipal school of music which he would also head. Later,
remarking on his rejection of the position, he said:

> I don't suppose I would ever have been able to
> bring myself to conduct a conventional symphony
> orchestra, because of my conviction that the
> value of the ordinary German-Austrian-Russian
> symphony repertoire is greatly overrated . . . .
> No American symphony board or audience would
> ever have been satisfied with such programs
> as I would have chosen.[20]

On January 6, 1919, Grainger was discharged from the
Army. Offers of concerts and solo engagements flooded
his manager. During the first concert season following
his military service, he appeared nine times with the New
York Philharmonic and five times with the New York
Symphony, in addition to solo engagements with Chicago,
Minneapolis, and Philadelphia.

It is interesting to speculate on the motives behind
Grainger's enlistment. He had fled England because of
the proximity of the war and, in some quarters, had been
severely criticized for it. It would seem that he had joined
the service for the reasons he gave publicly, but it is also
possible that his mother manipulated the circumstances
so that he might have a reasonably secure wartime position
and yet continue to grow in popularity as a performing
artist. In her book, "Songs at Twilight," his manager admits
that she had made an arrangement with the War Department to give 85% of his fees from the 1917-18 season to
the Red Cross and openly advertised his services as such.
This arrangement occurred about a week after Percy played
a benefit on June 23, 1917, at the Long Island home of
Henry F. Davidson, President of the American Red Cross.
At Mr. Davidson's invitation, Mrs. Sawyer traveled to
Washington, D.C., to confer with the War Department
concerning continuance of this type of concert. Although
Mrs. Sawyer implies Grainger was then already in uniform,

it was several weeks later when he actually presented himself to Resta for his audition. The alert reporter who discovered him playing in the band a few weeks later may or may not have been directed by Grainger's astute manager.

First American Tours

Although Grainger's personal income was reduced during the war, his manager had handled his absence well. Discussing the financial arrangements for his post-Army concert tours, Mrs. Sawyer informed Rose that "Now that he [Percy] is out of the Army, his fee is just double the amount and I think he should pay for the imprinting of his circulars and cuts."[21] Sawyer had managed to book the season full, from fall to spring.

A ten-year association with the Chicago Musical College began that summer. Grainger was contracted to teach piano for five weeks, both with master classes and with selected advanced students at a fee of $20 per hour. One of his students recalled that Grainger's tremendous energy could make an ordinary workday fade into nothing. Class would start when he strode "into the tenth floor studio, carrying a piano bench on his shoulder after walking ten flights of steps and would last for three hours, filled with new ideas, musical history, clean-cut criticism of playing and unpredictable happenings."

His interest in "modern composers" saw him master three hundred and fifty different selections, mostly by American, British, Canadian, and Australian composers. The more prominent of these composers were Scott, Delius, Mac-Dowell, Gardiner, Carpenter, Brockway, Stanford, Dett, and Mason; and, of course, his own compositions were

liberally included. Demonstration of the use of the sostenuto pedal was accomplished with Scott's herculean
Sonata, Op. 66. This first summer in Chicago was a success
and Grainger's students presented him with a silver ciga-
rette case — a curious gift as "My mother asked me not to
smoke, drink, or go with whores, and I behest-heeded her
strictly."[22]

Normally Grainger played to capacity audiences but
occasionally, when the house was disappointing, he took
the lack of patrons as a personal affront to his own compositions. In the fall of 1919, it was his misfortune to be
booked into St. Louis the same day that Belgium's King
Albert and his Royal party were visiting. The newspapers
concentrated almost entirely on the Royal visitor and, as
a result, Percy's concert was poorly attended. Perhaps the
thought of having been offered the symphony position the
previous year prompted him to deliver his unkind remarks
concerning the concert arrangements. In the future, he
studiously avoided that city.

Grainger was a frugal, yet generous man. He had found
that his "Army togs" were long-wearing and inexpensive,
so his haberdasher became the local Army-Navy Store. The
coarse army clothes appealed to him and, even after his
discharge, he continued to wear the army underclothing,
thick boots, and even regular issue army socks under his
own silk socks. He dismissed any criticism of his dress
stating that, "Physical luxuries handicap efforts."

His contributions to charitable causes were numerous,
and he regularly gave recitals for the Red Cross, the Scandinavian charities, and the New York Music School Settlements. The Brooklyn Music School Settlement, which was
designed to develop "native music" among the Negro
masses in New York City, received special notice from him,
and in 1919 he was elected to its advisory board. Through
this organization, he became familiar with Negro composers
and helped foster performance of their works. Endorsing

their appeal for funds, he wrote: "Some of the deepest and most unforgettable musical treats that I have as yet experienced in this country have fallen to my lot at the Music School Settlement for Colored People."

He did not forget his friends, helping them financially whenever he could. In 1917, he had assigned a portion of the royalties from his *In A Nutshell Suite* to Karen, by this time Fru Karen Kellerman, still living in Copenhagen.

The demobilization was rapidly changing the military establishments in the New York area. Clappé, still head of the Army Band School of Governor's Island, was recuperating from an operation. At Clappé's suggestion, Grainger joined with several prominent New York musicians and sent a request to the Secretary of War to continue the operation of the Army Band School. Walter Damrosch was asked to intercede with Pershing. All efforts were unsuccessful. The following year, Clappé died.

Grainger's interest in bands soon came to the attention of Edwin Franko Goldman who had recently formed his own organization. In November of 1919, Grainger, John Philip Sousa, and Victor Herbert were invited to serve as judges for Goldman's American Competition, the first such contest for a new serious work for band. Sousa was unable to attend, but Grainger and Herbert selected Carl Busch's "Chant from the Great Plains." That first season Grainger served as guest conductor on the Goldman series and presented several of his recently completed scores. He also appeared with the Goldman Band as soloist in a performance of Liszt's *Hungarian Fantasy*, in an arrangement by his former Army leader, Rocco Resta.

The popularity of Grainger's music was not limited to the band movement or even to America. In post-war London, the most popular musical entertainment was Sir Henry Woods' Promenade Concerts. According to the American critic, Henry T. Finck, "Smoking was allowed and so was Wagner, but more often the music was Grainger's."[23] The unusual popularity of his folk-oriented selections can, in part, be attributed to the sunny contrast they offered to England's bitter involvement in the recent war. The musical climate had changed in England. Balfour Gardiner terminated his efforts to compose, for the music of the Frankfurt Group, save Grainger's, drastically declined in popularity.

In the spring of 1920, Percy and his mother made a three-month concert tour of Oregon, California, and New Mexico. They became interested in the city of Barstow, California and stayed several weeks, resting, composing, and studying the Spanish language. The isolated desert area reminded them of their native Australia and it always remained one of Percy's favorite spots. For a time, he considered a renewal of his interest in the folk songs of the area, but his mother's poor health prompted their return to New York City. As a memento Grainger selected an ordinary piece of brown wrapping paper which he labeled: "fell off the back of picture of Venice Canal (queer German-looking respectibles were helping women out of gondola) Room 4, Casa del Dicerto Hotel, Barstow." Any special significance of this odd souvenir went unnoted.

Grainger's concert tours forced him to be away from his home in New York City much of the time, but he seldom traveled Pullman. In his desire to save money he would ride coach class as often as twenty nights a month. He had explained that "The reason I travel second class is because there is no third class."[24] Rose was traveling with her son less and maintained a comfortable apartment at The Southern, 680 Madison Avenue, where her son stayed when he was in the city. Constantly worried about memory slips, Grainger practiced incessantly and purchased a "dummy" keyboard so that he might practice undisturbed whenever he desired. Lionel Barrymore, living directly below the Grainger apartment complained bitterly: "I don't mind his playing, but I can't stand his *damn* thumping."[25] On October 1, 1920, the Graingers moved to West 92nd Street.

The 1920-21 season was even more strenuous than the previous one and Cuba was added to his itinerary. In the midst of these heavy concert commitments, Cyril Scott arrived from England. The Graingers secured rooms for him close to their own New York apartment and his meals were taken with Rose and Percy. The reunion was a fruitful exchange of compositional advice, opinion, desires, and the recitation of limericks. The limerick which Cyril most enjoyed brought a slight blush to Rose, but Percy thought it splendid enough to save:

A Lesbian lass from Khartoum
Took a Nancy-boy up to her room,
When they'd turn out the light
She said, "Let's get this right.
Who does what and with which and to whom?

Rose had always liked Cyril and had often remarked to Percy that she should like to help his career if Percy might suddenly die.

Grainger's interest in chamber music prompted his participation in several concerts that fall with the New York Chamber Music Society, founded by Carolyn Beebe. He rescored his passacaglia, *Green Bushes*, for a chamber group and assisted by the clarinetist, Gustav Langenus, and the violinist, Scipione Guidi, presented it on the Society's November 15th concert. Its success prompted the rescoring of *Hill Song No. 1* for chamber orchestra. Grainger's most unusual appearance that year was his participation in a benefit concert for the pianist-composer, Moritz Moskowski. Fifteen distinguished pianists combined to promote the evening and to perform. The pianists — including Bachaus, Bauer, Casella, Friedman, Gabrilowitsch, Grainger, Hutcheson, Lambert, Lhevinne, Mme. Mero, Mme. Ney, Ornstein, Schelling, Miss Schnitzer, and Stokowski — played separately, two by two, and then all together;

Walter Damrosch conducted. The unusually large and
enthusiastic Carnegie Hall audience heard performances
of Schubert's *Marche Militaire*, Moszkowski's *Spanish
Dances*, and Schumann's *Marche des Davidsbündler*. Madame Alma Gluck presided as auctioneer and John McCor-
mick was high bidder ($100) for a program autographed
by all the performers.

After the bulk of the season was over, Rose and Percy
secured a large three-story home at No. 7 Cromwell Place
near the downtown area of White Plains, a thirty-minute
train ride north of Manhattan. The proximity of the home
to commercial transportation was necessary because Percy
had a definitive fear of automobiles. Only under the most
pressing circumstances would he ride in one. Walking was
his favored means of travel, but unfortunately much too
slow for his usual concert schedule. When on tour, if his
train was to arrive earlier than he desired, he would often
disembark at an earlier station and hike the remaining
distance. Weather was no obstacle. Flying was dismissed
altogether.

The veranda at No. 7 Cromwell Place was the location
of the Graingers' afternoon tea. There Percy and his mother
spent much of their free time. They would leave bread and
nuts for the squirrels who seemed not to fear them; Percy
even attempted to domesticate two toads living under the
porch until they disappeared in a storm sewer after a vio-
lent downpour. The main floor of the home, spacious enough
for formal entertaining, contained several pianos, a harmonium, numerous exotic percussion instruments and
stacks of music both in printed and manuscript form. The
four bedrooms on the second floor provided ample space
for overnight guests while the third floor was reserved
for storage. It was there that Percy practiced his tenor
sarrusophone. Marie Sawneons, a maid who had worked
for them for four years, came three days a week to sew and
do light housework, and two other domestics came on al-

ternating mornings to do the cleaning. Rose's duty was to prepare the simple meals and attend to her son.

Rose maintained a steady flow of important persons through the home whenever Percy was there, but the traffic was different than it had been in their New York apartment. She seemed content with the move but her health continued to be a problem. Mrs. Sawyer did not live far and although she had turned over the details of her agency to her niece and husband, she remained extremely fond of the pianist and his mother. She would often stop to converse with Rose on returning from the city.

On Percy's 39th birthday, the first in his new home, Mrs. Sawyer came by along with Miss Fanny Dillion, a composer and pianist from California, and Mr. Leonard, the English singer. After dinner and an evening of music making, the conversation became a discussion of Percy's future. It was Rose who proposed the idea that he should find a suitable mate to be his companion in his comfortable home. She suggested that she might live in New York where he could come and sleep, dress for concerts, or practice. Percy was reluctant to comment and seemed distressed at the idea. It appeared that he had no desire to create a separation or to take a wife. He would "rather go into the desert for a while," he said, "or go hiking through South America and travel steerage to out of the way places."

Rose was aware of his "taste for an unrefined life" and was not as opposed to his indulging as she once had been. She was happy to have lived to see him "almost independent." "Why not," she wrote, "He is a real man and no Fanny."[26]

The physical discipline Rose administered to her son did not diminish as he reached manhood. To her, he was still a little boy who needed to be instructed in his every action. Remarking later about this difficulty, Percy explained: "She would smack my face, which I found very annoying, the more so as I neared 40 . . . If I held her wrists, to prevent her doing so, she would say, 'Someday you'll

kill me, exciting me so!' " Even as late as 1919 or 1920,
Rose would feign death scenes, much to the frustration
of her son. She would "lie quite still and corpse-like, while
I would get distraught and beg her to speak to me," he
remarked. "As soon as she was convinced that I was not
at all indifferent she would say 'I see you do care for me,
allright,' and go about her affairs as if nothing had happened."[27]

Shortly after their arrival in White Plains, Grainger
was routinely interviewed by the New York *Globe*. The
scope of the interview changed from a report of an artist
moving out of the city to Grainger's views on free music.
For the first time the decision to compose beatless music was publicly announced. Prophetically Grainger was
quoted as "hoping to make it [free music] available by
mechanical means" and the article went on to predict that
"he looks upon it as holding the solution of many modern-
ists difficulties, and which he expects to see taking its
share, perhaps 1/2 of the music of the future."[28] He admitted that his irregularly grouped beats prior to this time
had been somewhat of a "half-way house" between his
goal of beatless music and ordinary rhythmic pulse.

Mother Died

For the spring of 1922 Antonia Sawyer arranged a major
tour of Canada and the Pacific Coast for Grainger; it was
to be his most lucrative to date. Rose, depressed whenever Percy was out of town, wanted to accompany her
son as she had done so often in the past. She said that she
was feeling better, for the "Kelloggs Parawls" recommended
by Henry T. Finck seemed to have regulated her bowels

for the first time in twenty years. But the planned trip would be long and strenuous, and Mrs. Sawyer convinced her that she should remain in White Plains.

One Sunday, several weeks after Percy had left, Rose called Antonia Sawyer asking to be driven into New York. She could not be discouraged and, after phoning her physician, it was decided that the trip might even be of some benefit. After a silent ride to the City, the two women arrived at Aeolian Hall and went directly to Mrs. Sawyer's office. Rose requested that the window be opened for she needed more air, then she asked for a glass of water. When Mrs. Sawyer returned with the drink, she found that Rose Grainger had plunged to her death. It was ironic that she chose the same building in which her son had made his American debut seven years before.

The news of his mother's death reached Percy at the conclusion of a concert on the West Coast, and the details were brought to him in a newspaper he read enroute to New York. The immediate shock temporarily disoriented him, and on the train he wrote Balfour Gardiner a letter of authorization concerning publication of all his existing manuscripts and requesting him to "Bring out everything, sketches, etc.... that, together, could place me as Australia's first great composer and make Australia's and *my mother's name shine bright*. I have delayed too long, worked too long, did not bring leisure to her early enough. I have used shocking judgement in all these things." He included a blank check, signed in the event of a "breakdown of my forces enroute."[29] In her last wire to Percy, Rose indicated that she was more upset than usual. "My heart and head alarm me and I wonder if I can live through it all."[30]

The panic that he might not be able to fulfill his mother's expectations cautioned him to further instruct Balfour to consider the vacant lot adjacent to his home in White Plains as a possible site "for building a small fire-proof Grainger

Museum."

Mrs. Sawyer met Percy in Cleveland and together they continued to New York. Many sensational reports and rumors circulated throughout the city, and reporters harassed both the pianist and his manager. A strictly private funeral, augmented to include only Frederick Steinway and Henry Junge, was held the next day.

The music journals speculated about the amount of money Rose's will contained. Thousands, and even a million, were suggested. Percy had always been careful of expenses (when his aunt in Australia needed $100, he would send her $99.99 because of the difference in the cable fee). He kept meticulous records but when he countered each query with a reply of three thousand dollars, no one believed him.

The death of Rose Grainger was an emotional shock from which Percy would never fully recover. He speculated that she had taken her life in order that he might be free to make his own decisions and not be burdened by her failing health. Both Rose and Percy knew that marriage for him was impossible while she was alive. Rumors that their personal relationship was incestuous may have been a factor. In addition, this added to the uncertainties surrounding her death, making her son all the more insecure.

The pattern of returning to the Scandinavian countries whenever he sought privacy would occupy him during his life. In August, after completing his regular summer teaching duties at the Chicago Musical College, he sailed for Denmark. No performances were planned. He was obsessed with Scandinavian art, music, and literature, so it is not strange that one of his first projects on this trip was the collection of folk songs with the Danish folklorist, Evald Tang Kristensen. Grainger had learned of Kristensen's work during his 1904 Danish tour. When he inquired of Hjalmar Thuren and Herman Sandby where he might find original sources of Danish folk tunes, he had been directed to the work of Kristensen. Kristensen, who had published

Danish folk songs as early as 1871, was known for the care in which he transcribed his findings. Whether Grainger's identical method of notating rhythmic irregularities and personal characteristics of the singers came through his knowledge of Kristensen's work or whether he arrived at similar conclusions independently, is not known. That he agreed with Kristensen is well documented.

Grainger's interest in collecting folk songs with a recording machine must certainly be attributed to Eugenia Lineva (1894). Her findings, complete with photographs and musical examples, were published in both Russian and English in 1904 and were known to Grainger. Lineva's research was an extension of the work of Julius Melgunn whose concern with devising an accurate method of notating folk songs was published in articles in 1879 and 1885. It is most possible then that Grainger's method of notating folksongs was a result of his knowledge of the work of Lineva and Melgunn on the one hand and that of Kristensen on the other. It was Grainger, however, who finally brought the methods into clearer focus and applied them to the rich heritage of the English countryside.

Grainger and Kristensen (then eighty years old) traveled through Jutland on three separate occasions, 1922, 1925, and 1927, collecting Danish folk melodies. As in earlier excursions in England, Grainger employed the phonograph to "study . . . the singing-wonts of the true folk-singer."[31] Two things were evident: the accuracy of Kristensen's early collections and the errors of the critics who had accused him of notating his findings incorrectly. Although fifty years had elapsed between Kristensen's first work and his efforts with Grainger, the findings were the same in spite of the fact that, in every instance, the singers were different. At the conclusion of the third trip, over two hundred discs made on these song hunts were deposited at Copenhagen's Royal Library.

It was no mere chance then that Grainger's first efforts

at composition after his mother's death were concerned
with settings of several of the Jutland Peninsula folk tunes
that he and Kristensen had collected. *The Power of Love*,
the first tune to be scored, had been collected from a Mrs.
Post, whose "Nordic comeliness, knee-slapping mirth, and
warmheartedness, paired with a certain inborn aristocratic
holding-back of herself, reminded me of my mother."[32]

A curious similarity exists between the folk song collecting careers of Grainger and Béla Bartók. Both men were
among the first to utilize a mechanical recording device
to collect folk materials from their respective countries
and both started at precisely the same time. A distinct
feature of their folk song transcriptions was the meticulous
notation of the singer's inflections, a technique which does
not seem to have occurred to other collectors of the period.

Storm Bull, a pupil of Bartók from 1933-35, recalls that
Bartók explicitly told him that "the idea for using this recording device (Edison Wax cylinder) came to him [Bartók]
through the reading of an article by Percy Grainger."[33]

According to Benjamine Rajeczky of the Magyar Tudo-
mányor Akadémia, however, Bartók's "first collecting
trip with the phonograph fell on 1907" and it had been
"made known to him by his friend Kodaly [who] also taught
him how to use the instrument."[34] And in addition to this,
Grainger's article describing his collecting with the machine
in 1905-06 did not appear until 1908-09 in the *Journal of
the English Folk Song Society*. Although Grainger must be
regarded as having used the machine earlier than Bartók,
it appears that it was not possible for Bartók to have been
influenced by Grainger in the use of a mechanical device
to record folk tunes. Unless Bartók was referring specifically to the Edison wax cylinder, his statement to Bull
contradicts present day evidence. Bull, unable to substantiate his statement, later qualified it by saying that he could
not "be sure that Bartók's memory may not have been
wrong in its chronology."[35]

In 1933 Bull showed his teacher an article by Grainger entitled "Melody Versus Rhythm," which was published in the *Chicago Music News* in September and October of that year. Bartók, taking issue with Grainger's assertion that melody was the higher form of folk-art music, replied in an article appearing in the same magazine the following January. Percy never forgave Bartók for the published rebuttal to his view on folk melody and rhythm. When Bull later tried to interest Grainger in Bartók's music, Percy answered quite strongly:

> Why do you want to interest me in Bartók's music? He belongs to the enemy group — that is all I know or need to know. Furthermore everything I know of his is energetic, harsh, ambitious. You know what I worship in music: The smoothness of Bach, the smoothness of Fauré. I rate all music by its closeness to *Peace*.[36]

Later he added the final denunciation.

> One cannot make a paying career on Bartók, who, whatever else he is, is hardly a melodist and, therefore hardly a man to thrill the (buying public).[37]

It is likely that the two composers never met. Although Bartók tried to contact Grainger through Delius in 1911, an actual meeting has never been documented.

On September 7, 1922, Frederick Delius arrived in Denmark. As if holding court, Grainger's friends began to arrive. Shortly after Delius, came Balfour Gardiner and finally Roger Quilter. Only Cyril Scott was missing from the Frankfurt circle. His condolences came in the form of an offer to contact Rose through a medium. Percy refused. To each of these close friends Grainger reiterated the story of his mother's death, and he began to plan memorials to her in the form of new compositions, articles, and essays about their life together and the development of his career as a composer, the first "major composer of Australia."

Suffering from an advanced case of syphilis and confined to a wheelchair, Delius insisted on being carried up an adjacent mountain to view the sunset on the distant hills. With Grainger on one end of his stretcher and Mrs. Delius and two servants on the other, the group made the seven-hour ascent, paused at the summit to witness the spectacle, and then began the difficult descent. At Delius' request Grainger sketched a dance movement to be added to Delius' incidental theater music, *Hassan*, which was to be performed that fall. Grainger assisted in the complete scoring, but the new movement was not completed in time for the performance.

A number of articles by Grainger on various aspects of his music began to appear in the popular journals of the day. They did not reflect the scholarship of his earlier efforts and appeared to be attempts merely to get into print. Messages from his close friends consoling him on the death of his mother were answered with a private printing of "Rose Grainger — Three Short Accounts of Her Life." This expensive volume, privately printed in Munich in 1923, contains her letters, a chronology of her life, and her photographs. Each year on the anniversary of her death, Percy's diary would contain the simple entry: "Mother died."

In 1923, *Hill Song No. 1*, which he had rescored for chamber orchestra, was tried out in Frankfurt under the direction of Alexander Lippay. At this same time, he also heard a rehearsal of his enormous score, *The Warriors*, which Balfour Gardiner had helped him rescore the previous fall in Denmark. A total of six orchestra rehearsals were held, each financed by Grainger. Delius attended all the rehearsals, even though he had to be transported by wheelchair from his house to the hall and then carried to the second floor rehearsal room. Through Delius' influence both the *Hill Song No. 1* and *The Warriors* were published. Grainger described them as "two of my most important, yet least saleable works."[38]

Before returning to the United States, Grainger began

a whirlwind tour of the Netherlands, performing 21 times in four weeks and accomplishing a total of 56 concerts in Northern Europe that year.

Many of the contradictory statements that Grainger made were not understood by the general public. Perhaps to understand the man, one has to examine both what he said and what he actually did. Writing shortly after the death of his mother he remarked that, although he disliked performing in public, he loved the restful isolation of the concert platform and even the comparative isolation he found in the railway stations. Although he made a great deal of money he did not save any, because he felt "an artist should use 25% and spend the rest on art, science, and friends. My *absolute duty* as an artist and as a communist."[39] There is no question that his political leanings were socialistic, but he openly professed to be an ardent democrat and never subscribed to any particular political activity in the United States. There was one instance in the early forties when his name, along with that of Howard Hanson, appeared on the letterhead of the "Nationalist American Music Society" as sponsors of the organization, but there is no documentation that he had authorized the use of his name. That same year, 1940, Grainger refused to serve as a judge of a composition contest, stating that he was unqualified because his music "was not nationalistically American."

The naive rationalization which dictated his actions often caused bizarre and eccentric consequences. His personal logic seemed to absolve his conscience of any social affront. He had often been imposed upon to attend the homes of the wealthy in London in order to earn his living, therefore, rather than waste time on the formal topics of social intercourse, he would discuss only those subjects which interested him. Icelandic history, the superiority of the Anglo-Saxon race, and folksong collecting were central themes of his conversation — even though a particular host might be ignorant of the subject or, at least, disinterested.

He suspiciously viewed invitations to dinner and would often neglect to answer even his friends when they would invite him. He preferred to associate with the working class and continued to be socialistic in his political feelings. He could have been independently wealthy but instead generously gave his earnings to those he considered needy. By 1927 he was supporting, in varying degrees, thirteen relatives and friends.

In addition to his performing tours and a recording contract with Columbia, Grainger had an agreement with Duo-Art to produce a series of piano rolls which would be used on their mechanical pianos. Percy and Rose had recorded two piano settings of *Hermundi illi* and *As Sally Sat a Weeping* to inaugurate the agreement. The early 20's saw the height of popularity of the Duo-Art reproducing piano and in 1923, competing only against the poor quality of the disc companies, Duo-Art had under contract twelve of the most famous pianists of the day. In addition to Grainger these included Paderewski, Hoffmann, Pachmann, Bauer, Gabrilowitsch, Busoni, Friedman, Ganz, Cortot, Lamond, and Bachaus. In spite of their many art-music rolls, the best selling piano roll of 1923 was a rendition of "I've Got the 'Yes! We Have No Banana' Blues," by Herbert Clair (then, and as yet, unknown).

Grainger's versatility knew few limitations. In the Spring of 1921 he had become the first pianist of international reputation to appear in a motion picture theater. During his one week engagement at New York's Capitol Theater Grainger discovered an ingenious use for the reproducing piano. Sandwiched between the screen novelty "Lyman Howe's Famous Ride on a Runaway Train" and "Officer Cupid," a Mack Sennett production, Grainger performed the first movement of the Tchaikovsky Bb minor Concerto. He appeared daily at 2:31, 4:31, 8:01, and 10:01 with a reproducing piano ably providing the orchestral portion.

A few weeks later he became the first soloist ever to appear at the Evanston, Illinois Festival. The Chicago Symphony substituted for his reproducing piano and Frederick Stock conducted.

During the summer festivals at New York's Lewisohn Stadium that year, Willem Van Hoogstraten conducted the Stadium Orchestra in a performance of the Tchaikovsky Bb minor, the soloist being a Duo-Art reproducing piano which had been prepared by Grainger in advance. Grainger applauded the performance of the players from a secure position in the audience.

Grainger continued to teach during the summer in Chicago and for a short time he was in charge of the orchestra. He would often use multiple pianos, combining a most cosmopolitan array of pieces on a single program. He constantly encouraged piano ensemble playing and would assign single voices of a Bach fugue to several pianos playing in ensemble. His unorthodox teaching techniques attracted an unusually large body of students, and his summer teaching schedule was full to overflowing. But he did not really care for teaching, since he had little patience with students who were not as gifted as he. Percy continued on the staff, however, for the money was good.

The popularity of Grainger's light pieces was extraordinary, and they were arranged and performed by almost every conceivable organization. Even Sousa "pinched" them. Writing to Grainger early in April of 1921 he confessed that: "I have probably played your compositions a greater number of times than any conductor in America, and there is something about all of them that makes a very strong appeal to me and to my public. I heard *Country Gardens* on the Ampico 16 months ago and made an arrangement from your piano copy which I played this year on tour about 200x."[40]

Early in 1924 Grainger and Balfour Gardiner traveled to France to visit the ailing Delius. (A note from his American manager cautioned him to "Be sure and dress up when you go to Paris.") It was the two musicians' wish to perform for Delius and cheer the man they both respected and loved. Gardiner prepared for the visit as if he were scheduled to appear at the finest recital halls, and Grainger offered a body of literature which he rarely performed. The two pianists performed 8-10 hours a day for 10 days, in behalf of their audience of one. Their departure brought tears to the eyes of the grateful host.

The sociability within the Frankfurt group knew few limitations, for the compositional devices employed by one member were freely borrowed by the others, and no one person was given credit for originating the idea. In many instances Grainger used his ideas to influence Scott, and Scott saw no harm in borrowing certain techniques, to use in his own pieces. This pawning of material was not confined to the Frankfurt Group, however, for Scott wrote: "The most honest and conscientious bit of plagiarism was perpetrated by Eugene Goosens who incorporated a bit from (I think it was) my Symphony *The Muses* at the end of his opera *Don Juan*. He told me quite frankly 'I thought it would be nice there, so I pinched!" Well, I have no objection," remarked Scott.[41]

It is interesting to note Grainger's response to a query from the *Etude Magazine* that year to list the "ten great musical masterpieces." Differing in approach from the other 27 eminent musicians who were included in the survey, Grainger listed one work for each of ten styles and compositional forms he deemed significant: Oratorio — Bach *St. Matthew Passion*; Opera — Wagner *Tristan and Isolde*; Nature Music — Delius' *Song of the High Hills*; Symphony — Tchaikovsky's *Pathétique*; Religious — Franck's *Three Organ Chorales*; Sonata — Chopin's *B minor, Op. 58*; Harmonic — Grieg *Op. 56*; Polyphonic — Bach's *Well Tempered Clavichord*; Chamber work — Fauré's *Piano Quartet, Op. 15*; Descriptive Orchestral Work — Debussy's

Prelude to the Afternoon of a Faun.

Each of the musicians who responded, modestly left their own works off the list with the exception of John Philip Sousa whose tenth choice was his own *Stars and Stripes Forever.*

In April Grainger organized and financed two concerts which were of special import. He had long considered the possibility of utilizing the Bridgeport Oratorio Society to present a series of his favorite large choral and orchestral works. Because of his growing income from royalties and his successful concert tours, he was now able to finance such a project. He extended an offer to Mr. Warner, the president of the Oratorio Society, to provide the orchestra for both a Bridgeport and a New York performance. But Mr. Warner accepted the offer only in part, since he generously underwrote the bulk of the expenses for the Bridgeport concert.

With the dream of his Anglo-Saxon Scandinavian concert realized, Grainger set in motion the details of hiring an orchestra of 94 musicians to complement the 250 voice chorus. The first concert was scheduled for April 28th with a repeat of the program in Carnegie Hall two days later. Grainger planned to conduct, although he "had grave doubts as to how I would shape as a conductor." His fears proved ungrounded for "I found all the musicians, whether professional or amateur, sympathetic from first to last. They did not seem to laugh at me unduly."[42]

Grainger discovered his role as a conductor of pieces other than his own to be a difficult task, but it was his own *Marching Song of Democracy* that gave him the most concern. "I made a sorry mess of a place near the beginning (got muddled up with the changing bars), and if the performers had paid too much attention to my beats it would have been a catastrophe."[43] A wealth of publicity was generated by the advance notice that Delius was expected in New York for the second performance. Grainger, who was writing his own press releases, informed

Delius that he was "laying the jam on pretty thick, as USA needs this."[44] It is questionable if Grainger really believed that Delius would make the trip, and during the week prior to the concert, it was announced that Delius' doctors had cancelled his plans to attend.

The New York performance, given on the second anniversary of his mother's death, was dedicated to her memory. Reviews of the unusual concert were generally favorable and Grainger's conducting was applauded by the critics, although the *Christian Science Monitor* wanted to reserve judgment until he had conducted music which he was less "fond of or familiar with." At least one reviewer speculated as to how much it must have cost Grainger to produce the gigantic project.

That summer Grainger returned to Australia on a holiday, his first extended absence from the concert stage since the beginning of his career. In June he arrived in Sydney aboard the *Tahiti*. While reporters searched for him in the ship's first class section, Grainger easily avoided them by slipping from his second class accommodations to the street and hailing the shabbiest cab available. "Artists have to travel first class as much for advertisement as for comfort," he lamented, and when he had amassed sufficient funds he would always "either walk or travel second class." This was his first trip to Australia in 15 years and no concert appearances were scheduled. He planned to visit many of his relatives and gather material for a biography of his mother.

His love of the outdoors and "a boyish dream" to tramp the Australian desert was indulged when he hiked 80 miles in three days from Tailem Bend to Keith. His pack contained a sleeping bag with a Red Riding Hood sort of wired tent and a couple of rugs. Two packets of dates, a tin of brown bread, a packet of rusks, and some nuts were the extent of his food supply. Boots and personal luggage brought the pack to 42 pounds. The first day he covered 27 1/2 miles, the second 29 1/2. Discovering that his boots had chafed a vein on his right foot until it had broken, he slowed the pace to 22 miles on the third day. Since his foot continued to bother him, he "rejoined the train at Keith and continued my journey in a more conventional fashion."

As he "humped his swag" through the desert, he was mistaken for a detective at one hotel whose owner later apologized, stating: "You have to be careful of tramps anyway, and the police are always getting up some new dodge over the Early Closing Act." She also suspected that he might have been a piano tuner for he could "thump the keys quite smartly."[45]

Although he gave no public performances, Grainger held six private gatherings of friends and musicians at which he played and lectured on modern music in general and English-speaking composers in particular. In Sydney and Adelaide he lectured and demonstrated the Duo-Art reproducing piano which was then gaining popularity in most of the larger Australian cities. Through his lectures the music of Carpenter, Guion, Brockway, Dett, and Sowerby was introduced to the Australian public. Each piece was outlined as to its content and intention. The "Sydney Bulletin" described his presentation:

> The Grainger voice being as musical as the fingers, the talk was nearly as pleasing as the solos and one felt if more of this sort of intimate recital were given here, our concert halls would be better filled. Few expected to find so much charm in Grainger as a speaker; it all lies, however, in that simple and sincere directness which distinguishes also his playing.[46]

Grainger's visit brought him in contact with musical organizations in Adelaide, Melbourne, and Sydney and amid promises that he would do a professional tour in 1926 he left for the United States to begin a concentrated season of touring.

Commencing on October 16th, the 1924-25 American

concert season was an especially active one. The management of Grainger's tours was taken over in 1925 by Toni Morse (Antonia Sawyer's niece) and her husband. Fred Morse was a skilled photographer and he assisted his wife in handling the publicity and mailings. The couple moved into Percy's large home at 7 Cromwell Place, and together they served as Percy's cook, confidant, and advisor. Three programs, conducted in part and subsidized by Grainger, proved to be especially significant. On January 18th Grainger joined forces with the Harvard Glee Club, under the direction of Dr. Archibald T. Davison, and the Peoples Symphony Orchestra of Boston to present a number of his own compositions. Boston had always been a city which was fond of the Australian and hundreds of patrons had to be turned away. Not since Monteux conducted had the demand for tickets been as brisk.

The program included the first performance of three pieces from his *Jungle Book Cycle* — *Danny Deever, Tiger-Tiger* and *The Widows Party* — scored for male chorus and orchestra. The reviews were generous and Grainger's conducting was favorably compared to that of Monteux. The program included *Mock Morris, Irish Tune from County Derry, Colonial Song,* and *The Warriors;* and at the end of *Shepherd's Hey,* the enthusiasm of the audience was so great that an encore was demanded.

The quest for proper texts with American roots led Percy to contact Vachel Lindsay. In October of 1924, he wrote inquiring if Lindsay would consent to recite a poem or group of poems during a chamber music concert he was playing in Spokane. The idea of an article for the *Musical Quarterly* concerning "Musical Elements in Vachel Lindsay's Poetry," was also being considered. The partnership, however, did not mature.

In 1898, while a student in Frankfurt, Grainger had begun his extended *Kipling Jungle Book Cycle.* He referred to these pieces as being scored for "large chamber music."

They consisted of eight to twenty-five solo performers
providing instrumental backgrounds for single voices or a
small chorus. The basis for this type of orchestration was
later explained by Grainger in a letter to the pianist-composer, Harold Bauer.

> . . .the music Kipling Settings which I send you
> separately, hoping that it may interest you as
> an outcome of the influence emanating from the
> vocal-solo numbers-with-accompaniment-of-solo-
> instruments in Bach's Matthew Passion, as I
> heard it when a boy of 12, 13, 14 in Frankfurt.
> These sounds (2 flutes and harpsichord and
> mixed chorus accompanying a solo voice) sound-
> ed so exquisite to my ears (so much more *seemly*
> than a full orchestra accompanying a single
> voice) that I became convinced that large cham-
> ber music (from 8-25 performers) was, for me,
> an ideal background for single voices or a small
> chorus. On this assumption (all rooted clearly
> in Bach's procedures) I began my "Kipling Jun-
> gle Book Cycle" in 1898 and such compositions
> as: "Love Verses from the Song of Solomon" in
> 1899.[48]

This attempt at scoring for smaller instrumental groups
which would perform in smaller concert halls was vividly
demonstrated on April 26th and May 3rd of 1925 when
Grainger produced two evenings of "Room Music" at the
Little Theater, 238 West 44th Street, in New York City.

The first evening was an all-Grainger Program including *English Dance* (6 hands at two pianos), *Hill Song
No. 1* in its revision for chamber orchestra, seven settings
from the *Jungle Book Cycle, My Robin is to the Greenwood Gone* (flute, English horn and 6 strings), and *Scotch
Strathspey and Reel.*

The second evening featured Franz Schreker's *Kammer-
symphonie, Negro Folk-Song Derivatives* of R. Nathaniel
Dett, *Memories of New Mexico* by Natalie Curtis, *Lost
in the Hills* of Edvard Greig, and Paul Hindemith's *Kam-
mermusik No. 1.* The Hindemith selection, it's "dashing

ending produced by the fantastic instruments and percussion, moved the audience to mirths of laughter and held it lingering in the aisles, to comment upon the prankishness of the spirit of modern music."[49] All works were presented in their original form — a rather unique production which was enthusiastically applauded by the capacity audience.

Summer was spent as usual at the Chicago Musical College. Percy's master classes had grown to such popularity that students applied months in advance for the opportunity to study with him. His classes included (1) Repertoire-Interpretation-Teachers classes, (2) Piano-ensemble, (3) "How to Study," and (4) private lessons of 15 minutes in groups of four students each.

To meet the demand for enrollment a limited number of auditors were granted permission to attend the class lessons. These auditors could "not participate in the lessons" nor "interrupt the instruction of the four students by asking questions."

The teaching rates for Grainger's lessons were growing each year and at $125 for five thirty-minute lessons, students paid two to four times as much as with any other keyboard instructor on the staff. Prestige determined the tuition rate and only Leopold Auer charged more. Grainger's classes were packed and their popularity even exceeded that for the class offered in Motion Picture Organ, which hinted that its graduates might make $300 or more weekly in theaters throughout the country.

Plans for a return to Australia on a professional tour were progressing well. The Tait Agency of Melbourne assured Grainger that he would be booked solid for several months beginning in June of the following year.

In December, Herman Sandby arrived to present a series of concerts and to visit Grainger. To help him and to push the music of his Frankfurt friends, Grainger appeared on several of Sandby's programs, accompanying singers and instrumentalists in performances of his own work and that

George Percy Grainger
Age 4, Melbourne, Australia

Rose Grainger and Percy (on the left) at "Pension Pfaff," Frankfurt, Germany, 1895 or 1896

Travels in Europe

Rose and Percy
Frankfurt, Germany, c. 1899

A watercolor by Percy Grainger
Karl der Grosse Bridge, Frankfurt, Germany, June 6, 1896

Grainger (center) with Danish cellist
Herman Sandby and fiance, c. 1907

Karen Holton, Percy's
"playmate over the hills"
Svinkløv, 1909

Edvard Grieg, Grainger, Nina Grieg,
and composer Jules Röntgen
Troldhaugen, Norway, July 1907

Arrival in America

Shortly after his arrival, 1914

Grainger in New York, c. 1920

With Rocco Resta (left) in a
U.S. Army Band, 1916

In 1910

Rose and Percy

Fort Hamilton, N.Y., 1917

White Plains, N.Y., July 1921

Grainger the Outdoorsman

Wrestling with his secretary, Frederick Morse
White Plains, N.Y., 1923

In hiking clothes
Australia in the 1930's

Rowing at Grez-sur-Loing, 1925(?)

No concert singer I have ever heard approached these rural warblers in variety of tone-quality, range of dynamics, rhythmic resourcefulness and individuality of style. For while our concert singers (dulldogs that they are — with their monotonous mooing and bellowing between mf and ff, and with never a pp to their name) can show nothing better as slavish obedience to the tyrannical behests of composers, our folk-singers were lords in their own domain — were at once performers and creators.

P.G.

Grainger with folksinger A.J. Knocks
Otaki, New Zealand, Sept. 16, 1924

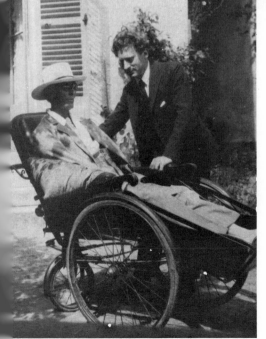

When Delius and I first met, in 1907, we felt a very close compositional affinity... And this was not unnatural; for although, up to then, we had seen nothing of each other's works, our melodic and harmonic inheritances came from much the same sources: Bach, Wagner, Grieg, and folk-music.

Percy Aldridge Grainger
Remarks about his Hill-song No. 1
September, 1949

Grainger with Frederick Delius
at Grez-sur-Loing, 1925(?)

Photo by Jean De Strelec

Ella Ström
London, c. 1915

Miss Ström is the very prototype of a radiant Nordic — as lovely as the morning to look upon, and a regular Amazon to walk, run, swim, and dance and play games. At the same time she is one of the most deeply and many-sidedly gifted artists I have ever met, and it is hard for me to say what charms me the most in her — her bewitching beauty or the philosophical and emotional depths of her nature as shown forth in her arts and thoughts.

P.G.

Percy and Ella

Percy, Ella, and conductor
William Durieux in the 1930

Percy and Ella in
rehearsal, 1950's

Shortly after their marriage in 1926

Ella and Percy

At their home in White
Plains, N.Y.
September 3, 1958

Photo by Frederick Fennell

Grainger in Milwaukee for the *Lincolnshire Posy*
premiere performance, 1937

Photos by The Milwaukee Sentinel

The Grainger Museum
November, 1938

Photo by Ella Grainger

Ella and Percy with Burnett Cross

The Later Years

Visiting Kneller Hall, England's Royal
Military School of Music
May 28, 1957

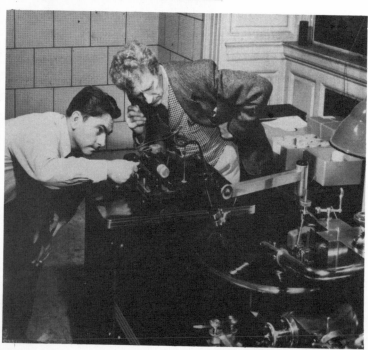

Transferring folk-
song cylinders
to acetate at the
Library of Congress

Ralph Vaughan Williams with Percy and Ella Grainger
White Plains, N.Y., 1954

Cyril Scott in 1951(?)

Grainger with Henry Cowell
White Plains, N.Y.

of Sandby, Quilter, Scott, and Gardiner.

In addition to appearing with the major orchestras during the fall of 1925, Grainger began to concertize more extensively for smaller audiences. He was even engaged for a week at the newly opened Keith-Albee's Hippodrome in New York where he was high-lighted between the Hippodrome's Ice Skating Girls and Lina-Basquette, billed as the "former Premier Danseuse of Ziegfield's Follies." The dancing act of Wallace, Cappo Brothers and Pastor ably assisted both presentations. Except during Grainer's engagement at the Largest Playhouse in the World, each patron that month received $15 discount on Charleston lessons from Arthur Murray.

Before sailing to Australia Grainger appeared as guest conductor with the Los Angeles Oratorio Society in the premier performance of his *Marching Song of Democracy.* This experimental piece, scored for chorus and orchestra, used "nonsense syllables" for it's text. Grainger's original plan had been to use voices and whistlers with only the rhythmic accompaniment of the chorus' tramping feet. The first rehearsals of the piece in Frankfurt three years before brought about the concept of the present orchestration.

The use of nonsense syllables was an effort by Grainger to achieve "a more varied and instinctive vocalism than could be obtained without the use of words in music of a polyphonic nature."[50] The concert was an amazing success and, although there were many empty seats, the critics and patrons alike were unusually generous in their applause and remarks. "Our Universities alone should have sent a contingent of listeners to have occupied every seat at Philharmonic Auditorium were they, indeed, the centers of culture they purport to be," remarked critic Bruno Ussher. He went on to add that "Grainger has grown into a conductor of technical sovereignty and irresistible personal power."[51]

In addition to the experimental *Marching Song of De-*

mocracy, Grainger included his *Irish Tune* for unaccompanied chorus which also utilized the novel "nonsense syllables." *Father and Daughter,* a Faeroe Island folk dance song set for male vocal quintet, double mixed chorus and orchestra concluded the concert. Its reception was so great as to demand that it be repeated. The exquisite oratorio chorus was prepared by John Smallman whom Grainger spoke of as being one of the most competent choral men in the country. The purpose of the concert was to "emphasize the return to an intrinsically vocal attitude toward the chorus on the part of several modern composers."[52] The Los Angeles public agreed that it had been accomplished.

Grainger's final appearance before departing to Australia was especially arranged for youngsters. Appearing at the West Coast Uptown Theater the next morning, he mesmerized the children with the most popular of his recital pieces.

Notes

[1] Antonia Sawyer, *Songs at Twilight* (New York: Devon-Adair Co., 1939), pp. 128-129.
[2]*Ibid.*
[3] Henry T. Finck, *My Adventures in the Golden Age of Music* (New York: Funk & Wagnalls, 1926), pp. 391-392.
[4]Letter to Frederick Delius from Grainger, Aug. 8, 1915.
[5]Letter to Grainger from Oscar Sonneck, editor of *The Musical Quarterly,* no date.
[6]Letter to Oscar Sonneck from Grainger, Oct. 22, 1915.
[7]Telegram to John Grainger from Rose Grainger, no date.
[8]John K. Sherman, *Music and Maestros* (Minneapolis: University of Minnesota Press, 1952), p. 137.
[9]*Ibid.*
[10]*The Christian Science Monitor,* Boston, Mass., June 9, 1917.
[11]"Percy Grainger," *Canon,* IV (Nov., 1950), 183.
[12]Grainger, "Deemths" (unpublished typescript, no date).
[13]*Ibid.*
[14]Grainger, "Bird's-Eye View of the Together Life of Rose Grainger and Percy Grainger" (18-page typescript, dated 1947).

[15]"Percy Grainger," *Canon*, p. 180.

[16]Letter to Balfour Gardiner from Grainger, Dec. 12, 1917.

[17]Grainger, "Notes on Hill Song No. 1" (unpublished typescript, Sept. 1949).

[18]Letter to Frederick Fennell from Grainger, White Plains, New York, dated 1959. (Quoted in the program notes compiled by Fennell for the record jacket of Mercury MG50219).

[19]*Ibid.*

[20]Letter to R. Clarke Ewing from Grainger, May 16, 1945.

[21]Letter to Rose Grainger from Antonia Sawyer, Mar. 15, 1919.

[22]Grainger, "Round Letter to Kin and Friends," Feb. 15-17, 1942.

[23]Finck, *The Evening Post Magazine*, New York, Oct. 11, 1919, p. 8.

[24]Letter to North American Lines from Grainger, White Plains, New York, May, 1951.

[25]Robert Lewis Taylor, "The Running Pianist," *The New Yorker* (Feb. 7, 1948), 39.

[26]Grainger, "Photos of Rose Grainger and 3 short accounts of her life by herself, in her own hand-writing" (Munich: privately published, 1923).

[27]Grainger, "Bird's-Eye View . . ."

[28]*The New York Globe*, Sept. 17, 1921.

[29]Letter to Balfour Gardiner from Grainger, May 3, 1922.

[30]Letter to Percy Grainger from Rose Grainger, 1922.

[31]Grainger, "Program Note" to *Danish Folk Music Suite* (G. Schirmer, 1928).

[32]*Ibid.*

[33]Letter to author from Storm Bull, Dec. 12, 1969.

[34]*Ibid.*, Sept. 15, 1969.

[35]*Ibid.*, July 28, 1970.

[36]Letter to Storm Bull from Grainger, Nov. 16, 1940.

[37]*Ibid.*, Feb. 1941.

[38]Peter Warlock (Philip Heseltine), *Frederick Delius* (reprinted with additions, annotations, and comments by Hubert Foss; New York: Oxford University Press, 1952).

[39]Grainger, "The Life of My Mother and Her Son" (75-page typescript located in the Library of Congress, dated 1934).

[40]Letter to Grainger from J.P. Sousa, April 22, 1924.

[41]Letter to Grainger from Cyril Scott, Nov. 25, 1949.

[42]*Musical Life and Arts*, I/2 (Oct. 1, 1924).

[43]*Ibid.*

[44]Letter to Frederick Delius from Grainger, Nov. 11, 1914.

[45]*The Advertiser*, Adelaide, Australia, July 24, 1924.

[46]*The Bulletin*, Sydney, Australia, Sept. 11, 1924.

[47]Grainger, comments to *Frederick Delius* by Warlock.

[48]Letter to Harold Bauer from Grainger, White Plains, New York, Aug. 26, 1947.

[49]*The New York Evening Post*, May 4, 1925.

[50]*Los Angeles Evening Express*, April 29, 1926.

[51]*Ibid.*, May 8, 1926.

[52]*Los Angeles Examiner*, May 1, 1926.

New Directions

Charisma

Grainger's arrival in Sydney on May 28th, 1926, aboard the *Aorangi* coincided with that of Chaliapin, the Russian basso; both had been booked by the J. & N. Tait Agency for extended Australian tours. Accompanying the pianist were four Steinway grands, especially designed and built for the tour. Grainger's voyage had been an active one; he played a recital enroute at Honolulu and finished editing the *Marching Song of Democracy* (which had received its revised premiere in Los Angeles a few weeks earlier). Upon his arrival he posted the manuscript to his publishers in Vienna.

Initial press interviews stirred a great deal of interest in Grainger's flippant attitude toward his hands. "I do not care a straw about my hands," he was quoted. "The main thing with a pianists hands is to harden them . . . . He [the pianist] is like a prize fighter — his fingers have to be hard to stand constant hitting."[1] But the most arresting description of Grainger appeared in the Sydney *Times*. "Percy Grainger, the Australian genius of the piano, does not walk. He trots — the kangaroo trot. His hands are priceless, but they're not insured. The world calls him genius, but he calls himself a democrat. And he never wears a hat."[2]

His love of the outdoors, his democratic attitudes, and his acclaim of the local country, made Grainger a national hero in this, his first professional appearance in Australia since 1909. The story of his recent sixty-five-mile hike between Pietermaritzburg and Durban, South Africa had preceded him. It amused his countrymen to know that when he had arrived at his South African hotel and could not locate his suitcases, he played the recital that evening in "running shorts." His interviews with the New Zealand press, where his ship had stopped four days earlier, were equally charming. His wide range of interests and ideas on composing beatless music, the development of a complete percussion family in the orchestra, and his fondness for polyphonic music were detailed. He struck the eastern coast of Australia, that June, like a tropical storm.

Grainger's marathon tour opened in the Melbourne Auditorium on June 5. Between that evening and June 22, he performed eight solo recitals, each played to a capacity house and each with a different memorized program; often seven or more encores were included. The critics were enthusiastic and the effect of his appearances prompted the following assessment: "Here is the genuine sweep and fire and elemental flame of youth. He is a whirlwind of dramatic fire."[3]

Chaliapin, who opened four days later, was overshadowed by the unusual reception afforded Australia's prodigal man-child. At Grainger's farewell concert on the afternoon of June 22, each patron received a printed slip containing a list of fifty-nine selections from which they might choose their favorites for inclusion on the program. This feat of memory did not fail to impress the Melbourne citizenry.

On the 24th of June, 1926, Grainger returned to Sydney and presented the first of five concerts at Town Hall, all but the first were aired on the Farmer's Broadcasting Station. The local press contained interviews, statements, and speculations about the merit of his freely offered ideas. He had come out openly for jazz and was suspect for it.

"I think the beauty and subtlety of the best jazz is going
to revolutionize music or form the basis of a new school."[4]
That he did not insure his hands was again of interest, until
Grainger offered that "the bulk of singers and players who
insure lavishly are simply admitting a weakness — making
a gesture, as it were, to cloak a mass of shortcomings."[5]
As for his athleticism, he explained that many great artists
were interested in exercise. "Chopin and Bach were great
walkers," he offered, while "Wagner was a great tree-climber."
The source of this interesting analogy was not questioned,
and Grainger continued to court the best publicity available
by merely appearing to shun it.

His casual stage deportment was widely applauded by
his audience, and his brief introductory remarks about the
selections were well-received. On one occasion, when "Grainger came onto the stage . . . he found the instrument not
placed just to his liking. Refusing to summon aid, he gave
it a smart heave. The heavy instrument yielded to his
tugging, and he settled down at the piano without more
ado. Though his ability as a piano mover had been impressive, the audience was apparently even more impressed
with his piano playing — since they called him back fourteen times!"[6]

The appearance of the controversial pianist varied from
immaculate attire to the most slovenly of dress. It probably
did not occur to him to be consistent in his dress — after
all, his public statements were contradictory as well. He
described each organization he appeared with, for instance,
as the "most responsive choir (or orchestra) he had ever
heard." Through his exaggerated statements and dress, he
was accepted by both critics and public, and his flair for
the theatrical was accepted as a mark of his personality.

> There is something irresistibly spontaneous
> about him. Pose is an unknown quantity to him.
> For instance, he never wore a hat for years, un-
> til it was said that his idea was to pose and show

off his luxuriant head of golden hair. On Wednesday he wore a felt hat jammed down firmly on his head as he left the Melbourne Express. That is to say, it was jammed down as firmly as the unruly golden mop would allow. He wore an old sack suit and a heavy overcoat, and boots that were too uncompromisingly broad and plain to be anything but comfortable.[7]

Grainger's hair was "doubtlessly admired by the ladies," whose recent coiffure fashion of shingling had not been well-received by the male population. One Aussie remarked that a woman's neck was usually a place to kiss, but now "one could strike a match on it."

The hearty physique of the pianist was a trait especially appreciated by the Australians, and he was described as "most typically Australian in his justification of the physical side of his art . . . Grainger has none of the effeminacy that the ignorant associate with handsome profiles and womanish tresses. He is a man's man — a good fellow, and an athlete, active beyond the concept of the average,"[8] commented a Brisbane reporter. He was "of Grecian build, and with a classic, clean-cut countenance, he impressed with a quiet, ingenious manner, and yet with a vitality which revealed a strength of purpose and understanding."[9] To the Australians, both musically and physically, Grainger was a "smasher."

After Sydney came Adelaide, his mother's home. Although not the size of his two previous tour-cities, its welcome was equally enthusiastic. Percy's Aunt Clara Aldridge had made his coming known and the few days preceding his appearances had been spent in meeting the musical public at small receptions. A large audience was almost assured.

Five concerts in eleven days drew laudatory reviews. "One can scarcely imagine a better artist than Percy Grainger to attract the business man, tired or fresh, to listen in at the musical game. He plays tunes 'rippingly' . . . as a boy whistles a tune, with lots of swing and rhythm to them, and he gets a thrill out of a good tune and passes it along to the listener in great shape."[10] Even the most cynical of audiences were captivated and a particularly revealing column stated: "There was quite a personal touch in Percy's playing of 'Tomorrow You May Be Wed,' [Grieg]; but he has been too well chaperoned, by his aunt, for it to be possible. 'Turkey in the Straw' gave Adelaide audiences a chance to show their culture and they seized it with both hands."[11]

Commenting on the remainder of the program, the same writer continued:

> "One More Day, My John," was a sea chanty, which ought to have as great a vogue as "Shenandoah," which was sung here by the massive Clara Butt after the fashion of an anthem.
>
> A Chopin bracket on Saturday proved Grainger's uncanny versatility. There is something essentially manly in his playing itself. He neither bobs nor shingles, and, with another week's growth on his golden locks, could qualify as a Christian Israelite.
>
> Every time he comes to Adelaide, one of our swankiest "coiffeur de dames" is called on to trim the sacred curls.
>
> At the Town Hall the light glinted on the pale, passionate profile of Percy Grainger, somewhat roughened by a recent argument with a chest of drawers, and found a few gleams of gold in his hair despite the years.
>
> Percy knows what the people want, and he gives it to them. The critic who remarked that he "was in the first flight of the world's pianists" might have added that he could give most of them fifty yards and a beating.
>
> He interpreted Bach in a different musical idiom from any that the younger generation had ever heard. Later on, quite a number in the gallery held hands in the belief that they were at Waterfall Gully, so cool and clear was the splash of tumbling waters in the Gavotte.

Then, just to show that he was at home, and
all matey like, Percy sat down as it might have
been in the bar of a pub parlor, and dashed off
what the reviewers called "a careless burst of
scale passages," which sounded like Henley on
the Torrens expressed in musical fireworks.
He won in a duel with the Town.[12]

After only a month in his homeland, Grainger was acclaimed a success. Not in Australia's recent memory had a
single performer captured the fancy of the public as had
Grainger; and that public included not only the music
critics and the regular concert goers, but the farmer and
the laborer as well. Each felt that he was their personal
artist and fellow Australian. No previous success quite
equalled what was happening to him now.

Following his triumphs in Adelaide, Grainger retired to
the countryside, visiting relatives and preparing scores for
his next project. Before he left Australia he wanted to
present his larger works, in which his "democratic and
Australian feelings were prominent." Adelaide was chosen
for the first presentation of these scores, and in September
he returned to his home town for two concerts with the
South Australian Orchestra and the Adelaide Bach Society
Chorus. This time he appeared as conductor and soloist
with the results equaling the success of his solo recitals.
In addition to the Kipling setting, *We Have Fed Our Seas*
for chorus and orchestra, the *Irish Tune* for unaccompanied
chorus, and *I'm 17 Come Sunday* for mixed chorus and
brass, he included pieces by Grieg and Sandby. Grainger
appeared as soloist in the Tchaikovsky B♭ minor Concerto
and the program closed with his *Colonial Song* and the
Gumsucker's March.

The second and final chorus and orchestra concert contained music by Grainger and Grieg. The *tour de force* was
reserved for the conclusion of the concert, when Grainger's

"The Warriors" for three pianos and full orchestra
was presented by the composer.

The composition is a tremendous experiment
in musical possibilities. It suggests, rather than
completes, trying the effects of swiftly-shifting
rhythms and cross tonality. Snatches of individual
melody, widely diversified, lose themselves in a
seeming chaos of dissonances, which would give
the temporary impression that the musical mass
was without form and void, were it not for the
guiding hand of its creator, who out of chaos
evolves the musical cosmos.

It was a terrific ordeal for conductor and conducted, and not the least for the audience, who
followed, breathless, but the gigantic proportions
of the novel composition incited the hearers to
the highest pitch of enthusiasm, and the composer, dominant and apparently unwearied, had
to submit to a great ovation. . . . [13]

Before leaving Adelaide, Percy attracted attention and
approval by donating L500 to the city to initiate a fund for
the South Australian Orchestra in memory of Rose Grainger.

Traveling North to Brisbane, Grainger found that news
of his Adelaide success and his generosity to the state
orchestra had preceded him. He was greeted with a reception
in his honor, hosted by the Brisbane Australian Choir, with
whom he was to conduct two concerts. In a room decorated
with blue and gold curled streamers and pedestals holding
bowls of Iceland poppies, he spoke of the wonderful reception in his native country. As a memento he received a
"walking stick made of Queensland timber and a book
containing views of Brisbane."

The public adulation was unusually competitive, and
Grainger made the rounds of various music clubs and organizations. The minutes of the Queensland Music Teachers
Association reprinted the following day, gave a detailed
account of the composer's address, noting the frequency
of the applause and the abundance of laughter.

It was Grainger's purpose to use this Australian tour,
not primarily as a means of making money, but rather to

promote his compositions and those of his friends. He used his reputation as a performer to draw an audience and then would return as a conductor of choral and orchestral pieces with complete control over the selection of the program. He continued to speak to the press detailing his ideas on composition, programming, democracy in music, and polyphonic choralism. It would not be unfair to compare his evangelism with that of his contemporary religious brethren. The main ideas of his cause recurred throughout his tours and, except for becoming more intense in later years, they would never really change.

Two more major concerts were scheduled before he was to return to America. Early in October he journeyed to Hobart, Tasmania — a distance requiring over four days of travel, to conduct and perform an additional pair of choral and orchestral concerts. His release from the Tait Agency to appear in such a remote outpost may indicate that the financial arrangements, unlike those for his Adelaide appearance, were guaranteed by Grainger himself. The popularity of his programs must certainly have matched the break-even point, for in Melbourne a few weeks later, he made an additional donation to the Lady Northcote Orchestra Trust Fund for the promotion of orchestral concerts. This generous offer, in addition to the success of his appearances, gave Grainger a farewell unknown to any previous visiting artist.

The most arresting work on the two Melbourne farewell concerts was again, *The Warriors*. It was acclaimed as Grainger's most important orchestral piece and the press noted that it was the first twentieth-century score "to provide for a complete percussion group."[14] Thorald Waters of the Melbourne *Sun Pictorial*, remarked that

> In an orchestra I have heard real cannons fired
> in place of the clashing of Brobdignagian drums
> to heighten the effect of Tchaikovsky's *Overture*
> to the "Burning of Moscow," but that was fairy-

tread music compared with the cataclysm of sounds in Percy Grainger's *The Warriors*, which startled the unwarned in the audience last night.[15]

Cornfield Hair and Cornflower Eyes

While returning to the United States Grainger met Ella Ström. Miss Ström, thirty-eight years old and a mature woman of exceptional beauty, was returning to England by way of America. Seated with the ship's captain at dinner one evening, she heard Grainger practicing in the next lounge and inquired as to the identity of the performer. Thinking of Percy's recent success in Australia, the captain remarked, "Why that's our Percy Grainger!" Assuming that this meant Grainger was the ship's pianist, Ella did not pursue an introduction. In the next few days, the reputation of the pianist became known to her, and Ella approached him with the pretense that he help her tune a hastily purchased ukelele. By the time the ship arrived in San Francisco, the two travelers had become close friends and journeyed together to New York. When Fred Morse met Percy at Grand Central, he recalled that he had never seen him so deliriously happy, and during their short ride to White Plains, Percy could speak of nothing but marriage.

A new tour had been arranged by the Morses and, beginning in January, Grainger bounded into the concert circuit in earnest. Whenever possible, he would barter performances of his own music in exchange for a reduced fee; and, as a result, the Minneapolis Symphony programmed *The Warriors* on two successive days in April. That same month Grainger joined forces with the New York String Quartet in concerts at Oakland and San Francisco. He performed a set of Chopin pieces in addition to the Schumann piano quintet with the New York group. One memento of the bay area was a copy of *Fanny Hill*, purchased in a local book store.

In the meantime, he had been sending numerous cables and letters to his intended. They were finally answered with a cautiously worded reply, received early the following year: "Patience rewarded, consent given, Loving preparation for August reunion can be proceeded with." On October 1, 1927, Percy arranged with a London bank to create a Trust Fund in Ella's name. One month before the wedding ceremony, a deposit of L1200 completed the settlement.

Ella Ström, born in Sweden, May 1, 1889, was raised by foster parents whose surname she adopted. An unusually beautiful girl, she was sent to England at the age of sixteen. Her beauty did not go unnoticed and, at an early age, she began an active social life. Art studies in London and later at the studios of André L'hote and the Grande Chaumiere in Paris eventually produced paintings, tiles, and reliefs which were well above amateur offerings. Possibly because of her humble beginnings and transient home life, Ella placed great importance on the titles and positions of her many beaus. Her recall of these pleasant London times is vivid and her wit sharp. A delightful example is the story of her first meeting with James Joyce:

> I attended a meeting of the Pen Club in London with some older friends at which James Joyce was to speak. The noted and very famous writer, Galsworthy, refused to introduce Joyce, fearing a mar on his own reputation and indicating his disapproval of Joyce's works. Another member introduced Joyce rather eloquently, as a forerunner of modern literature, etc. Joyce stood to acknowledge the lengthy and complimentary introduction with a "Thank you," followed by the comment, "Under the circumstances, I have nothing to say," and was seated.[16]

Ella was always fascinated by Joyce and his work and tried to read him on occasion. She had attempted *Ulysses*, but admittedly did not understand it. When *Ulysses* was finally filmed, she attended several showings, remarking that she had "left as innocently as I was when I went in. Because of my poor hearing, I didn't hear a word of the movie."[17]

With occasional side trips to Sweden, Ella divided her time between London and Paris, being a favorite at many of the most fashionable parties in both countries. In her diary, she stated boldly: "Feb. 27, 1926. *Learned in Paris*: Never to stay in Paris more than 10 days."

The marriage was scheduled for August 9, 1928, in the Hollywood Bowl, to be performed during the intermission of a Concert of the Los Angeles Symphony and the Smallman a cappella Choir. In her reply to a birthday wire a few weeks before, Ella unknowingly gave her consent to the gigantic nuptual. "Loving thanks for cheerful birthday wire — Bowl wedding most attractive. No objections. Harmless church ceremony. Greetings from Brisbane. Ella" The evening of the wedding Grainger conducted on the first half of the program and, following the nuptuals, appeared as a soloist. Included on the program was *To A Nordic Princess*, an orchestral work written especially for the occasion and dedicated to his bride. Although his shyness seemed inconsistent with a marriage before 22,000 people, he explained that, "I did it as a favor to my manager."[18] Ella was mildly disturbed about the garishness of the ceremony and remarked that she had consented to be wed in the Hollywood Bowl because she thought it to be a "grotto in the woods."

The role Ella was to fulfill as Percy's wife was quite different from the life-style to which she had been accustomed. That she was, in part, to replace Rose Grainger was plainly stated by Percy in a press release prior to the ceremony.

> After the great spiritual cut-offness and loneliness
> I have borne since the death of my beloved mother
> in 1922, it is an unspeakable boon to me to have
> this soul-satisfying comrade to commune with
> by letter and to look forward to sharing my life
> with in so near a future.[19]

In January, the couple sailed for Sweden and during the next few months visited Percy's Frankfurt friends and spent a few days with Delius whose health was rapidly failing. In February Grainger finished the orchestral setting begun in 1919 of the American folk tune *Spoon River*. The tune had been passed on to him by Edgar Lee Masters, and he had wanted to meet with Masters to show him the completed score, but the poet replied: "I am in bed, running a fever, cannot possibly come [unless] I could cure this luck."[20] Before filing the note, Grainger commented across the bottom: "These light-hearted meat-eating anti-prohibitionists!"

Grainger did not become a "meat-shunner" until 1924, although he had long been associated with vegetarian proselytizers. Among his Frankfurt friends, both Herman Sandby and Cyril Scott advocated a non-meat diet for health reasons, but Grainger rejected their suggestions with simple logic: "Why should I be healthier than other men? I felt all right as I was."

Early in 1924 in Scranton, Pa., he was approached by a stranger and asked whether he considered George B. Shaw's "Wars will never cease as long as men kill animals to eat them," a valid statement. Shaw's position seemed plausible and from that day on he totally eliminated meat from his diet. It was not an unusual sacrifice as meat had never been a particularly favorite food, and it was probably more of a humanitarian gesture than a health motive that made him a vegetarian. When questioned about the inconsistency of his enjoyment of war-like and violent-mooded literature and his concern for the senseless killing of animals, Grainger replied: "One answer to that is that since war has ceased to be hand-to-hand fighting, its appeal to the savage side of our nature doesn't amount to much; it isn't sporting."

Although Percy later contributed an extensive article to *The American Vegetarian*, he seemed to have no particular taste for vegetables either. He once indulged in an eating contest with Vilhjalmur Stefansson, the arctic explorer who was under contract with a meat-packing firm to eat meat exclusively for one year. The two-hour luncheon provided no decided winner, but Grainger charitably remarked that, "As a vegetarian I think there is much to be said for his all-meat diet."[21]

The self denial involved in the lack of a balanced diet and his embrace of vegetarianism may not seem so strange when one considers Grainger's penchant for the middle ages — a time when fasting and flagellation were considered acceptable methods of martyring the flesh and of penance. After all, he has written in one of his letters, "the 9th century is the chief source of my inspiration."[22]

From time to time, the close bonds of the Frankfurt Group were tested, as they freely criticized each other's work. No member escaped castigation. Balfour Gardiner, who had remained close to Percy throughout the years, did not agree with Grainger's compositional practices. He wrote the Australian rather severely condemning his methods and directions.

> You have formulated with regard to a number of alien matters that you have arbitrarily brought into connection with music in your own mind. You have spun this web for years, and for all I know may still be spinning it. At any rate, there is no question of your disentangling it now. You talk quite rightly of your being engaged on a 'campaign for life.' I am sorry, for your campaign is not likely to succeed, and there are many grievous disappointments in store for you.[23]

The frustrations Grainger felt toward his own composing,

now joined by the admonishment of a close friend, began to cause him to doubt his ability. By 1936, the year before his *Lincolnshire Posy* masterpiece, he was to confide in Cyril Scott that "I have allowed theories and experimentalism to grow like fungus."

During their 1929 trip to Northern Europe, Grainger supplied a series of articles to the *Musical Courier*, entitled "Impressions of Art in Europe." These articles contained references to his favorite composers, authors, and artists who were then the center of cultural life in their respective countries. The Graingers attended many of the musical festivals in England and Scandinavia, and Percy reported to the *Courier's* readers his impressions of the developing musical climate. On July 25, Percy heard a first performance of his *Hill Song No. 2* at the Harrowgate (England) Music Festival, with Basil Cameron conducting.

Whenever he traveled to familiar cities he would endeavor to rent the identical rooms he had used when he and his mother had stayed there. Even in marriage he remained frugal and kept his standard of living meager. Concern for his physical condition found him constantly weighing himself. His diary noted that this year he had "weight'd 147# (Guessed right, Money back.)".

While in Oslo, Grainger met Sparre Olsen the Norwegian composer and violinist who was then supporting himself by playing in the house orchestra at the Grand Hotel. His interest in the Norwegian began when he discovered Olsen's "Six Old Rural Songs from Lom," while browsing at the Norsk Musikkforlag. The beginning of a warm friendship, lasting over thirty years, was initiated by this chance meeting.

In England, Grainger and his wife often stayed at Pevensey Bay in a small cottage which had belonged to Ella. It was in this rural setting that many of Grainger's compositions were reworked and rescored, although his habit of composing while traveling did not subside. His capacity for work was unusual and, coupled with his strenuous exercise program, left little free time. A normal Grainger day started at five a.m. with a light breakfast at seven, composing and practicing were then alternated throughout the day. Refreshing swims, strenuous hikes and side trips to historical places in the neighborhood, with reading and music in the evening, completed his 18-hour day.

Often when Cyril Scott would journey from London to spend a few days or a weekend, the evening routine was altered to include the trying out of new compositions. On occasion, Scott would entertain by seating himself at the reed organ and placing a newspaper in front of him. He would then chant, in Gregorian fashion, the market prices, stock quotations, and even the advertisements.

Grainger never appeared to be interested in investments, preferring instead to have cash available. It was most inopportune, then, for him to have selected 1929 to break that custom and acquire a modest amount of shares in the LaQuaria & Carcus Railroad, the Bengal & Northwest Railroad, and the Corboda Central Railroad. The names and types of companies he was interested in did not, however, seem that unusual to him.

In September, they returned to the States and Percy left immediately on a tour. During his absence, Ella visited at the nearby Bigelow estate at Malden-on-the-Hudson. She had known Poultney Bigelow before her marriage and would often stay there while Percy was traveling. In fact, she had first met her husband while enroute to visit Poultney. Bigelow's father had been Ambassador to France under President Lincoln, while Poultney had enjoyed an unusual career as an author, explorer, and world traveler. He had been expelled from Russia in 1892 for his political writings and for a short period was a correspondent for the London *Times* (1898). His magazine, *Outing*, was the first·American magazine about amateur sports. His love of sports appealed to Percy, and the two men developed a strange bond of friendship and respect.

Poultney was the antithesis of the Anglo-Saxon type which Percy applauded, and it was perhaps their opposing idealogies as well as their compatible love of exercise which brought them together. Bigelow was fond of swimming nude in the Hudson, but a female neighbor had complained to the authorities. He was known to have personally cut down the trees which blocked his view of the river and on one occasion, he and Percy even competed to see who was the best lumber jack.

The frequent parties at the estate were large affairs, often attended by important government officials. The Graingers were usually invited but were often unable to accept because of Percy's concert schedule. Whenever Grainger was able to attend, his arrival would be loudly announced by Bigelow: "Here is Percy Grainger, who will tear the guts out of the piano."

Throughout the early 1930's, Ella Grainger assisted in her husband's concerts. Although she had no formal musical training, Percy found her to be very adaptable. Inasmuch as many of his compositions and arrangements included parts for unfamiliar percussion instruments, it was more expedient for his wife to learn the parts than it was to train different players for each concert. The mallet percussion parts were often difficult for an experienced player, because Grainger would rearrange the keyboard of the instrument to facilitate technique. Although this would make the part easier for a neophyte, this "percussive scordature" had a devastating effect on traditionally trained performers. When they traveled together, Ella would shoulder her share of the baggage, which often consisted of several large pieces containing the extra percussion instruments. In accordance with his plan of frugal living, no red-cap was ever utilized and the handsome couple often struggled in rail stations under their unusual loads. In recalling this scene, Eugene Goosens commented:

An athletic type, he could often be seen carrying

some of these instruments on his back whenever they were needed at his concerts. Later when he was married, his wife, a dignified handsome woman, often volunteered to relieve him of this chore. One day, meeting him at the train in Cincinnati, I asked, "Where's Ella?" Glancing down the platform, he replied, "She's coming right along with the staff-bells." Sure enough, she was.[24]

Ella Ström Grainger was a perfect mate for the iconoclastic musician. She stayed in the background for the most part, working as a percussionist, music copyist, and foil to the general public. Her own artistic inclinations were in painting. She did numerous sketches of her husband as well as portraits of him and their friends; and several of her ceramic tiles were exhibited in small shows (the most notable being at the Ferargil Galleries in New York in 1930). She also wrote two books of poems, *The Pavement Artist* and *A Wayward Girl*, which were printed through Percy's backing and two songs which he scored and harmonized. When Ella was asked to speak before the Saturday Morning Club in White Plains, Percy accompanied her to the Library to research her Australian subject. He wrote a special arrangement of several Australian folk songs and even checked at the Hotel Seville a day before the scheduled lecture to see if the piano was available and tuned. They were a delightful couple who were described by an associate as "children, of course, but they are simple, warm-hearted, wonderful children, and they've both got a great deal done. Sometimes I think they're the only entirely natural people I've ever known."[25] Percy seemed content with marriage although he had often condemned family ties when he had been single. After ten years of marriage he stated: "Personally, I feel my marriage to be one of the few really successful deeds I have done in my life."[26]

Albert Stoessel, who was associated with the Worester, Massachusetts Musical Festival and several music organizations in White Plains, became interested in Grainger's music. It was Stoessel who promoted and conducted the orchestra premiere of *Spoon River* on October 3, 1930 at the Worcester Festival. An additional audience delight that evening was the appearance of the composer and his wife as participants in the performance; Percy at the piano and Ella at the handbells.

The history of the root form of the folk-tune *Spoon River* goes back to a country dance in Bradford, Illinois, where it was heard by Captain Charles H. Robinson in 1857. The appearance of Edgar Lee Masters' *Spoon River Anthology* in 1914 prompted Captain Robinson, then 90, to send a copy of the tune to the poet. Masters, in turn, loaned it to Grainger who, in 1919, began a variety of settings of it. It became the lone entry in a projected series entitled *American Folk Music Settings*, an obvious compositional parallel to his earlier *British Folk Music Settings*. A setting for the New York Chamber Music Society received its premiere December 14, 1930. This performance at the Plaza was staffed by members of the New York String Quartet assisted by clarinetist Gustave Langenus and oboist Bruno Labate. In both of these unusual settings, Grainger draws abundantly on percussive instruments. Many precedents for the rash of percussion writing witnessed in the 1950's and since can certainly be found in Grainger's use of mallets, tuned glassware, and unusual instrumental sounds. Rhythmic freedom is yet another aspect of his work which heralded developments to come.

An article Percy prepared for the *Pult und Taktstock* on new percussion instruments appeared in January of 1926 and brought a great deal of response from musicians and, more especially, composers. Editor Erwin Stein wrote Grainger asking for more information regarding the price and availability of the new instruments, for Alban Berg had long wanted to use a bass xylophone and a bass glockenspiel but none were known on the continent. A request for

an additional article on Grainger's use of the chamber-
orchestra was presented, but Percy's activities did not
permit him to prepare the desired essay.

On April 12, 1931, Grainger participated in a unique
concert of band music at the American Bandmasters Association Convention in Boston. The program, dedicated to
the memory of Patrick Gilmore, was held for the benefit
of the Musicians Mutual Relief Society. The band of over
four hundred members was conducted by twenty-six leading conductors and composers of band music. Among the
most distinguished musicians appearing were John Philip
Sousa, Walter Smith, Frank Simon, Herbert L. Clarke,
Edwin Franko Goldman, Henry Fillmore, Karl L. King,
Thomas M. Carter, Leo Sowerby, Carl Busch, A.A. Hard-
ing, and Percy Grainger.

That fall the premier of Grainger's *Tribute to Stephen
Foster* occurred at the 72nd Annual Worcester Music
Festival, Albert Stoessel conducting. This unusual score,
begun in 1913 was composed as a birthday gift to his
mother in 1914 and 1916. The final scoring, dated 1930,
was for five solo voices, mixed chorus, solo piano, orchestra and one-hundred musical glasses. The glasses, each
filled with varying amounts of water, were played by members of the chorus who rubbed their fingers about the rim
of the glass to produce the desired overtones. In describing
his most recent composition, Grainger wrote:

> In my 'Tribute to Foster' I have wanted to give
> musical expression to these Australian memories
> and to my love and reverence for this exquisite
> American genius — one of the most tender, touch-
> ing and subtle melodists and poets of all time;
> a mystic dreamer no less than a whimsical
> humorist.
>
> Thinking as I do, of "Camptown Races" both
> as a dance-song and as a lullaby, I have treated it
> in both styles in this composition. First of all
> Foster's tune is heard in its original lively charac-
> ter, using Foster's original words. Then follows

a lullaby section mirroring a mood awakened by childhood memories of my mother's singing, in which the Foster tune is treated very freely indeed and in which six solo voices (singing doggerel verses of my own) are accompanied by 'musical glasses,' bowed metal marimba and a few other instruments. The original lively dance movement is later resumed. The piece then ends with a tail-piece which suggests a countryside teeming with rural dance-music (different tunes issuing from many shacks), gradually lapsing into silence. In my mind this symbolizes the fading away of those untutored forms of Negro folk-music from which Foster drew inspiration for his art songs.[27]

The unusual use of tuned glass-ware to produce musical effects again exhibits Grainger's interest in indeterminacy of sound. It seems fair to assume that Belgium's Ethnological Museum, which provided the germ for *Random Round* and its use of planned inexactness in 1913, was also the source of the musical glasses. Sustained octaves moving in and out of a phrase were produced when a moistened finger was rubbed over the rim. Ella described the search for the original set of musical glasses:

We went to many stores and warehouses that specialized in glass, and there we had to explain our problem of finding glasses of the right note. Hence a great number of glasses were assembled and offered for us to try out. Assistants in the various warehouses and shops were really quite intrigued and helpful. When we also demanded buckets of water for use in tuning, they were equally willing to rush around with pots and cans for that purpose. They were patient with us. Each glass that we tried had to be either one note or another: C sharp, D sharp, E sharp, F sharp, G sharp, A sharp — all six sharps in several octaves. Eighty (80) glasses, one each for a chorus of eighty, and more, if needed. Each glass had to have a small amount of water, for

the sake of dipping the finger tips, because one
had to have a wet finger with which to rub the
rim of the glass. Also, water was to be added to
make the note of the right pitch, more or less,
to make it sharp or flat . . . . Hence our labor
lasted some hours. That the assistants in the
shops were willing to give us so much time and
serious attention was due to their kindness and
perseverance, plus the 'Grainger charm' perhaps?
Percy had this invincible quality of charm (plus
insistence) that was very difficult to resist. I
experienced it from time to time in many various
ways. And, when asked by some friend if Percy
did not mesmerize me, my answer was, Yes, if
someone very clever and charming persuades
one into doing something one would not otherwise do, then indeed he mesmerizes me.

Thus a great many glasses were gradually
assembled, and they had to be tuned, as I said
above, and the tuning waterline had to be painted
on each glass in black oil paint, which was an
easy task for me, who had been an art student
and therefore glad to wield a paint brush . . . .[28]

When the eighty or more glasses enter during an orchestral
lull (bars 77, 81, 91, 102, etc.), they produce quite a breath-
taking effect, something like the drone of insects on a summer's evening. Adding to the ethereal effect was a string bass
bow drawn across the metal bars of the mallet instruments.

The Absence of Applause

In 1932 Grainger was appointed associate professor
and chairman of the music department at New York
University. Already on the staff were Marion Bauer,
Gustave Reese, and Phillip James, who had known

the pianist and would champion him in later years. It was an unusual arrangement, and although Grainger apparently "enjoyed his actual teaching and contact with the students," it was not certain that he "found pleasure in his administrative duties."[29]

Grainger's teaching duties included a series of thirty lectures entitled, *A General Study of the Manifold Nature of Music.* The weekly two-hour lecture ran from September 20th until May 9th, and its title posed the question, "Is Music a Universal Language?" This gargantuan project of discussing the field of art music outside the "comparatively few [well-known] compositions by a small number of composers from a small group of European countries, active between 1680 and 1900,"[30] was addressed in the usual aggressive Grainger manner. The exotic music of the Orient, in addition to native music from Asia, Rarotonga, Madagascar, Australia, and Cuba, was illustrated by grammophone recordings that Grainger had made in the field. Pre-Bach polyphonists were included, as were Schönberg, Scott, and Riegger, and jazz was discussed as "the most classical of popular music." The focal point of the series was to point to the process of musical development as "steadily moving towards free music — music that will tally the irregularity and complexity of nature."[31] Guest lecturers were invited to participate and to augment Grainger's thesis. Among the prominent musicians who appeared, were Ralph Leopold, Joseph Yasser, Henry Cowell. D.G. Mason, William Durieux, Wallingford Riegger, and the Duke Ellington Orchestra. Ellington's organization drew the most attention, and the students "nearly broke down the doors trying to get in."[32]

The lectures were unconventional and the subject matter crossed every culture and civilization, with special emphasis on native and folk music. The Yasser

lecture, "The Music Scale of the Future Historically
Evolved from the Scale of the Past and the Future,"
directly embraced Grainger's search for codification
of his "free music" theories and Cowell's interest in
percussion instruments echoed Grainger's cause.

The summer following his first academic year, Grainger
became visiting professor at the School of Education,
then resigned his position to journey to Europe. He
explained that he had accepted the chairmanship, "because I was well paid [$5000] (I wanted to apply the
money to building my museum) and, because I wanted
to study the subjects I was to lecture on. I like everything to do with music education,"[33] he stated. "I like
the building, the resources, the chance to present 'unpopular' music, and the absence of applause."[34] He was
known later to remark that, "I'm not against education
— it's harmless."[35]

One positive effect of the year at New York University
was the contact Grainger had made with composers
whose music was experimental, new, and relatively
unknown. Using the same persuasions as he had for
his Frankfurt friends, Grainger began to champion
their music. His friendship with Frederick Stock prompted
him to encourage Stock to hire Henry Cowell as soloist
for a performance of Cowell's piano concerto. William
Durieux, whose all-girl string sextet illustrated many
of the lectures, found many concert connections through
Grainger's influence and often appeared with him in
programs long after Grainger had left the academic
world. Years later it would be his colleagues from NYU
who would initiate offers of honorary degrees and propose
him for membership in the prestigious National Institute
of Arts and Letters.

Henry Cowell and Grainger had known each other
before these New York University days, for both men
had often attended New York percussion recitals and

lectures. Cowell, then editor of the *New Music Quarterly*, and active in New York music circles, was a staff member at the New School for Social Research. A series of nine records, produced at the New School by Grainger for use in his University classes, was arranged in conjunction with Cowell. This series was an attempt to widen the historical range of music study to include pre-Bach and post-Brahms composers. It was an ambitious undertaking and had the support of both Cowell and Charles Seeger (also on the New School staff) who acted as engineer. The recordings, eighteen sides in all, were not meant to be released commercially but were to be purchased by students and used in conjunction with their class notes as a substitute for a textbook. Each record had to be cut separately from the master and could only be played with non-metal needles.

Grainger used the performers who helped illustrate his lectures and, together with the Durieux String Quartet, Merle Robertson, and Ella assisting on mallet-percussion, the project was completed. These crude cuttings contain some of the earliest recorded examples of Claude Le Jeune, William Byrd, and Paul Hindemith.

While at New York University, Gustave Reese, Grainger's colleague, played a recording for him which had been prepared by the noted English musicologist, Dom Anselm Hughes, for a 1932 American lecture tour. At this time a recording of medieval music was unique and brought to Grainger's attention a body of literature which would occupy much of his time during the next twenty years.

Grainger was so enthusiastic that he wrote Hughes asking to meet with him to hear more about this promising field of investigation. Grainger's experience in folksong collecting, allied to his natural faculty for penetrating below the surface of pretentiousness, meant that he would find himself quite at home in the unsophisticated atmosphere of 13th and 14th century polyphony.

The two men met at Nashdom Abbey in 1933 and examined the monastery's deposits of early music. It was Grainger's suggestion that a joint publication should be formed for the use of choral societies, schools, and concert groups. Sixteen items were picked to form an album, with an introduction and musicological notes as to original sources and other matters of interest. *English Gothic Music* was selected as a title for the venture and the duties of editorship were divided. Hughes was to supply Grainger with the text and music copied from the original manuscripts. The editorial decisions about the presentation, arrangements, and suggestions for dynamics were to be Grainger's part; Hughes would make all necessary Latin translations.

Only twelve of the original sixteen were prepared and, over the years, only seven were released. Hughes explained this delay as a result of "Grainger's system of putting down part of the capital cost and drawing a higher royalty . . . [he] would not publish a work until he had heard it sung in various key-pitches or (if for instruments) various combinations."[36]

Perhaps the finest example of Grainger's editorial practices may be seen in this series. It presents early English music in transcriptions for "practical music-making." Every intention of the original music is presented. Alternate instrumental and vocal combinations are listed, while any editorial corrections or additions are clearly marked and the source of the original manuscript is noted. This scholarship reflects the care Grainger exhibited in his composing, arranging, and collecting. In his earliest gathering of folk songs, he carefully notated inflections and nuances of the singers and presented the alternate versions in his comments to the printed tune. And instead of placing the tune in a prearranged meter, he notated the rhythm exactly as it was performed. Any textual additions were clearly indicated.

Although the published versions were vocal settings in three and four parts, Grainger experimented with the music in settings for wind instruments. Dom Anselm Hughes commented on his experiments:

> PG always visualized instrumental accompaniments to these motets where available. The best results I heard were, however, with the Dolmetsch family and such people, recording for the History of Music in Sound. We worked mainly on the recorder/oboe/bassoon type of orchestration. I do not remember clearly what PG used for his instrumental performances, but believe he was more ready to use brass than I should have been.[37]

Hughes and Grainger respected each other's abilities and their partnership was an excellent combination of supporting forces. The body of early music that Grainger examined influenced him to expand his programs to include a wider range of styles and periods. In a note describing their efforts, Hughes stated that Grainger had

> . . . soon found that they [the manuscripts] had a value which [was] quite outstanding in music, and not merely antiquarian. Their immense importance was realised by such scholars as the late Charles Van Den Borren, and after I had published some academic sources in *Worcester Mediaevel Harmony* (1928), Arnold Dolmetsch, who was a great friend of Percy Grainger, also came to know and value them. But it was high time that they should get more widely known, and available in practical popular performing editions.[38]

His many visits to England and his custom of spending time at Pevensey Bay brought Grainger into frequent contact with the Dolmetsch family at Haslemere and their annual Festivals. These concerts of early European music were performed by the family on traditional instruments constructed by and under the direction of the father, Arnold Dolmetsch. Grainger and Dolmetsch became fast friends and Dolmetsch, like Grieg before him, served somewhat as a father figure to the Australian who was always welcome in the family circle. They met often and engaged in playing the traditional music which held such a fascination for Grainger. This friendship resulted in an arrangement whereby Dolmetsch supplied Grainger with several scores of 16th- and 17th-century English consort music. Grainger published three of these scores for modern string instruments under the title *The Dolmetsch Collection of English Consorts*. Often, when he was engaged as a conductor, he would perform this music as well as selections of the *English Gothic Music* series in arrangements for different wind combinations. The printing of the Dolmetsch pieces was the beginning of another projected series, but Dolmetsch's death in 1940 and a myraid of other Grainger projects prevented him from carrying out his plans.

One of the regular commitments which prevented Grainger from devoting the full depth of his interest to any single pursuit was his association with the National Music Camp at Interlochen, Michigan. After a brief visit to the Camp in 1931, regular summer engagements began in 1937 and continued until the war. Grainger was initially attracted to the Camp by its salary and intrigued by the lack of travel and the absence of applause. Yet it did not prove to be a totally satisfactory experience.

Percy and Ella occupied a cabin within "hearing distance" of the shell and rose early each day. A round of tennis at 7:00 a.m. was customary, with private teaching beginning at 8:00 a.m. and continuing until 6:30 p.m. Evenings consisted of rehearsals until 10:00; Percy would often practice until 1:00 or 2:00 a.m.

Their daily schedule was strenuous but Grainger

seemed to thrive on work; he rarely slept more than a few hours and could refresh himself by dozing five to ten minutes during the day. His lunch period was spent standing in line for he refused to eat in the faculty section of the dining rooms, stating that he felt it an undemocratic thing to do to the students. The lake was nearby and he frequently swam although he complained that he "felt as if he were drowning." He felt, however, that it was good exercise, but more important, "I do it mainly because I want to be ready to save myself if shipwrecked."[39]

Usually Percy could be found wearing the stiff and uncomfortable white canvas pants he had purchased at an Army surplus store in White Plains. It was these same trousers which later caused his arrest in Wausau, Wisconsin, on suspicion of vagrancy, while there for a recital appearance.

The Interlochen years were frustrating for Grainger, since he felt his audience was slipping away. The younger players did not seem to like the selection of literature he was promoting, and he remarked that he felt like "a lonely old crow on the bough."[40] He wanted to quit but worried about money, and he often complained of never having heard a talented student there. Technique was quite natural to him, and he could not understand why a pianist should need such efforts to cultivate it. "You can get more keyboard skill out of Bach's 48 Preludes and Fugues, than out of a boatload of studies by tone-deaf nit-wits like Czerny,"[41] he remarked to one persistent student. And to another who insisted on playing a particular passage faster than he was capable because he had heard Horowitz play it "like a blue streak in his recording," Grainger explained "There likely wasn't room on the recording at the right speed, so he had to hurry it up."[42]

He later wrote of these years: "Why do all the young

folk at Interlochen yawn at their rehearsals, why do they not want to hear new tone-art, why don't they want to know older-than-Bach masters, why do they never ask a living ask-ment, why can they never play or sing one loud note? Because they are sissies thru and thru — *all frenzy having been ruled out of their life."* At the end of each season, he would seem pleased that "all the young blighters had left."[43]

One aspect of the Interlochen summers in which he became interested was the camp saxophone choir directed by Rollin Silfies. He began to arrange pieces specifically for this group and continued his interest in it after he was no longer a member of the Camp's faculty. He even coaxed Ella into playing the baritone saxophone, which she did until he criticized her playing by requesting: "And now, play it in tune."

No reasonable request from the students was neglected, and Grainger interrupted his practice one evening to accompany a fledgling soprano in a rendition of "Trees." The unusual combination of a very bad singer and a superb pianist attracted several of the camp personnel with Grainger explaining that she had asked him if he knew who could play it, and he did not.

Grainger was popular with the students and impressed them with his athletic abilities. He could leap from the ground to the stage of the outdoor shell, a feat no student could equal. He formed a club among the students called "Grainger's Rangers," and to be accepted for membership, a student had to leap to the stage of the shell in the manner of the group's founder. Inasmuch as no one ever accomplished the leap, Grainger offered associate membership to those who could master the porch of the Hotel Pennington, a jump of considerably less difficulty.

The rehearsing and teaching became too strenuous, and Grainger became increasingly upset when other conductors would extend their allotted rehearsal time on musical "chestnuts." With Grainger, everything went by the clock. He had complained repeatedly to Joseph Maddy that the condition of the pianos was unbearable and accused the Camp of being afraid to do his *Lincolnshire Posy.* Each year he had become more embittered toward both the staff and the students. The summer of 1944 was the last of his Interlochen association. "I shall never teach again. This summer was my last. I earned well. I earned almost double my guarantee."[44] His wife shared his lack of enthusiasm for she commented, "It would have been so nice there if it wasn't for all those horrible children."

The Sojourner

In March, 1934, Grainger and his wife arrived in Australia to begin a series of public concerts and broadcasts sponsored by the Australian Broadcasting Company. The one hundred day voyage from Copenhagen was made aboard the *L'Avenir,* a four-masted barque which had once served as a training ship for the Belgian Navy but, more recently, had been one of the picturesque sailing vessels that annually participated in the Australian Wheat Races.

Grainger took advantage of his time at sea and scheduled the days to accommodate his writing and study interests. He did not find cause to neglect his exercise merely because the area was limited, and an early morning climb to the crow's nest seemed to fulfill this need. Current work included preparation of notes for the coming Australian lectures and a study of Dom Anselm Hughes' recent *English Gothic Music* findings. Grainger desired to make Scandinavian music better known in the Anglo-Saxon countries, and he hoped to program Sparre Olsen's chorus and orchestra piece, *Mountain-Norway*, on the up-coming tour. Earlier attempts to translate the Olav Ankrust text were frustrated by his inadequate command of Norwegian. But now, aboard ship, he could pursue this project with the aid of a dictionary and an analysis of the poem supplied by the poet's son.

Percy had hoped that this tour would be among the last he would have to give. He wanted to suspend performing and concentrate on his composing and speculated that "Ella and I ought to be able to retire in a few years now. This is what mother and I were longing for ever since I started this hateful virtuoso business over thirty years ago."[45]

During this fourth tour of the Australian continent, Grainger was to participate in 158 radio broadcasts and 56 public concerts which were to include 17 concerto appearances. In addition to personal appearances and broadcasts, Grainger was to contribute a number of articles to music magazines in Australia and New Zealand.

The tour began in Melbourne on April 14th, and amid the flurry of appearances, he found time to finish the lecture broadcasts for the Australian Broadcasting Company which were to commence in December. His contract, calling for twenty weeks with two one-hour broadcasts weekly, was for L800.

The news of Frederick Delius' death reached Grainger in June. The death of his close friend was a crushing event, and Grainger's letters to friends and kin were sprinkled with premonitions of his own end. Continuing his campaign for Delius' music, Grainger arranged a memorial concert for the following month in Adelaide. The program included *English Fantasies* by Henry Purcell and John Jenkins, Grieg's four *Romances*, and several works by Delius (the string quartet, cello sonatas, violin sonatas); all were favorites of the two men. A touching eulogy was delivered at the concert by Grainger.

Throughout his Australian touring Grainger continued to encourage local orchestras and choral societies. He even donated two special prizes of L5/5 in Sydney; one for the best vocal ensemble of three to nine voices and one for the winning string ensemble of the same size. Each group was to be tested on specific selections set by Grainger. The choice of pieces was limited to a selection from any of the following composers: strings from Purcell, Sandby, Jenkins, or Byrd; vocal selections from Lineva, Machaut, Natalie Curtis-Burlin, Grieg, Rachmaninoff, or any of the proposed *English Gothic Music* series. All the music was recently uncovered by Dolmetsch and Hughes or were pieces of distinct folk song derivation. Rachmaninoff was the single exception.

Grainger's popular radio lectures, "Music — A Common Sense View of All Types," began December 4th. They differed from his earlier recital broadcasts both in content and purpose. With the exception of Schoenberg's *Opus 19*, the repertoire was a reflection of the recital fare Grainger was then offering in the Australian concert halls. In the main, it consisted of Debussy, Albéniz, Brahms, Chopin, Balakireff, Bach, Schumann, Grieg, and music from the Frankfurt Group. Many of the selections were being introduced to the Australian public for the first time.

The lecture recitals covered the span of musical progress from the Middle Ages to the present and included music from many non-western areas. It seems quite possible that his previous lectures and research at New York University, his friendship with Gustav Reese, and his work with Dolmetsch and Hughes provided the background and sources for the amount and diversity of the material presented. Each lecture was illustrated by selected examples of the music being discussed. Grainger assembled the singers and musicians and for one broadcast organized twenty percussion players to illustrate music for "Tuneful Percussion."

The final lecture broadcast, "The Goal of Musical Progress," brought before the public specific examples of his Free Music. Although January 10, 1935, is generally regarded as the premiere date of his Free Music, Grainger had, on at least four previous occasions, discussed his Free Music ideas before an audience and attempted to demonstrate them at the keyboard. A note in his scrap book for 1930 gives priority to the Scarsdale Women's Club for an October 1st lecture on Art Music and Folk Music: "Illustration included Grainger's Free Music (first public performance)."

The example Grainger sketched on January 8th for his broadcast two days later did not satisfy him and the string quartet demonstration, directed by Percy Code, was not successful. In addition to Free Music, this final broadcast included examples of Jazz, gliding tones taken from Grieg, Sandby, and Scott, atonality from Schoenberg, quartertones from the American composer Fickenscher, and irregular rhythms from both Scott's piano sonata and his own *Hill Song No. 2*. In his book, *Australia's Music*, Roger Covell concluded that "the consequences of this tour (especially the lecture broadcasts) had more to do with simple astonishment than genuine enlightenment...any direct fruitful results it may have had have been slow to declare themselves."[46]

Grainger was concerned with historical priorities in compositional technique and was bitter that he had not been given credit for his innovations. "I think my melodic invention is poor, my orchestration clumsy and uninspired and my choice of subjects unpleasing," he wrote. "But as an innovator (irregular rhythm, etc.), I think I am first class and that no one has given me credit for these things I consider unfair to Australia."[47]

In 1934 a contract was negotiated between the University of Melbourne and Grainger which outlined plans for the construction of the museum he had been planning since before his mother's death. This museum was to be a library of music manuscripts and was to contain personal material of Grainger and the artists with whom he had been associated. These collections were intended to be a center for the preservation and study of early European music, to serve students of genuine folk singing, and to aid in the study of native music in and near Australia. Recordings of the folk songs which he had collected in England, Denmark, and New Zealand were to be included. The building was designed to consist of two separate wings. One portion was to be designated the "Music Museum," and the other, the "Grainger Museum." The latter would consist of Grainger's personal papers, manuscripts, first editions of his published music, and his collections of books, instruments, and folklore of the Northern European countries. The section of the building labeled "Music Museum" would house materials of a general nature as well as materials relating to Australian musical culture. In a letter to the Chancellor of the University, Grainger presented his reasons for building such a museum:

> As I see it, the purpose of the Music Museum would be to preserve and exhibit things of a *general* musical interest and things connected with the *general* musical life of Australia.[48]

Upon completion of the museum, a fund was to be set up to aid Australian composers and to provide a series of concerts in his name, which would feature a wide range of musical styles and types. The purpose of the project was the result of Grainger's convictions that: (1) art is a total effort on the part of its creator, and (2) to understand the artist and his work one should know as much about him as possible. To support his thesis that no work of art was created without influence from its environment, Grain-

ger planned to include physical artifacts as well as intimate
details of the lives of the composers that were represented.
He knew also that an artist was influenced, both consciously and unconsciously, by his contemporaries as well as by
tradition, and he was attempting to recreate that portion
of the artist's environment in which he himself had had
contact. He even planned to exhibit a number of wax figures which would represent composers in characteristic
dress. The complete financing of the project was to be met
by Grainger; Balfour Gardiner contributed L1000 to start
the fund.

In December, with the museum one-fourth completed
and their money running out, Percy and Ella returned
to the United States aboard the *Niagra*, for yet another
American concert tour.

*   *   *

Constantly critical of balance in symphony orchestras,
Grainger began to score for single instrumental lines early
in his career.

> I endeavor to achieve with larger groups of sin-
> gle instruments a tonal balance more delicate
> than that natural to the symphony orchestra,
> with its top heavy and ill balanced sonorities.[49]

In 1929, he spoke of his ideas: "We might as well look
upon the present time as one well suited to bold experimentation with orchestral and chamber music sound-
blends." One of his most important contributions to the
technique of scoring for wind instruments was his own
treatment of the individual instrumental line. His concern
with melodic development caused him to write inner parts
which exploited an instrument's individual character. Beginning with his earliest wind writing he scored for complete instrumental families. In the case of the double-reed
and clarinet families, scoring for such complete groupings
was truly original in regard to heterogeneous groupings
of wind instruments.

With the exception of the large orchestral wind sections of the previous century, this type of wind sonority had never before been considered. Explaining his position of writing for complete families of instruments, Grainger stated:

> But even on those colleagues who do not share my passion for the soprano saxophone I urge the supreme importance of keeping instrumental families intact. The French have shown deep wisdom in constructing their newer instrumental families (saxophones, saxhorns, sarrusophones) in close accordance with the range of human voices (soprano, alto, tenor, baritone, bass); for the whole development of European harmony (and with it everything we call "classical music") from Perotin le Grand (c. 1200) to Wagner or Cesar Franck, has been built up with an intimate adjustment to the *tessature* of human voices. To lack the soprano voice of an important instrumental group is a fatal handicap.[50]

Grainger's most drastic departure from contemporary practices of scoring was conceived in the early 1930's. In an interview with an editor of the *Musical Courier*, he outlined his concept of "elastic scoring."

> It consists of so arranging the "cues" in the orchestral parts that the piece may be played by any combination of instruments from 2 or 3 to 100 or so . . .[51]

Individual parts were written first, then reduced to a score. Speaking of the unusual properties of the score, Grainger added: "It takes thought to interpret these scores and use them properly, and I have found that people hate to think."[52]

The purpose of this type of scoring was commercial and was designed to be executed by amateurs. In the aforementioned interview, Grainger admitted that the scores were planned for schools or amateur orchestras which often lacked instruments, but added that he did not know the full marketing possibilities as it was then still quite new. Several subsequent works were published with elastic scoring, but the commercial possibilities he envisioned did not materialize and he soon abandoned the practice.

Early in 1937, Grainger scored a set of folksongs which he had collected in Lincolnshire during his 1905-06 folk song hunts. This suite conceived directly for the wind band, represents a major contribution to original wind band literature of the first half of this century.

Lincolnshire Posy was somewhat of a hybrid of folk song arranging and original composition. Its greatest influence, however, must be said to have been in the way Grainger scored for instruments, individually and together. The color and voicing of *Lincolnshire Posy* was to set a pattern of scoring for the wind band which has lasted well into the last half of this century. Grainger's general ideas as to the makeup of the instrumental structure of a musical body are made clear throughout the piece. Complete instrumental families abound, not only in the woodwinds and brass, but in the percussion as well. Several of his principals of Free Music appear, such as the use of sliding pedal point in an effort to depict gliding tones in the third movement. Unusual rhythms and directions can also be found. At the end of movement six, for instance, the trumpets are directed to reach their last note "at will" in a wayward rhythmic fashion. All directions are given in "blue-eyed English" (Grainger's anglicized approach to a pure language).

The scoring of this "bunch of musical wildflowers" was intended as a musical portrait of the original folk singers, to capture their personality and the exact way they had originally presented their song. Each movement was based on the original wax cylinder recording he had collected thirty years before. And in the score one can see the editorial considerations and niceties that Grainger provided. Included with each of the six movements was the history of the tune, the circumstances of its collection, and a listing of any other arrangements he might have made. In the Program Notes at the beginning of the printed score, he also presented an interesting biographical outline of the individual singers who had contributed the original tunes.

Two types of irregular rhythms may be found in the suite; those that are conveyed by changing time signatures (as in the "Rufford Park Poachers") and those marked "free time" (as in "Lord Melbourne"). When *Lincolnshire Posy* first appeared, the irregular rhythms proved to be a formidable obstacle to most conductors, but Grainger felt that they were easily within the powers of a normal high school band. In a note to band leaders he remarked that the only players likely to balk at those rhythms were seasoned professional bandsmen, "who think more of their beer than of their music."[53]

The premiere of *Lincolnshire Posy* under Grainger's direction, occurred on March 7, 1937 at the Annual Grand Concert of the American Bandmasters Association Convention in Milwaukee. Also included on this program was the first public performance of *Lads of Wamphray*. Glenn Cliffe Bainum, in charge of the rehearsal procedures at the convention, noted that prior to the first rehearsal, Percy and his wife went from stand to stand, each armed with needle and black thread, sewing together the pages of the manuscript. Mr. Bainum remarked that "with 'Lost Lady Found' in mind, perhaps Percy wanted no lost pages unfound."[54]

The Lincolnshire premiere delivered by Grainger and the Milwaukee Symphonic Band was enthusiastically received, although the irregular rhythms in the third movement gave the band somewhat of a problem. Writing to Grainger a few days after the premiere, Edwin Franko Goldman remarked on the problems that had existed in the performance.

> I am very sorry that the band had problems in
> the Poaching Song. After thinking the matter
> over, I would think that the bands would have
> considerable trouble with this number, unless
> they rehearsed it long and often. The constant
> change of time I believe will make it difficult
> for amateurs as well as professionals. After
> people once get it in their ears, it, of course,
> simplifies matters.[55]

The association between Grainger and Edwin Franko
Goldman had existed since the war. In 1918, The Goldman
Band had given the first performance of Grainger's *Gumsucker's March* (the fourth movement of his *In A Nutshell
Suite*), which he had rescored for military band while in
the Army. Thereafter, Grainger's music appeared on the
Goldman concerts with increasing frequency. As early as
1927, Goldman had the first movement of the Grieg piano
concerto arranged especially for Grainger's appearances.
In the summer of 1932, shortly before he joined the staff
of New York University, Grainger was invited by Goldman to conduct a benefit with the band. "I very much fear
that I could not take on a whole program," Grainger replied, "As I do not know a whole program of military band
music."[56] The following spring, at New York University,
the Goldman Band delivered the first performance of his
recently scored *Spoon River*.

Grainger often complained about the lack of complete
instrumentation in the Goldman organization, although
he knew financial considerations limited the band to a
specific number of players. Grainger especially wanted
them to add an alto clarinet, a second alto saxophone, and
a baritone saxophone, and he lamented that they had but
one bass clarinet. On occasion, when he conducted his own
music, he would pay the extra fees for hiring the additional players. He felt that it was necessary to have balance
in the low reeds and that the low reed sound in the band

was the most neglected area in composition and arranging. Furthermore, he felt that if composers would write for complete balanced families of instruments, the military band could be even more successful as an artistic medium than the symphony orchestra.

Intermittent work with the *English Gothic Music* series soon produced nine of the selections scored for band, which he tried out at the Williams School of Music. These were scored to broaden the repertoire of the wind band. As Percy explained to Richard Franko Goldman: "If the band is to go on being a stranger to all deeper, older music, band musicians will remain nit-wits and the best efforts made to form and improve bands will not have deep musical results."[57] At the younger Goldman's request, Grainger contributed the preface to his *The Band's Music*, incorporating in it his views as to the historical basis for the band and plans for its future development.

Referring to the arrangements he had made from the *English Gothic Music* manuscripts, Grainger wrote: "I do not attach any importance to these arrangements in connection with their skill (or lack of it) or personal qualities. But I attach much importance to them as showing which way band activities are going."[58] In 1939, Schott & Co. released four of his pieces for brass band based on English folk songs he had collected earlier.

The first serious break in Grainger's health came in 1937, and a proposed tour of England and Scotland was cancelled. At the time of the birth of *Lincolnshire Posy* and immediately following, depression was overcoming him and he often contemplated death. In a detailed sketch written two weeks after the *Lincolnshire Posy's* premiere, Grainger outlined his fears:

Thots I Think as I Grow Old

These are the thots I always think nowadays — now that I am nearly old, near the time when it is likely I will die:

I walk towards Denton Cothers [sic] & Daniels
(music Store; Steinway agents) in Buffalo (in
order to get in as much piano practice as I may,
when I am in the thick of concerts, I try to travel
by night & practice by day; thus if I am headed
for Duluth, Minn., from New York, I take a night
train from New York to Buffalo, spend the day
at D., C.&D's in Buffalo practicing, take a night
train from Buffalo to Chicago, spend the day
practicing at Lyon & Healy's Chicago, take a
night train from Chicago to Duluth) & I think:
Say that I come to Buffalo to practice like this
once a season; I may come 5 times more, or 10
times more, or even 15 times more — but if 15
times more, I will be 70, beyond the age when
man, as a rule, writes masterpieces. If I come
5 times, 6 times more, I will be as old as my
mother when she died. Already I am older than
she was when we came to New York. Yet how
much younger I feel, & how much older I feel,
than I think she felt then. Time is closing in
on me, with my master works unwritten. These
are the thots I think unless Ella is by me to
dispel my gloom, or other nice mindsters keep
my thots off myself, my failures, my guilt. Mar.
25, 1937.[59]

The guilt that plagued him did not subside. It had developed as a result of his inability to write the masterpieces
he felt were in his destiny and the knowledge that his personality disorders might prevent him from ever doing so.
He sought to explain his frustration by examining the lives
of other artists and, after reading a biography of Van Gogh,
he commented:

. . .see the likeness between the roughness and
cruelty of Van Gogh's cutting off his ear is the
same sort of stuff as my cruelty only in my case
it is the women I let suffer instead of myself.
And then the love life of us who write great art
is clearly gone wrongsome.[60]

Plans for a return to Europe were cancelled for Percy
was "too spent." He and Ella stayed two weeks at the Bige-

low estate, swimming and relaxing, while Percy tried to regain some of his earlier stamina. A score of the Free Music arranged for four Theremins was Grainger's product of the short vacation period.

A reception of one thousand people in honor of the German Ambassador, with President Roosevelt attending, occurred during the Grainger's visit. Bigelow planned the "unveiling of a bust of the great emancipator, *Luther*, which was to be unveiled with much ceremony unless blown up the night before by a Jesuit bomb!"[61] Through pressure by the American Federation of Musicians, a bid to get the West Point Band for the *Kaisermarsch* was unsuccessful. A White House appearance was arranged for Grainger by Bigelow for the coming January. Following this successful performance, a subsequent appearance with the National Symphony began a very busy concert season for the pianist.

Between tours, Grainger was assembling materials destined for his uncompleted museum. The fear of fire prompted him to construct two fire-proof vaults in the basement of his White Plains home; duplicates of his manuscripts were made and a copy deposited in each vault. Relegated to the basement were hundreds of photographs made by him and his mother and reams of memorabilia gathered over his long career. Among these were Wallingford Riegger's plea to join a musician's committee to aid Spanish democracy and to help form a musician's congress. These invitations were neglected but he did join other organizations, including the American Legion.

In July of 1938, the Graingers returned to Australia. As was his usual custom, concerts were given in the major ports of call and included a series of lectures in Honolulu. The writing project during this voyage was the two-piano setting of the recently completed *Lincolnshire Posy*. It was a leisurely trip which included stops at Tahiti, Samoa, and Pago-Pago. Arriving in Melbourne, Percy and Ella became involved in the final construction of their museum.

They had brought with them, John Grainger's 1894 painting, "A Running Flight," to add to the growing deposits.

For four months Ella and Percy worked at the construction of the museum. It was a difficult time for Grainger
who felt he had "gone through a terrible and tiring period.
We worked like slaves on my museum. We started at 5:30
in the morning and were not finished before 8:30 in the
evening, and how much money it cost! I had to borrow
money from many people, and now I have to earn money on
my forthcoming American tour. It starts in the western
part on Jan. 15, 1939."[62] On December 10, the museum
officially opened but it would take another thirty years
before it would be in a position to offer anything more than
a cursory service to the public.

A meeting between Robert Atkinson and Grainger was
arranged during this Melbourne stay. He had met Percy
in Tasmania in 1934. Their mutual bond was language
reform, or, as Grainger referred to it, "blue-eyed English,"
devoid of all foreign roots. Atkinson had been writing to
Percy in their new language and Grainger's response would
include a few L's to pay for Atkinson's time.

In January the couple returned to San Francisco and
Percy visited Henry Cowell, who was then serving a fif-
teen-year sentence on a morals conviction at San Quentin
prison. In an effort to comfort Cowell's parents, Percy
wrote them relating his own mother's reaction to his personal life and defending what he felt to be the artist's
prerogatives in private matters.

> I do not know for certain whether she [Rose] did
> so in despair because some friends thought her
> relation to me an unnatural one, or in despair
> because of the immoral acts of mine known to
> her but not to the world . . . I refuse in seeing
> anything bad in what we artists do. Our 'sins'
> are only 'sins of pleasure,' not sins of greed,
> hatred and falsehood.[63]

Cowell, who played flute and later conducted the prison

band, was actively writing for bands and correspondence between the two men was concerned with the technical aspects of proper wind scoring. Cowell, agreeing with Grainger's procedures, wrote:

> I have always felt that the band suffers from too much tutti, certain instruments apparently being added or not quite casually, owing to whether they happen to be there...I am interested in the band, and appauled [sic] at the lack of new works written originally for it, and the rut into which conventional arrangements for it have fallen, in many cases.[64]

Cowell's *Interlochen Camp Reel* was one of the products of this correspondence.

Richard Franko Goldman provided another source of encouragement to the imprisoned Cowell, and he and Grainger made sure that a continual flow of books, music, and support arrived at San Quentin. During the Goldman Band's appearance at the Golden Gate International Exposition in San Francisco in 1939, Richard Franko Goldman planned to program Cowell's recently completed *Celtic Set*, and wrote him that it would be broadcast at 4:00 p.m. on June 21st. In his reply Cowell requested that his work be played during the first part of the broadcast, because he would be returning to his cell at 4:15 and didn't know if he could receive permission to hear the complete program. Goldman complied and, under such conditions, Cowell was able to hear, for the first time, his newest piece for band.

In May, Ella and Percy sailed for Europe where they began to assemble materials for their museum from their Frankfurt friends and their many professional acquaintances there. Manuscripts and personal effects of Cyril Scott, Roger Quilter, and Vaughan Williams were collected. Arnold Dolmetsch contributed an old violin. A week was spent at the home of his former sweetheart, Karen Holten, and at his request she began to arrange, chronologically, their thirty years of correspondence. A visit with Dom Anselm Hughes renewed efforts on their *English Gothic Music* project and concluded the European visit.

That year, Rudolph Ganz offered Grainger a chance to return to the Chicago Musical College and take over direction of the 1940 summer band. Grainger's short reply only suggested that he anticipated a "busy season" and would not be available, although he "would enjoy doing any work with the bands (senior or junior) you might wish. My experience is that the main defect in all bands is a lack of complete saxophone families (lack of soprano) and lack of balance in the clarinet choir. Lack of alto and bass clarinet or hopelessly poor playing on these instruments."[65] It was the first communique from the Chicago School since it had offered Grainger an honorary doctorate in 1936. He had refused it.

> Please don't think me ungrateful when I say that I shall never under any circumstances accept a degree of any kind. 1stly, because I feel all distinctions to be undemocratic, and 2ndly, because I am opposed to all musical education as I have known it. I believe that composition is something that cries for musical experience rather than for teaching and I would not like to give the impression that music has connection with education, in universities music as it is taught universally, badly.[66]

Concert appearances in 1940 were unusually light but Grainger was occupied with preparing parts and reading proofs of the *Lincolnshire Posy* and *Lads of Wamphray* scheduled to be released that year. To compound his work load he now concerned himself with the cover design and accompanying art work; he had recently taken over these tasks from his publisher. Whenever he traveled he carried his work with him, writing in trains, dressing rooms, and rail stations, and occasionally missing his connections because he was engrossed in his work. Appearances with the National Symphony and a recital at Town Hall were the most significant concerts of that spring.

For Grainger it was unthinkable to cancel an engagement, and he met all disasters head-on, nearly always defeating them. On one occasion a torrential rain storm washed out a bridge, blocking his route to a performance at a Roswell, New Mexico military base. Arrangements were made for a military car to meet his train and he changed to formal dress in the station. Driving to a nearby rail bridge the Graingers negotiated the trestle on foot. A second car picked them up and deposited the couple at the concert hall, two hours late. A local violinist had kept the audience entertained while confidently awaiting their famous guest.

Expenses of traveling were closely scrutinized, and Grainger was careful to account for every item. His new obligations toward the Melbourne Museum made him spend less and save more. The little food he needed was provided at receptions given for him in each city and his usual habit of avoiding them was forgotten. He noted bitterly in his diary that at Mrs. Kennedy's reception in Omaha, there had been "nothing to eat." Whenever his contract called for a fee plus expenses, he would submit the cost of a hotel room and then leave on a late train, sleeping upright in a second class seat as he had become accustomed.

In March of 1940 Dom Anselm Hughes arrived in America and during the following months visited Grainger several times. Their time together was spent in the technical details of their *English Gothic Music* series which was awaited by Schirmer.

The first American performance of *Hill Song No. 2* by the U. S. Military Academy Band at West Point on April 28 was a turning point in Grainger's attitude toward his scoring. With the exception of the opening overture and the Grieg concerto in which he assisted, all the music that evening was original music for band by Grainger and Cowell.

The highlight of the concert, *Hill Song No. 2*, was described by Grainger as "perhaps the pleasantest compositional surprise of my life."[67] It had been written in 1907 and tried out at Percy Hall, Tottenham Court Rd. in London in 1911, with its premier at the Harrowgate Music Festival in 1929, under the direction of Basil Cameron. Subtitled, "Out of Hill Song No. 1 by 'Criticism'," it was scored for 22 winds. It was this West Point performance, however, which convinced Grainger that he no longer had to experiment with scoring in order to get the effects he desired. In his thinking, his scoring would produce the sounds he intended; he confessed to Howard Hanson that he considered himself "a notoriously bad score reader," and now he was overjoyed. Grainger's habit of trying out his writing before deciding on the final scoring had brought him in contact with Francis Resta* and the superb West Point band. The next decade and a half would find the composer coming more and more to the Point (which was only a few miles from his White Plains home), conducting rehearsals and hearing his music performed.

Through the joint efforts of Richard Franko Goldman and Grainger, Henry Cowell was paroled to Grainger, and in May, 1940, he arrived at 7 Cromwell Place, White Plains. Percy had considered housing him at the Roger Smith Hotel, located only one block away and had written inquiring about the price of accommodations. In answering, the hotel had noted that it seemed unusual, writing to someone who lived closer than the post office.

At a salary of $42.00 per month plus room and board, Cowell began to assist Grainger in preparing an index of the folksongs Grainger had gathered in England some thirty years before. The collection of wax cylinders was destined for the Library of Congress, but Grainger had insisted on supervising the organization of the enormous collection himself.

*Brother of Rocco Resta, Grainger's Army band leader.

The fever of war was everywhere and the Graingers considered a move from the East Coast, for they felt an invasion by Germany to be a distinct possibility. In that event, his home would not be safe for "the rabble would take over White Plains." In late June he removed a considerable portion of his more valuable papers and manuscripts to a security vault in Springfield, Missouri. Plans were made for a more complete move to the Willshire Apartments in Springfield later that year; Henry Cowell would continue to live in the White Plains home and help manage his busy concert career.

Cowell and Grainger continued a close friendship, both as business associates and as fellow composers. Grainger would often accompany Cowell to rehearsals of his music and included him in concerts whenever possible. On December 13, 1940, they joined in a Carnegie Hall "Bundles for Britain" benefit with Marjorie Lawrence and the Durieux String Ensemble playing piano and guitar accompaniments to Grainger's compositions. They were both interested in music for band and much of Grainger's work at this time was concerned with scoring for that medium. The final reworking of *Immovable Do, Marching Song of Democracy, Prelude in the Dorian Mode,* and arrangements of the *English Gothic Music* for winds, which were to find performances in the next few years, date from this period.

In June, Grainger refused an invitation from Phillip James to serve as a judge for a contest of new compositions, explaining that he was not qualified because his "music was not nationalistically 'American'." He had rejected a request to appear at the Australian Pavilion at the World's Fair and confided to John Alden Carpenter that "as to riches, I have many blessings, but few dollars."

By September the task of cataloging the four hundred wax cylinders was finished and Grainger took them to Washington, D.C. He had requested, but had been denied, official backing in England for transferring the sound track

of the wax cylinders to longer lasting discs and hoped that
the Folk Song Division of the Library of Congress would
make the transfers.

Appearing at the door of the Library in his hiking clothes
and with his burlap sack of cylinders, he was detained at
the guard's station until appropriate officials from the
Music Division interceded and he was allowed to enter with
his gift. While in Washington, he visited Pete Seeger, and
together the two collectors discussed folk song notations
and collecting with the phonograph. Seeger's interest in
Grainger's projects had prompted him to visit White Plains
the previous July, so this D.C. visit was only a continua-
tion of the conversation that had been cut short by professional commitments.

Early that fall, Eugene Goossens requested that Grainger supply a new piece to coincide with an appearance with
Goosens and the Cincinnati Orchestra scheduled for November. The two men were both fond of folk songs and,
with Goossen's approval, Grainger rescored his 1905 woodwind quintet, *Walking Tune*, for the winds of the Cincinnati
Orchestra. Although not based on a folk song, this score
with its folk-like melody, is one of exquisite charm and was
received with enthusiasm by the Cincinnati public.

Excepting the "Frankfurt Group," Grainger had made
few intimate acquaintances and he remarked that he had
not made a new "friendship [in America] in 27 years."[68]
Both he and his wife had few social contacts although invitations were available from time to time. Besides a basic
disinterest in the public, Grainger's unpretentious attitudes were disarming to them. Returning from a private
appearance in Connecticut one afternoon, he explained
to his wife, who thought the program had been a bit short,
that he had "dropped the middle of the second and third
movements so he could catch the 4:12." In Sioux City,
Iowa, the audience discovered the pianist asleep on the pi-

ano bench when they arrived for the concert. He had been practising and apparently decided on a pre-concert nap.

By January of 1941, the move to Springfield was complete. From this point, Grainger traveled throughout the United States giving concerts and lectures, and continuing to turn out a veritable mountain of written materials. The amount and variety of work he managed to do was exceptional; his eighteen-hour days would have exhausted men half his age.

Always generous, he continued to be active with British War Relief concerts and even assigned his fees from the Society of the Performing Arts to war charities. The insults he received from people who thought him insincere or from colleagues who misunderstood his intentions, were suffered without revenge.

He added the University of Kansas Summer Music Camp to his schedule and was a frequent guest at Gustavus Adolphus College in Minnesota; the Burrell Symphony Orchestra in Columbia, Missouri was a favorite. Wherever he went, he delighted audiences and pricked the balloon of stuffiness which was such a part of American concert routine.

In April he joined the musician's union after an official met with him to explain the benefits. Two weeks later he and Henry Cowell visited a rehearsal of Stokowski's; the new union member was evicted, while Cowell was permitted to remain. Yet Grainger had been considered acceptable to Fritz Mahler when he and Cowell attended his radio orchestra rehearsal of Henry's *Fair Irish Tales*, a short time before.

Nineteen forty-one was a busy and successful year. ASCAP informed him that he had 538½ minutes of music in either printed or available manuscript, and his fee continued to grow. His diary's last entry of that year stated: ". . . So ends the best musical year I've ever had."[69]

Notes

[1]*The Sun*, Sydney, Australia, May 28, 1926.

[2]*The Sydney Times*, Australia, May 28, 1926.

[3]*The Evening News*, Sydney, Australia, June 23, 1926.

[4]*The Brisbane Sun*, Australia, Sept. 26, 1926.

[5]*The Labor Daily*, Sydney, Australia, June 24, 1926.

[6]Robert Lewis Taylor, "Matter of Kicking Out at Space," *The New Yorker* (Jan. 31, 1948), 32.

[7]*The Advertiser*, Adelaide, Australia, July 8, 1926.

[8]*The Sunday Mail*, Brisbane, Australia, Sept. 26, 1926.

[9]*The Register*, Adelaide, Australia, July 19, 1926.

[10]*Ibid.*, July 5, 1926.

[11]*The Truth*, Adelaide, Australia, July 22, 1926.

[12]*Ibid.*

[13]*The Gossip*, Adelaide, Australia, Sept. 22, 1926.

[14]*The Herald*, Melbourne, Australia, Oct. 27, 1926.

[15]Thorald Walters, *The Melbourne Sun Pictorial*, Oct. 27, 1926.

[16]Interview of Ella Grainger, 7 Cromwell Place, White Plains, New York, by author, August, 1966.

[17]*Ibid.*

[18]Robert Lewis Taylor, "Top Notes Glassy," *The New Yorker* (Feb. 14, 1948), 36.

[19]Press release written by Percy Grainger, Mar. 13, 1928.

[20]Letter from Edgar Lee Masters to Grainger, Nov. 23, 1929.

[21]Robert Lewis Taylor, "A Matter of Kicking Out at Space," p. 37.

[22]Letter to Basil Cameron from Grainger, Mar. 19, 1957.

[23]Letter to Grainger from Balfour Gardiner, June 11, 1922.

[24]Eugene Goossens, *Overture and Beginners* (London: Methuem & Co., 1951), pp. 94-95.

[25]Robert Lewis Taylor, "Top Notes Glassy," p. 43.

[26]Letter to Robert C. Bristow from Grainger, Aug. 11, 1937.

[27]Program for Worcester Music Festival, October, 1931.

[28]Ella Grainger. Unpublished typescript, n.d.

[29]Letter to the author from Gustave Reese.

[30]Course description catalogue, New York University, College of Fine Arts, n.d.

[31]*Ibid.*

[32]Taylor, "A Matter of Kicking Out at Space," p. 38.

[33]*Ibid.*

[34]"Percy Grainger," *Canon*, IV (Nov., 1950), 184.

[35]Taylor, p. 38.

[36]Letter to author from Dom Anselm Hughes, Nov. 30, 1965.

[37]*Ibid.*

[38]Dom Anselm Hughes, O.S.B., "Medieval Harmony — English Gothic Music" (n.d.), p. 4.

[39]Grainger, "Round Letter to Kin and Friends," Sept. 3, 1943.

[40]*Ibid.*

[41]*Ibid.*

[42]Grainger, "Round Letter . . ." 1944.

[43]Grainger, "Round Letter . . ." Sept. 3, 1943.

[44]Grainger, "Round Letter . . ." 1944.

[45]Letter to Frederick Delius from Grainger, Jan., 1932.

[46]Roger Covell, *Australia's Music* (Melbourne, Victoria, Australia: Sun Books Pty. Ltd., 1967), p. 99.

[47]Letter to Thomas Armstrong from Grainger, Oct. 17, 1958.

[48]Letter to the Chancellor, University of Melbourne, from Grainger, Aug. 24, 1938.

[49]Grainger, comments to *Frederick Delius* by Peter Warlock (Philip Heseltine) (reprinted with additions, annotations, and comments by Hubert Foss; New York: Oxford Univ. Press, 1952).

[50]Grainger, "Program Notes" *Lincolnshire Posy* (New York: G. Schirmer, 1940).

[51]"A Talk with Grainger," *Musical Courier*, CI/24 (Dec. 13, 1930), 7.

[52]*Ibid.*, p. 18.

[53]This note, which appeared inside the front cover of the published version of *Lincolnshire Posy* (Schirmer, 1940), was probably inspired by the beer-loving Milwaukee musicians — whose premiere performance of this work was far from perfect.

[54]Letter to author from Glenn Cliffe Bainum, Oct. 16, 1968.

[55]Letter to Grainger from Edwin Franko Goldman, Mar. 9, 1937.

[56]Letter to Edwin Franko Goldman from Grainger, Apr. 29, 1932.

[57]Letter to Richard Franko Goldman from Grainger.

[58]Grainger, "Preface" to *The Band's Music* (New York: Pitman Publishing Corp., 1938).

[59]Grainger, "Thots I think as I grow old" (unpublished typescript, Mar. 25, 1937).

[60]Grainger, "Thunks," (unpublished typescript, dated March 25, 1937).

[61]Letter to Grainger from Poultney Bigelow, Oct., 1937.

[62]Letter to Sparre Olson, Summer, 1938. Quoted in Sparre Olson, *Percy Grainger* (trans. by Bent Vanberg, ed. by Stewart Manville; Oslo: Det Norske Samlaget, 1963), p. 19.

[63]Letter to Henry Cowell's parents from Grainger, Aug. 15, 1937.

[64]Letter to Grainger from Henry Cowell, Sept., 1937.

[65]Letter to Rudolph Ganz from Grainger, Nov. 6, 1939.

[66]*Ibid.*

[67]Grainger, personal Daybook entry dated Apr. 28, 1940.

[68]Letter to Ellen Bull from Grainger, Jan. 3, 1941.

[69]Grainger, personal Daybook entry dated Dec. 31, 1941.

The Final Years and Beyond

Looking Backward

In 1942 Grainger celebrated his 60th birthday. In describing the event at the year's end, he recounted: "You know what the last loud outburst in *Tristan Prelude* is deemed to stand for. Well, I had 70 of them in 1942."[1] His physical accomplishments were, however, balanced by the nagging presence of age. "I've grown awfully old-looking," he complained, "not merely scrawny & crow-like, but with such a devilish bad tempered fact-look."[2] He could not seem to make up for a small loss of weight and felt that "death is lurking — maybe just round the corner, or maybe far off. But he is nearing."[3] He was pleased with the extraordinary number of recent laudatory reviews but cautiously offered that "This may be all part of my being 60 or part of the war-mood. I do not take these things to heart."[4] He felt rather like Delius, who "on the morn of his 60th birthday was rung up by his young friend Alexander Lippay (Hungarian tone-write & blend-band time-beater; dead some years ago in Manila — long before the war) who asked Delius, 'Have you seen the lively theme-write ((article)) about you by Paul Bekker in this morning's paper?' and went on to read Delius part of it — very glowing. Then he asked Delius what he thought of it. 'You see,' retorted Delius, 'I remember what he wrote about me before.'"5

The "crowning delight" of the year was a Gustavus Adolphus College performance of his complete *Jungle Book Cycle*, a compositional project which had occupied him since the turn of the century and which was written expressly as a protest against civilization. Confessing that he had "never written a part I didn't sing myself when writing it," Grainger described the set of pieces based on Kipling texts as being a long work. "All for choir in one form or another . . . I thought it very wish-worthy to have one number for a single voice as change-shock from all the choral pieces. And *The Only Son* is the one. I pride myself that it is really singable . . . Tho it may not seem so at 1st glance. It is, in fact, a real aria."6

An unusual amount of concert activity was booked that year, and Grainger attacked his schedule in a frenzy. "As this season ran on from the last without break I just kept on playing last season's program."7 Performances were almost daily and his usual four-to-eight hours of practice was divided among the keyboards he found in his path. He complained of the demanding bus and train schedules, the unfavorable climates, and the frustration of having concerts often scheduled in a direction opposite to which the trains ran. He laced his published scores with the problems of travel and chided the Anglo-Saxon for "so chaotic a joke as non-nation-wide daylight-saving time."8 He continued his frantic pace for "the glory of Australian music and the glory of Nordic music," for he wished to continue to publish his music and to finance his experiments. He was fond of quoting Cecil Rhodes' remark about a man "being able to afford his ideals."

Ella continued to accompany her husband whenever possible, but Grainger carefully excluded her from most of his concerts at military establishments. He encouraged her instead to stay at the Bigelow estate for "anything deadlier than Ft. Riley, Hancock, Dix, I cannot mind-see."[9]

During a trip through Kansas and Missouri that year, Grainger formulated plans for a four-month tour featuring an ensemble of six pianists. This interest in piano ensembles appears to have begun with Grainger's participation in the 1921 Carnegie Hall benefit for Moritz Moszkowski, although Grainger's 1916 score, *The Warriors*, had called for pianos in multiples of three. During the 1930's, while teaching at the Chicago Musical College, Interlochen, and in presenting his lecture-recitals, Grainger had utilized massed pianos. This practice, popular in America in the mid 19th century, was handicapped by the very obvious problem of physically arranging a number of instruments on one stage. The proposed tour never materialized although much of the music was selected and several transcriptions were made.

The majority of Grainger's time away from the keyboard was spent in scoring for the band; he often wrote sixteen hours a day. Appearances as a guest conductor of bands began to take precedence over his engagements with choirs and orchestras. "I would not be paid to time-beat all these bands (over the country)," he wrote, "If I could not offer tone-fare for band that no one else had. Still, that is not my goal in doing all this band-scoring. My goal is merely to have the joy of hearing the rich sounds come out of the bands."[10] When he had rescored *Lads of Wamphray*, he had felt "a joy, wallowing in the scoring-thought of 38 years ago. The end of the ballad prov'd maybe, the mightiest crest ((climax)) I have ever heard from my own pen."[11]

Cyril Scott continued to remain Grainger's confidant and their exchange of correspondence exhibited Grainger's strength of purpose and Scott's subtle coaxing to interest him in Yoga and theosophy. Scott's recommendations of natural health remedies were occasionally sampled and, for a time, Grainger tried exercises to help his failing eyesight.

It was Grainger, however, who supplied most of the correspondence — letters filled with pointed criticism of Scott's
"playboy" attitude and abstinence from composing, all
the while accusing Scott of exhibiting the flaws of the English middle-class. "You go around like vacuum cleaners,"
he complained, "always yearning to suck up more and
more." Apparently the greediness of the English had passed
Grainger by. "I am wholly satisfied with myself as I am,"
he wrote. "It is true: I don't get on very well with the world.
But that (in my view of it) is because I am always right and
they are always wrong. But on the whole I have a good
time."[12]

Grainger's meticulous repair of old European friendships was partly due to his inability to form new contacts
in America. His unusual personal philosophy and asocial
mannerisms led him to be rebuffed by many he met. The
social amenities which he had carefully cultivated in England were no longer practiced and his total energies were
consumed by performance, writing, and traveling. Even if
he had wished to pursue a personal relationship, there
would not have been time. His main social outlet was his
correspondence and in this way, he kept in regular contact
with his friends. The lack of new friendships caused him
some concern and, to Ellen Bull, he admitted: "I have
formed no friendship in the 27 years I have lived in America, because no one here talks art to me and I can only form
friendships with those who talk art (all the arts) to me."[13]

The lack of communication between Grainger and other
American musicians grew more intense as Grainger became
older. His decision to continue concertizing was not applauded by the younger performers who viewed his ability
as much over-rated and passe; his eccentricities only wid-
ened the breech between them. The country which he long
had lauded became the brunt of his frustration. "As I have
found it, America is an utterly barren field to till, musically speaking," he wrote Scott. "I do not know of a single

man, on this continent, who has the key to my thoughts, my musical and human hopes and goals . . . & this in spite of *my* great worship of so much American art."[14]

Grainger's chauvinistic attitude toward English-speaking people in general, and the Australians in particular, became a prejudice which grew more narrow during these later years. He was intent on purging the English language of all foreign words and their derivations and, early in his student days, he began to substitute English for Italian in describing tempi and directions in his music. Cyril Scott abhorred his "culinary and golfing expressions, such as 'louden lots,' 'hold til blown', 'bumpingly,' and 'well to the fore,' "[15] but no matter how peculiar they might appear, it would be wholly inaccurate to say that they did not describe his intentions.

His cause for language reform found expression in the series of Round-Letters he frequently sent to his "friends and kin." These letters described his work and performances, his attitude toward concerts and composition, and generally provided an easy method of keeping in contact with a number of people he would not have the time to correspond with individually. Each letter was laced with examples of his "blue-eyed English," with each word or phrase followed by their normal equivalent set off in double parentheses. After a word was used several times, he would drop the accompanying translation, obviously satisfied that the reader had incorporated the term into his expanding vocabulary of "blue-eyed English."

Finally, Grainger's interest in language reform resulted in an attempt to codify the salient points of his new language into dictionary form. Spurred by his correspondence with Robert Atkinson, he began to assemble his Nordic-English, American slang words, and Atkinsonisms to form the basis of a new and more direct approach to communication. After working on the dictionary for over a year, he set it aside and labeled it for his museum.

Another interesting Grainger project was a quest for

proof of the historical independence of England expressed
in James MacKinnon Fowler's *False Foundations of British History,* which Grainger personally financed. Privately
printed in 1943, this curious work sets forth two unusual
conclusions. First, that "neither a Celtic population nor
Celtic forms of speech ever existed in the British Isles,"
and second, that "the so-called Anglo-Saxon invasion and
conquest of England never happened." Fowler's son,
Richard, the editor of this slim volume, worked for a time
in arranging the contents of Grainger's museum in Melbourne and gives credit in his preface to "Percy Grainger —
that helper of a thousand lame dogs over a thousand stiles."

During the years which immediately preceded America's
entry into World War II, Grainger produced a number of
unusual documents. Some he planned to publish while
others were destined only for his museum. A draft of his
"English Speaking Leadership in Tone-Art," takes a gen-
eralized sweep at history and gives credit to England,
America, and Australia, for nearly all progress in social
justice, music, and philology. The figures of Marx and
Lenin were dismissed because they had spent time in England or America, while Naziism was explained as "simply
boy-scout-ism, invented by Baden-Powell."[16]

The cradle of artistic civilization, according to Grainger,
could be found in the Nordic countries, the countries from
which he believed the English race had sprung.

> Everything is done to belittle the Prussians
> and North Germans (as everything is always
> done to belittle superior races) while everything
> nice is said of the South Germans and Austrians
> (because everybody feels comfortable in the
> presence of *inferiority*). "They are so artistic."
> "They are so music-loving." What are the facts?
> That all Austrian composers (Haydn, Mozart,
> Mahler. Maybe Schubert is an exception) are just
> ruthounds, chewing the cud of superior North-
> German music & inferior Italian music. Compare

with them the towering figures of North-German music: Handel, Bach, Beethoven, Weber, Wagner, Schumann, Brahms — all of them bristling with size and spirituality. And of these, the *Saxon* composers (Handel, Bach, Wagner, Schumann) show a marked emotional superiority over the other North German composers. And not without good reason. The Saxons were *North Sea dwellers*, until they were moved South and East by Charlemain (I know that the modern Saxons are deemed to be full of Wendish and other Slavic blood. There is seemingly enough Northern-ness left in them to allow them to easily overtop the other Germans, in music.) No one in his right senses could compare a Bavarian like Richard Strauss with Saxons like Bach and Wagner.[17]

Grainger believed English-speaking people to be a hybrid of the Nordic races and, of these, Australians to be the most superior. South Germany remained at the bottom of his artistic scale.

The summer of 1943 saw the second public performance of his 1912 chance music selection, *Random Round*, and in the same year Albert Spalding was complimented by Grainger's description of him as a "highly gifted fiddle-scraper." Except for the free music ideas which still remained foremost in his thinking, nearly all of Grainger's compositional activities were concerned with reworking materials he had begun twenty and thirty years before. The initial scoring of *Random Round* was basically improvisational, and the difficulty in performance prompted Grainger to rescore the piece in a second version. This "set version" was to be used as a guide to performers who were unaccustomed to the improvisational nature of the original. Programmed July 30th at a student concert in the Interlochen Bowl, it was described as "A study in improvisational canon for soprano, alto, tenor, flute, xylophone, marimba, piano, violin, viola, cello, contrabass, mandolin, or ukelele."

It was not the only experimental work by Grainger which found difficulty in initial performance; even *Lincolnshire Posy* had slow acceptance. Conductors were reluctant to try it because of its use of irregular barrings. Grainger, however, continued to promote it whenever he chanced to conduct a band. In a round-letter from this period, Percy described the problems he encountered when he tried to program this work.

(for Wind Band) Lincolnshire Posy

I had a great struggle to do the letter *whole*. The man in charge of the band & everybody else, all wanted me to leave out the two hard movements. But I had no craw ((stomach)) for that & will-forced the giving of the whole work. I hate forcing my will on the folk. But still more do I hate shielding-the-wind from all these milksops of sissified mother's darlings who sit there yawning in the band, thinking they've played everything & know everything. If they want *me* to do anything with them I'll jolly well see to it that they get something to chew on & taste some of the rocks on the rocky road of now-tiney tone-art. Not that the young folks *do* want me to do anything with them, much. When I draw near the wind-band or the string-wind-band I always think I hear soundless groans from the young folk themselves & from their loving guides. Everyone (outcounting me) wants the young folks (poor dears; they may be in the Army next year!) to have so much *joy* in their tone-art. Not me. If I can twist their tails, show them how backward they are (still 50 years behind an Australian of 50 years ago), & show them what a little real tone-art-y work is like — that's all I ask. As I said to them, at the last rehearsal of *Lincolnshire Posy*, anent the changing bar-rings: "Don't mind if you play a few wrong notes;

don't mind if you get the rhythms wrong. Please
don't think I will suffer if you do. My job is to
show you what modern music is like. These
irregular barrings were started over 40 years
ago, so its about time you begin to get used to
them. I'd much rather hear you make a mess
of typical modern music than to hear you tootle-
ing forever at a lot of baby's stuff." (That's one
thing the young folks don't like: to think that
they are fed baby's stuff!).[18]

In consultation with his managers, Fred and Toni Morse,
Grainger made his decision to give up teaching and concentrate on better paying solo engagements. It was his
continuing desire to retire and devote himself to experimental composing. Reflecting on this decision, he wrote:
"I know only one thing; the era of special effort is over
for me. No more teaching at Interlochen. No more working
early and late. No more tenseness. The concert business
which was in the doldrums because of uncertainties created
by the war is very brilliant again and I'm told I have an
unusually fine season ahead."[19] In an effort to expand his
touring or perhaps because of the inability of his amateur
agent, Grainger acquired both a mid-west and a west coast
manager; Fred and Toni Morse continued to be his east
coast contact.

Before reporting to Interlochen for the last time, Grainger had added the Gershwin *Concerto in F* and the Morton
Gould *Concertette* to his repertoire. In learning the two
new pieces Grainger wrote out the orchestral line for harmonium, recorded the accompaniment, and then played
with the recordings to insure "steadiness under fire."

He preferred the Gershwin over the Gould and condemned the latter stating: "Gould's Concertette (it's careless wrong note chords) brings the blush of shame to my
cheeks — that I, at 61, can earn my living as a piano-play-
er only by playing such muck!"[20]

The use of the two concertos was more of a concession

to his public rather than a search for new material. He still continued to present the same works with which he had long been associated. In less than three months he performed the Grieg, Tchaikovsky, and the Saint-Saens twice each, as well as the Franck *Symphonic Variations,* the Liszt *Hungarian Fantasy,* the Delius *Concerto,* Gershwin's *Concerto,* and Gould's *Concertette.*

An offer from Harms to write the solo piano version of the Gershwin concerto for only a 5% royalty angered him. He had already prepared several transcriptions for them but had vowed no more "hack work." Yet in refusing he left negotiations open by hinting he might do just one more if they would give him 7½ %.

It was impossible for Grainger to accept as many engagements as he desired, for his hayfever was bothering him considerably and from time to time he became nauseated. In consideration of his health he occasionally took a berth when traveling. In March he remarked that: "1st sleeper I've slept in for many years — great balm!"[21] His shy nature had not changed and his mother's influence was still apparent. Each year on her birthday, his diary would note how old she would have been. He continued to dislike crowds: "I am so utterly a woman-trained man that I am ill at ease in men's clubs and the like."[22]

Grainger's effort to place himself before the public was based in part on a concern for his place in history, and he was discouraged by exclusion from the more reputable music texts. He considered moving back to Australia: "I must [return] to lawfully dub my tone-works Australian."[23] Earlier he had failed to interest the Melbourne firm of Allan and Company in issuing several of his pieces. He had selected *Australian Up Country Song*, a 1928 creation for mixed chorus based on material he had used in *Colonial Song* and the *Gumsucker's March*, as a suitable first publication for Australia. He received a negative response from the firm. "I'm afraid it's too difficult," they replied, "to be a big seller in Australia."

By the end of the war Grainger's concert career was once again a major activity, and he accepted all engagements he could physically accomplish. Everything he could save was set aside for the museum which was completed but unstaffed and, as yet, not regularly open to the public. In an effort to further reduce his expenses Grainger wrote Cyril Scott explaining: "I have written Balfour Gardiner asking if he could be your money prop for a while."[24] He discontinued subsidies to friends and relatives who had long relied on him for financial support. He did arrange trust funds for them, but he cleverly constructed them so that the principal would eventually serve his museum goal. "I have made irrevocable life-time settlements on composers, other artists, and my dependents to the extent of about L10,000 which capital will revert to me or my heirs on the death of the beneficiaries."[25]

To celebrate Poultney Bigelow's 90th birthday, Grainger personally mowed a large meadow for use as a parking lot for the party. Grainger's physical activities continued but he did not feel well, his throat and tongue remained sore and his stomach often upset. "Perhaps it's cancer — I must have it looked into," he remarked. "But I'm not long enough in one place for a leech to treat it and watch what happens. I must, tho."[26]

Facing the uncertainties of his health Grainger continued to write and that year reaffirmed his conclusions about his scoring. After attending rehearsals with the West Point band for an all-Grainger program, he remarked: "This was the most satisfactory day of my life as a wind composer. Fearing that things won't sound well, of having to try everything out because of doubting my scoring, that has lasted so long is over for good."[27] He was happy he had not followed Balfour Gardiner's suggestion that he revert to the 1907 scoring. He described the West Point performance as the "most up-heartening comp-concert of my life,"[28] with *Hill Song No. 2* still the "pleasantest compositional surprise of my life."[29]

The period during the war had brought mixed blessings to the pianist. His performing in behalf of war relief programs had taken him on extended tours where he graciously gave of his talent. In typical generosity he returned the Steinway which was on loan, because he felt that the company would have trouble securing instruments during the war. His participation during these years in the Williams School of Music Summer Camp at Saugerties, New York influenced Henry Cowell and his wife to secure a home in nearby Shady. Interlochen had now ceased to be a part of his summers and his mood seemed to be lighter. Even the hay-fever which plagued him was stoically accepted: "What I have now is just fun — the fun of a now and then roofshattering, pipe-bursting sneeze."[30]

Grainger replaced his Interlochen summers with short stays at a variety of summer music camps that became popular after the war. In 1946 he became associated with the Pacific Music Camp in Stockton, California and continued at the Mid-Western Music Camp in Kansas. Camp atmosphere, with its outdoor activities, appealed to him and for these few weeks he did not have to travel. In addition, he was free to perform the music of his choice and was usually well paid. His demanding, yet benign nature continued to assert itself. At one such camp he closed the final rehearsal of his *Marching Song of Democracy* with the following remark: "For a group of excellent musicians, you play very badly."[31]

The first performance of *Youthful Suite* occurred in 1946 under Hans Kindler and the Washington National Symphony. Conceived in Frankfurt in 1898 and reworked many times, it was a work of which Grainger was especially fond. Its use of "tuneful percussion" called for an inordinately large group of percussion instruments, but Grainger defended his complete family of mallet instruments and his solution for their limited keyboards.

> The trouble with the wooden marimba has been that most of them do not go lower than to F (below C) though some go to the C below that, and that the tones lose body & quality as they get lower. As early as 1913-or 1915 I had hoped that piano strings drummed by marimba mallets would offer a use-worthy bass to the marimbas.[32]

But he doubted that these scores would find acceptance. "For one cannot take the bulk of my tone-try-outs earnestly. I do, but then I am gifted with *quite unwonted foolishness,*"[33] he concluded. He had refused to follow the traditional directions of his English colleagues because "so many home-trained Britishers became shillsters and mob-mongers in tone-art (hanging round the smell of the church or the Royal Family — like Bax, Vaughan Williams, Elgar.)"[34] It was comforting to him then when Henry Cowell wrote expressing his confidence: "I am sure you know that I consider you one of the great composers of this age. One who has had a great deal of influence on the thought and style of me, and of many others (most of whom probably don't realize where it came from)."[35] And Stokowski added, "He's a wild man, who breaks down all our pet conventions."[36]

When Storm Bull arranged Grainger's *English Dance* for two pianos, he wanted to dedicate it to Vera Gillotte and Vincent Micari. Grainger refused for he held all performers in contempt but toward a select few, he was especially vindictive.

> 1) This composition belongs manily [*sic*] to my teens and if I dedicated it at all it would have to be to someone of that period.
>
> 2) I have made a strict resolve all my life (and kept to it) never to dedicate any composition to a performer of any kind — whether soloist, conductor, choir, orchestra, band, etc. I refused to do so to Madam Melba when she asked

me. I believe in keeping the "class distinctions"
between creative and executive musicians very
strictly. I have always begged my composer-
friends (alas fruitlessly) never to dedicate their
music to nincompoops such as Sir Henry Wood
or Sir Thomas Beecham.[37]

Late in 1947 Grainger recieved his first commission;
he was then 65 years old. The commission, commemorat-
ing the 25th anniversary of the League of Composers,
was in honor of the 70th birthday of Edwin Franko Goldman. Calling for an original work for band, it posed a
new problem for Grainger. His most recent work had
been experiments in free music and arrangements for
winds, and it had been ten years since his last major
work, *Lincolnshire Posy*, was completed. Grainger's no-
toriety as a composer of band pieces had been achieved
largely through performances by the Goldman band, but
these pieces had, for the most part, been written many
years earlier. He admitted that his recent creative energies had not been in writing new pieces and complained
that "my tonery has been growing more & more commonplace ever since I was about 20 or 22 [but] Hillsong 1 & 2,
English Dance, Tiger-Tiger, and Greenbushes all seem
to me masterpieces."[38]

Faced with a deadline and nothing yet on paper, Grainger
decided to rescore *The Power of Rome and the Christian
Heart* for the occasion. Openly admitting what he had
done, he explained: "As it takes me about 20 years to
finish a tone work, the best thing I could do was to fix
up my *Power of Rome* so it could be played without
strings."[39]

The premiere of Grainger's "fixed-up piece" was held
on January 3, 1948 with the composer conducting. The
program consisted exclusively of original band pieces
coming from such respected composers as Milhaud,
Vaughan Williams, Cowell, and Schoenberg; Walter
Hendl conducted. When asked how he had reacted to

the mixed reviews, Grainger replied: "But I didn't see
[them] either — why should I, seeing that I do not write
my music for my daily bread?"[40] He did, however, accept
Milhaud's *Suite Française* as "a delightful part of the
program."

Grainger accepted the lack of enthusiasm for his new
piece and settled into the celebrity role he had so vig-
orously rejected in his earlier years. "I am utterly happy,"
he declared, "I like to be kow-towed to, & I like all the
treatments that come to one with old age."[41] He even
welcomed the younger group of conductors who were becoming the center of the developing band movement. A
year later he would comment: "I am jolly glad that I
have lived long enough to see a younger batch of time
beaters arise who are more friendly to my tonery than
their fathers were and that I can now wash my hands of
the whole dirty business."[42]

Snobs and Prigs

The firm of G. Schirmer was the primary outlet for
Grainger's music in America. His loyalty to them seemed
unusual in an era when composers would frequently change
their business agents, but it was a loyalty that he used
in forcing his will on the editors to get his less popular
pieces into print.

Grainger's demands were so stringent that each editor
had to conform to his wishes regarding the layout of
the parts, page turns, and color in the cover design. But
above all, they had to defend any decision to discontinue
even minor items. Gustave Reese, who served briefly as
head of the publishing department, was no exception and
the friendship Grainger had extended to him during his

student days found repayment in the patience afforded
his demands. Schirmer's decision to release the four movements of the *Danish Suite* as separate items brought a
lengthy rebuttal from the composer. His rationale, though
unsuccessful, exhibited his keen mind and shrewd business sense. He felt that everything he wrote fitted into
a total artistic plan, and to effect a change in any portion
of this extensive and craggy collage, the firm had to deal
with the composer.

Grainger's suspicion of publishers had begun very early.
Universal Editions had published *Hill Song No. 1* and the
Marching Song of Democracy in 1923, even though they
were not admittedly salable works. Delius had recommended them to Dr. Hertzka, the editor, who did not
care what the compositions were, only that Universal's
catalogue had a few English composers represented. Mr.
Boosey had received Grainger's contempt on an earlier
occasion when he had explained to Roger Quilter that
the firm did not care to reissue many items for "we prefer
them to be replaced by 'new blood'." Grainger viewed such
policy as parallel to the fate of works which received a
first performance quite easily, but were never played
again. His intense democratic viewpoint was equally critical of pieces which were repeatedly performed at the expense of other deserving works. Even the popularity of
a few of his own pieces was embarrassing, although he
judiciously used the income to promote concerts of lesser-
known music, both his own and that of his friends. He
recalled how Novello had rejected *Country Gardens* and,
as a result, lost considerable revenue. Publishers, he
thought, should rely on the judgment of musicians, and
he could not understand why they were reluctant to do so.

Grainger's goal was to interest his publishers in printing his more daring pieces in deluxe editions. To this end
he offered to purchase a number of sets of the first edition and to relinquish royalties for "esthetic" considera-

tions. In the process of these negotiations he accepted a raise in the royalty rate from 10% to 12½% for his setting of "Hard-hearted Bar'bra (H)elen." To Scott he confided: "As long as I make synopses of concertos and the like that sell, Schirmers will go on pandering to my wishes, to some extent."[43]

There was a limit to what Schirmer was prepared to do for Grainger. When Percy began to pressure them to issue *Hill Song No. 2* and *The Power of Rome and the Christian Heart*, Nathan Broder sent a copy of the *Hill Song* to William Revelli for consideration as a part of the University of Michigan Band Series. "But Mr. R. did not approve — which I think quite reasonable . . . I was delighted that Mr. R. rejected *H.S. II*, as it is *by far* my best wind piece & I would much prefer to see it appear as a single piece & not in a 'series'."[44]

The one and a half year delay caused by the inaction of Schirmer bothered Grainger, as he realized that age was becoming a factor in his master plan. "But the effect of submitting these things to Revelli," he wrote, "is to hold up publication, with the result that *just in these years when I am still in the concert field* & could do something for these pieces if they were published, I cannot (in some cases) even program them, because the material is with Schirmers."[45]

In an effort to get the two pieces published and yet continue a working relationship with the firm, Grainger made one last offer. He conceded that, because of the publishing congestion caused by the war, they were probably overwhelmed by fine works from prestigious composers eager to publish with the "world's leading publishing house," and he offered "to do for Schirmers such 'hack work' as it really pays to publish — such as piano solo arrangements of piano concertos." His major goal was to see all his larger works issued before he died, and to that end he was willing to compromise. Leeds had made an

offer for the *Hill Song* and Mills for the *Power of Rome,*
and it was Grainger's idea to let them take such financial
"white elephants" off Schirmer's hands. Then, he suggested, Schirmers could address themselves to his other
scores. Replying for Gustave Schirmer, Nathan Broder
felt that, "under the circumstances," there was no objection to either the Leeds or the Mills offer.[46]

As early as 1920 Grainger had complained to Oscar
Sonneck, then chief editor for Schirmer, about their
inconsistency in advertising. "For a species of publicity
of a transcontinental kind," Sonneck replied, "this would
be the very worst time of year. It would resemble the actions of the Russian Army at the end of 1914 when they
were in the habit of shooting their ammunition by day
& night although the enemy was not showing any signs
of attacking."[47]

To sell copies of his music and that of his friends,
Grainger would go to great lengths. In order to stir interest in Delius, he would respond to every inquiry. To
the younger musicians who wanted to know more about
Delius than the invalid tradition, Grainger was available to provide something more juicy. "They are delighted
to know that he really had syphilis," he remarked, "and
was a selfish lustful man."[48] At Stokowski's request he
re-orchestrated several of his pieces to fit recording limitations for an album that was planned. "A nice insult to
offer me at the age of 67 — that my orchestrations are
not fit to record," he complained. He knew, however, that
royalties would be forthcoming and he set himself to the
unpleasant task. "But there is no abuse of shame and
belittlement I will not submit to if it leads to money —
for music, and fame — for Australia."[49]

In late January and February of the following year, a
profile of Grainger appeared in the *New Yorker* which was
not well-received by the composer. The three-part article,
emphasizing his eccentric qualities and dismissing his

serious work, helped to more firmly establish his humorous side. The author who had interviewed the couple
became *persona non grata* at 7 Cromwell Place.

In the spring of 1948, Ella and Percy returned to their
cottage at Pevensey Bay for the first time since before the
War. Scott, Quilter, and even Gardiner had advised them
not to travel to England because of the food shortage. But
Percy circumvented this post-war inconvenience by carrying his own meals. The main purpose of the English trip
was to take part in the first orchestral performance of
his *Danish Suite* under Basil Cameron at the London
"Proms." He would also attend a scheduled performance
of his recently rescored *Marching Song of Democracy* by
the Royal Air Force Band.

The reassurance brought by these two performances
strengthened his goal of devoting the bulk of his time to
composition and to the promoting of works which remained
in manuscript or limited editions. Returning to America
in the fall, his first task was to try to arrange for a recording of the Grieg piano concerto. His offer to Dimitri
Mitropoulos to perform without fee brought no response.
He had made a similar offer to Frederick Stock in 1940,
but Stock had not been interested in such an arrangement
either. He was extremely disappointed, for he had wanted
to record the Grieg, and he was growing old.

Renewed bitterness set in, and an offer of an honorary
Doctorate of Music from the New York College of Music
was refused. In answering the invitation, he explained
why he did not feel he should accept it.

> Dear Warner Hawkins,
>
> I was very much touched by your letter of
> February 7 in which you express the generous
> wish of the New York College of Music to con-
> fer the degree of Doctor of Music upon me. To
> have the good opinion of such a deeply musi-
> cal colleague (and such a fine composer) as your-
> self is highly flattering to me, and I am extremely

proud to be thought worthy of honor by so admired an institution of music as the New York College of Music.

Unfortunately, I am not able to accept such a degree. To begin with I am not a well educated musician, and therefore not deserving of a distinction rightly reserved for those who have been studious. And apart from that, I am not able to identify myself with the musical (or other) culture of the white man. I feel myself closer to the music of the South Seas, China, Japan, Java, Africa than to the music of Europe, and I would be insencere [sic] if I took upon myself a distinction that identified myself with the art, culture and opinions of the civilized world — my own trends being so very different. It is not that I do not *admire* and *love* the music of Josquin des Pres, Dunstable, Adrian Willaert, Skyabine [sic], Fickenscher. But they are not of my world, as the savage people are. Several universities and other institutions of music and learning have been kind enough to offer me degrees, but while I have appreciated the kindly thought most warmly, I have always had to decline the honor — for the reasons set forth above . . .[50]

In 1945 he had refused a similar offer from McGill University in Montreal, stating that:

1) the democratic Australian viewpoint of my early years makes me unable to accept any distinction, and 2) the fact that I regard my Australian music as an activity hostile to education, and civilisation leads me to regard myslef [sic] as one to whom educational honors cannot apply. Also, as I have had only 3 months schooling in my life, I feel that my music must be regarded as a product of non-education.[51]

The success of postwar movies drawn from the lives of popular musicians and artists prompted an offer from one studio to produce a film based on his career. Grainger dismissed the idea because it would force him to continue his concert career; the producers had insisted that he still be active as a performer when the movie was released. In rejecting the offer, Grainger informed his New York agent that

> . . .mere pianists are not worth making films of, for they interest only a comparatively small public. So if the film people are concerned with whether I am concert-playing during a certain season, or not, they must be very misguided, & in that case it is better to have as little to do with them as possible. I am quite willing to do something with the film people, if the payment is big enough & there is no nonsense about the film being contingent upon continued concert work.

His conditions were rejected.

By 1949 Grainger's health began again to limit his activities, but he scorned various medical authorities who had advised an operation. Cyril Scott directed his attention to nature-healers and convinced Grainger that "one's ailments likely are rooted in mineral deficiency." On Scott's advice, his diet began to include "black strap molasses."

Constant touring was now over, but shorter tours and selected appearances could still be fulfilled. The bulk of his time was spent at his White Plains address arranging his personal papers for the Australian museum and working on free music. His assistant was a physicist, Burnett Cross, whom he had met at Columbia University in 1942. Cross' home in adjacent Hartsdale was close enough for almost daily work sessions and for a while Grainger retained him full time so he could help develop a "performer's machine." The two men became friends as well as colleagues. In the evening Cross would join in the music-making sessions which were a part of Percy and Ella's routine. At Grainger's urging, Cross practiced the folksong, "Bold Will Taylor," until his singing was "the living spit of that old singer." Grainger then recorded a harmonium accompaniment one half-step lower than the original to accommodate Cross' voice, and played back the resulting tape one whole-step higher to capture the timbre of the original singer. On at least one occasion, he performed this recording to the accompaniment of two clarinets and strings.

The decade of the '50's was spent "happily working on my free music," and trips to Europe in search of artifacts for his museum became more frequent. In June of 1950, while in Stockholm with Herman Sandby, the Graingers learned of the death of Balfour Gardiner whom they had planned to see in London. After a pilgrimage to the grave of Ella's mother and a visit to Copenhagen, they arrived in London. One of the completed projects in England was a collection of color photographs of Scott, Quilter, and Friederick Austin, and a promise of one from Vaughan Williams. Grainger had become convinced that blue eyes suggested creativity and set about in an orderly fashion to collect sufficient photographs to substantiate his theory. In 1948 he had written: "One of the most unusual signs of genius (this is not my idea, but has been noted by many) in music is a flaming, wide open eye and brilliant coloring."[52] It was his grandmother, he recalled, who first drew his attention to the phenomena. He was convinced that all British composers had light eyes and extended his theory to Austrian and German composers after having examined contemporary paintings of them. It did not appear that the eye coloring of performers embraced this consistency.

The projected content of the museum was unusual, especially in Grainger's desire to totally represent the composers he had selected. Like the care he had exhibited in collecting folksongs and detailing the dialects and habits of the singers, this was another example of Grainger's concept of the artist as a total being. The thrust of the museum was to be a representation of people and circumstances with which he had been in contact during his career.

For each of his Frankfurt friends, he attempted to present a mannequin in perfect replica, exact in size, and dressed in clothing actually worn by that person. In a letter to Quilter, Grainger was specific as to the kind of apparel he wanted:

> *Today's Letter is an S.O.S. for a Suit of Your Clothes*, to be hung on an effigy in the museum. Mrs. Rodgers, the lady who is making the "effigies" or dummies for me has already made 2 (one of Ella, one of mother) which I think are quite satisfactory. She is very anxious to get on with the other figures — of you, Cyril, Balfour, as it is cheaper for her to do them all at about the same time. I mean, it is *cheaper for me too,* if she can do them at the same time, about. Some months ago (before you went to the hospital) you kindly said you would do what you could about a suit of clothes, but you explained [how] dear it was to buy newr [sic] clothes for your very big size, so that you were hanging onto your old things.
>
> I do not know what to say about that. Of course, we want *seemly* (not *seamy)* clothes of you to be seen in the museum; so the suit musn't be too worn out. If you cannot spare a suit, without having a new one made to replace it, how would it be for me to pay half (or whatever division you say) of the cost of the new suit, which suit you would keep, sending me in its place a suit already worn, to this address so that Mrs. Rodgers can get on with the figure?
>
> Do you remember the suit you are wearing in the Harrogate Festival photo of you, Cyril & me, of 1927 (I will try & send you a print of the photo to refresh your memory of it & some other photos)? That seems to me a very suitable one, or something like it. Anything that seems suitable to you & is characteristic.

I will want suit, underclothes, socks, necktie, hankerchief, walking stick, hat, shoes.

Perhaps you would prefer to send me the *new suit* you have made (me sharing the expense)? But in that case *be sure to wear it for a month before sending it* & be sure to label it "worn clothes", as otherwise I have such awfully high duty to pay (on Cyril's suit, for instance).

Please be a darling & deal with this *suit of clothes* problem as soon & as quickly as you conveniently can!! It will be so much easier & cheaper for me if I can get the suit soon. *And so much hangs upon it.* I have so many proofs that might schemes & plans *are wight* [*sic*] *& work well*. So please, darling Roger, help me to get this *clothes-on-effigies* job done!

Yesterday, for the first time, Ella & I ran all the 8 graphs (needed to play 8-part Free Music — something like a string eight-some) at one & the same time. It went awfully well. and we are both very well. We hope you are too beloved friend.

I wrote you that Cyril had got from his taylor his measurements (Cyril's) height, leg, waist, leg & arms lengths, width of shoulders, wifth [*sic*] of hips, etc. Could you give me that too — from your taylor?[53]

An offer from Delius' widow to sell her husband's correspondence for $50 a letter was refused.[54] "I have too many expenses in preparation for my museum," he explained. He was discouraged that Jelka Delius would suggest such an arrangement.

In September he returned to the states. Since his lumbago was bothering him, a few scattered concerts within easy traveling distance of his home were all he could handle. The greater portion of his time was spend studying and working with Burnett Cross on his free music machine.

By January of the following year, Grainger had resumed limited touring, but his attitude toward programming had drastically changed; he was no longer trying out his compositions to see if they sounded as he wished. From January until May, he concerned himself merely with selling as many copies of his works as possible. He even devised a graduated scale for his fees so he might force more sales for his publications. A low fee was quoted if he conducted a chorus; if he could choose the program it would be even less. His highest fee was reserved for the occasions when he would have to perform the Grieg concerto in its "King James" version.

> On this tour I was not (as so often before) trying to test out my pieces as to their art worth, or as to their scoring. I was merely trying to sell as many copies as I could to keep my forth-printers ((publishers)) happy; for if they should wake up some day & find that nobody is buing [*sic*] my tonery ((music)) they would simply stop reprinting my stuff. So I have been doing all I could to boost *sales*, uncaring of the art-some outcome. Thus if I hear that Miami is doing Ella's *Love at First Sight* with 300 voices, I give inner thanks for the many copies sold & I dont allow myself to say: "It would sound better with only 30 voices". And when they do my *Youthful Suite* & tell me that they are leaving out the best tonebout ((movement)), which is *"Norse Dirge,"* I say to myself "At least they have *bought* the whole Suite, even if they dont forth-play ((perform)) it all."[55]

And from this business tour he had learned three things, "Once and for all:"

> 1. That no matter how much the forth-players dislike my tonery ((music)), I can always force them to do it at least middling well, if I am on the spot (there for rehearsals) long enough.
> 2. That the sound of my tonery is always more or less pleasing; so there is no longer any need for further testing, trimming & titivating. All my tone-works *can just stand as they are.*

3. That my tonery (out-counting little tones like
Molly & *Country Gardens*, which *I didnt write
myself*) is unfailingly unpleasing to listen-hosts
((audiences)) everywhere.[56]

He began to feel that conductors disliked his music and
did not attempt to understand it, for the groups he guest
conducted were often poorly prepared. If only he could re-
hearse them long enough, he felt that he could convince
the performers that it was worthwhile. In Peoria he complained that the conductor and business manager had "vied
with each other in telling me how much the singers & players disliked working at *The Lads of Wamphray*, how badly
it was going, how badly it was written for the voices, and
the like."[57] But after he started rehearsals, Grainger felt
that:

The groups are willing and friendly. *It is mainly
the leaders, the timebeaters, who are against
the new works.* The only thing wrong with the
men voices was that they had taken everything
too slow. They were stuck in their slow speeds,
like a cow in a bog, & I couldn't quite drag them
out of it. Nevertheless, after the tone-show ((concert)) was over the time-beater of the men's
sing-band said to me: "This is the best thing
that has happened to the Orpheus Club in their
40 years existence" — he who had been so
against the whole thing! But nor he, nor anyone
else, tells me that he *likes* the work. And the
coolness of the listen-host ((audience)) is
unmistakeable.[58]

Although he was selling more copies, Grainger was de-
spondent about the lack of acceptance of his more difficult works. His dislike of the musical aristocracy recalled
his early concert career in England. His age was against
him now and his health was becoming a major concern.

So what is there to hope for — since neither
time-beaters nor listen-hosts like our British
tonery? As I see it, the thing to hope for is that
the snobs & prigs (who have always ruled tone-

art ((music)) with an iron hand, & who are always browbeaten by tonery that is hard-to-do
& hard-to-like) will sooner or later ram our tone-
art down the throats of the simple & helpless
rank & file, as they have with Bach, Beethoven
& Brahms in the past. My job is to keep my
tonery in print (hinder the forth-printers ((publishers)) from losing heart) thru forth-playments
((performances)) until the snobs & prigs catch
on. For if one cannot please listen-hosts, the
snobs & prigs are one's only hope! The only
thing I ask is: How long will it take before the
snobs & prigs catch on. For I am too old to keep
on with these sales-boosting tours for ever. Yet
the outlook seems too good to quit wholly just
yet. I do draw great crowds in some places (who
want to hear me do the Grieg concerto or who
want to *see* the tone-wright ((composer)) of *Country Gardens*) & snobs & prigs are always swayed
by the power to draw crowds.[59]

His only real consolation was that his free music work
with Burnett Cross was progressing well; traditional composition no longer interested him. "In the meantime I am
unspeakably thankful that my *inner* puzzle-tasks ((problems)) as a tone-wright are over — mainly the askment
((question)) of whether my tonery as it stood *pleased
me*. All my compositions, I hope, will be in this state —
that they *please me,* however little they please anyone
else."[60] Grainger seemed relieved that his problems with
traditional composition were over and he could "now throw
myself into my yet-to-do other jobs: *Free Music,* blue-
eyed English, the noting down of folk songs & South Sea
tonery."[61]

The Albert Morini Agency, which had handled most of
Grainger's tours since the war, began to limit his appearances to the first few months of the year. By limiting them
Grainger could command top fees and gross nearly as much
as if he had worked all year. Nevertheless, he still insisted
on playing with many of the small community orchestras.

Except for a now-and-then appearance with Kindler and the National Symphony, none of the younger conductors of the major orchestras seemed interested in him. He hadn't played with the New York orchestras for over ten years, although he had received a standing invitation to perform with them when his schedule permitted. The relationship had been strained when, after tiring of Grieg and Tschaikovsky, he had offered to do "Turkey in the Straw" free.

Piano recitals were still the core of his performing although he was becoming more widely accepted as a conductor of choirs and bands, a task he enjoyed more than "thumping the piano." On one occasion, during a recital performance in Washington, D.C., he had been brought back for a number of encores. After tiring of the accolades, he returned to the stage, looked directly at his audience, and announced: "I shall now play for you that great American classic, 'Nola'," and he did.

Although Grainger's memory was considered exceptional, he began to doubt his ability to deliver full recitals without the music. His inventive spirit took command, and he designed a music desk roller which sat on the piano and could be activated by a foot pedal. Snatches of tricky passages and, at times, whole pages, would roll into place at the press of his foot. He was pleased with his machine and commented: "I have never had so easy a concert season, thanks to the music desk roller . . . Those who are interested in my music could listen to me; those who were not interested in my music can watch the piano desk roller: everyone is happy."[62]

In the fall of 1952, after a shorter performing season than usual, Percy and Ella returned to Oslo for three months and were considering leaving America permanently, but as yet were unsure. In his 1952 letter to Quilter, he wrote:

> My tours are now over, for the time being, &
> I now can give myself wholly to the jobs I have

at heart — work for the museum, Free Music
& preparing music for publishers, etc. . . . In
1952 I have played the Cyril Scott Sonata 17
times & in many places it was more enthusiastically received than any other pieces on the
program. That shows what "the passage of time"
does for progressive music. In my opinion, the
time is just ripe *for every phase of the Frankfurt group.* When I have cleaned up my various
obligations (to publishers & newly published
works) in USA & done my museum work in
Australia, we will then give up our American
life (which will not mean that I cannot come
to USA for pianistic tours (if we need the money)
or composition-promoting tours) & try & live
mainly in those countries where I have the most
artistic interests & the dearest friends — Australia, England, Ireland, Scandinavia. And in
those countries I will try (as far as my finances
permit) to show forth the achievements of our
group, or any other music specially dear to me
— very often in the form of "large chamber-
music" concerts, no doubt.[63]

Free Music

In his final years Grainger devoted his greatest efforts
to free music and the creation of a mechanical device to
realize it. The goal of creating music which could "glide
about freely into every cranny of tonal space," and eliminate "beats occuring [*sic*] simultaneously in different
voices," had concerned him since his childhood in Australia. It was also Grainger's intention to eradicate the
"tyranny of the performer" by developing a composer's
performing machine which could transfer music directly

from the composer to the listener. Where other inventors were producing performer's machines, his goal was a composer's machine which would completely eliminate the performer. A machine which could realize intervals of all gradations of tones was needed, yet no available instrument met his requirements.

Originally Grainger had attempted to achieve free music through conventional notation and his experimental scores, which date from 1897 and shortly thereafter, contain examples of these ideas. The *Love Verses from the Song of Solomon* of 1899 contained a wide variety of irregular rhythms and barrings which almost defied accurate performance. Shifting meter patterns of 2/4, 2½/4, 3/4, and 3/8, although common today, were revolutionary for that time. Many of these patterns were derived from Grainger's notation of the speech rhythms in Quilter's readings of Biblical texts. His 1902 *Hill Song No. 1* admitted that barrings were provided only for ease in reading and did not imply stress or pulse. This lack of rhythmic simplicity is one of the basic elements in all Grainger's experimental pieces. With Grainger's permission, the use of these irregular rhythms was adapted by Cyril Scott in his *Sonata, Op. 66* for piano, and the wide performance of the piece may have influenced other composers of the period. It is interesting to note that the type of rhythm used by Stravinsky in the *Rite of Spring* (1913) was already being used by Grainger twelve to fourteen years earlier.

In May of 1907, prior to his visit to Grieg's home and only three months before the completion of *Hill Song No. 2*, Grainger sketched four bars of another approach to his ideal of beatless music. This approach was then expanded in *Sketch for Sea Songs Style*, which was completed in Denmark, August 30 and 31, a few weeks after his important Grieg meeting. Originally two versions were made showing "the differences between: A) regularly barred music, and B) irregularly barred music. Scored for strings, the melodic line was extremely chromatic avoiding any hint at a tonal center. Rhythmically, version B's fourteen measures presented the following subdivisions: 3/4, 2½ /4, 3/8, 7/8, 2½ /4, 3/8, 5/8, 7/8, 2½ /4, 3/4, 2/4, 7/8, and 2½ /4. On May 4th and May 26th of 1922, Grainger added C) beatless music. This version was the most complex of the three and was intended to be performed on a pianola — "if possible mechanically played." The unusual barrings contained usage of 1/4, 7/32, 5/64, 5/16, etc., easily the most complex rhythmical notation Grainger had yet attempted.

One year before this third sketch, Grainger publicly announced his progress in realizing beatless music. In an interview with the New York *Globe*, he admitted the difficulties he was facing but "he was hoping to make it available (free music) by mechanical means, which he looks upon as holding the solution of many modernist difficulties, and which he expects to see taking as its share perhaps one-half of the music of the future."[64] Rhythmic liberation was calculated to strike the hearer as the most drastic musical development of the era, "and as likely to give to musical form and rhythm, a liberating stroke no less considerable than that given to harmony by Arnold Schoenberg and his followers."[65]

Prior to 1921, Grainger had carried out his experiments within his close circle of friends and, in most instances, the realizations of his compositional experiments were unpublished. *Random Round*, his 1911 attempt at chance music, was one of the side paths he explored and then left. Although he later prepared a simplified version to facilitate performance, Grainger never developed the aleatorical concept. One has to look to his unpublished scores and sketches of the period to see the variety of approaches he used in his attempts to achieve beatless music. His views toward free music and how it should sound remained basically unchanged from his youth, and he continued to be frustrated by conventional notation and performer's limitations. He differed from Busoni and his 18-tone scale and, much later, from Harry Partch, who based his work on a scale of 43 divisions. Grainger's concept was to embrace all intervals and to be able to move between them in a glide or by the more familiar leap. He did not accept intervals or scales arranged in a predetermined way.

The use of a prepared piano roll to eliminate the technical limitations of the human performer originates from Grainger's familiarity with the Duo-Art reproducing piano of the period. Grainger made many piano rolls for the Aeolian Duo-Art piano, but, more than that, he had expert understanding of how the player piano roll functioned. He even cut by hand a piano roll of part of his *Sea Song Sketch*. The experiments in piano roll composition by the American composer, Conlon Nancarrow, which attracted so much attention in the mid-forties were therefore not as original as they first seemed. Most of what Nancarrow proposed had already been suggested and tried by Grainger twenty years before.

In 1924 Grainger summarized his views in an interview published in the *Australian Musical News*, reporting his progress in attempting to free music from its man-made shackles:

> A long time ago — about 1899 — I began experimenting in beatless music; a liberation of music from regular durations. In beatless music not only are there no beats in the sense of regular durations on which one can rely for absolute rhythms. We can understand a single phrase partaking of pulses which occur quite irregularly, and in this music the pulses occur at different moments in the different parts. Not only are they irregular within themselves in each part, but the rhythmic pulses do not occur simultaneously in the different parts.[66]

He admitted that he had been unable to actually compose

a work embracing these principles "because of the complexities of the notation involved, but I hope to do something in the next few years."

Although he did not consider rhythmic liberation more important than harmonic liberation, he could not understand why composers of the "ultra-modern Continental school" had addressed themselves only to the latter. He admired Schoenberg for his work in atonal writing, but cautioned that "he [Schoenberg] is not liberating us from harmony but only from the inevitability of harmony." Grainger predicted that "any sensitive musician who has heard Schoenberg's work on these lines once is likely to be compositionally an altered man. The more gifted he is the more altered he is likely to be, for the simple reason that freedom is always preferable to the reverse."[67]

The rhythmic, pitch, and dynamic complexities that Grainger planned would be humanly impossible to execute, so the need for a machine — a performing machine — was obvious. He openly admitted that it probably "cannot be conducted at all. How it is to be done I don't profess to know. If the conductor remains, he will remain merely as an emotional stimulant. His object might also be to control the balance of sound in some cases; to bring out some parts and repress others."[68]

In summation, he outlined his main compositional goal:

> The big object of the modern composer is to bring music more and more into line with the irregularities and complexities of nature and away from the straight lines and simplicities imposed by man...we should follow nature and allow ourselves every possible freedom of expression.[69]

Along with rhythmic difficulties, two missing ingredients in realizing free music were the ability to perform micro-intervals and to pass from one tone to another by means of gliding. It was logical, then, that Grainger should

next attempt to demonstrate his free music by providing
a sketch for string quartet such as that used to illustrate
his lecture on the Australian radio broadcast in 1935; it
was possible to glide between pitches on string instruments
and still have a fair amount of rhythmic control. The sketch
Grainger prepared on January 8, for the broadcast two days
later, was thirty seconds long and conservative in its technical demands. He stated that, "In free music all the musical elements will be wholly free; the intervals will be free
of all scales or fixed intervals of any kind; the rhythms
will be quite free of same-beatishness in the various parts
(the beats — if any — happening othersomely in each part);
the many-voiced texture quite free of harmonic thought."[70]
But the examples for this lecture were more simply written; "No out-of-tune intervals (closer than ½ step) are
used (as will be in free music, of course) to help speed in
rehearsal. For the same reason the rhythms bear a closer
relation to the barring (which is purely arbitrary — the
melodic lines carry no beat feeling. The bars and beats are
simply like a yardstick by which the irregular durations —
lengths of the tones — may be gauged and readily read)
than they will in fully fledged Free Music."[71]

This approach to his free music, though simplified, still
gave the performers difficulty. The flaw was that it was
humanly possible to perform only rudimentary examples
because of the music's innate complexity. Grainger was not
deterred and, on October 6, 1935, while returning to the
States aboard the *M.V. Wanganella*, Grainger reworked
his short sketch moving closer to his goal of liberated
sound. In revising the sketch he attempted to notate intervals of less than one-half step gradation by the use of ob-
long or square shaped notes whose stems would be posi-
tioned according to the direction of the desired out-of-tune-
ness. Slides between pitches were indicated by slanted lines
between notes. "All notes (except the long ones) throughout this piece should be slid, all intervals (except the long

ones) being everlastingly in a state of slow drift. There should be no intervalic sunderedness between notes," he wrote.[72]

By 1937 Grainger turned his attention to the use of the Theremin as a suitable vehicle for free music. He had become interested in the instrument after its inventor, Russian physicist, Leon Theremin, had presented several Carnegie Hall concerts earlier in the decade using a variety of electronic instruments that he had constructed. Percy initiated a meeting with the Russian and asked about the possibility of a Theremin-type machine that would play free music without the use of a human performer. Theremin admitted that such a machine was a possibility, and Grainger produced a graph score for six Theremin entitled "Free Music Nr. 2." Although *Baker's Biographical Dictionary* states that Theremin constructed "an automatic musical instrument for playing directly from specially written musical scores (constructed for Percy Grainger)," there is no evidence to support this claim.[73] Shortly after his meeting with Theremin, Grainger stated that "Theremin disappeared into Russia, and I never heard from him again."[74] If such a machine was constructed, it never reached Grainger and Grainger was forced to abandon the idea of using the Theremin. It was a direction which would lead nowhere he concluded, although Cross later felt that the idea of a modified Theremin was a good one. It should not have been difficult to devise an automatic Theremin at that time. For instance, a sheet of foil of varying height passing close to the Theremin's pitch control rod would surely have affected pitch. Rhythmic freedom was yet to be achieved.

In February of 1943, Grainger produced a short document regarding his most recent thought in notational attempts at free music. In this essay he reverted to the practices of the folk singers he had come to know some thirty years before. He rejected the string instruments he had recently experimented with and planned to develop free music by using his own voice, recording each line on a crude gramophone disc, and gradually adding voice lines until he got a satisfactory result. Then, with a product of three or four voice lines, he would attempt to notate what he had created adding conventional instruments as desired.

Free Music ideas, Cedar City, Utah, Sunday
Feb. 21, 1943.

1. *"Curve-tone backgrounded by roll-tone-line"* for 2 voices (both to be sung by me) Roll-tone-line-goes 〰〰 lower than curve-tone. Curve-tone keeps (in the main?) above roll-tone-line and is slow, mournful, with very gradual tone-hight-changes. Should it some-times veer off into short (staccato) coloratura tone-sprays, like Spanish Gypsy and Northern Indian (music of the Orient) singing? First I must sing the roll-tone-line onto one tone-disc (grammophone record). I tryout, many times, singing my curve-tune on top of this sound-disc, till I get quite wonted to it. Then, into a new tone-disc, I sing my curve-tone — the tone disc also taking up the roll-tone-tune from the first disc. In order to be able to note down the outcome exactly (on paper) I must first add a ticker (with bell on 1st of every 4 ticks, to the twaid (2nd) tone-disc. (Will it be needful to put all this on a 3rd tone-disc.) Then I note from the pitch at every tick and then get my tone-height bearings for my down-write-ment (notation).

2. *"Feelingful tone-lines with upwellment-&-plunk background."* 3 or 2 theremin (or 3 or 2 voices, or 3 or 2 strings) playing "upwellment," followed by "plunk" on sliding-tone kettledrum, marimba-mal-leted low piano string, (bass drum?), low-tones (3½ tones next to each other?) on wooden & metal marimbas: again-sounded over & over, like a flower pattern on a Far-Eastern Fabric.

Upon this 2 or more he-highish voice's sing tense, mournful, many voicedness, & maybe a trumpet

play an off-tone call like

Each time this is sounded the tone-step's must be
othery. Sometimes (as in birdcalls) the last note
(high d#0 can be left out. Sometimes the mournful "feelingful tone lines" should run in triads(?).
In tonefeasts the end-some (final) tone-disc would
be used, or printed copies be on hand.[75]

Basically, however, Grainger felt that "It would be out
of the question to play *Free Music* by human players . . .
It could only be played mechanically." Thinking only
in terms of constructing a machine which could produce
the sounds he had heard in his head since childhood, Grainger and his technical consultant, Burnett Cross, began
just such an undertaking.

One of their most interesting experiments was with three
Solovoxes linked to a Duo-Art reproducing piano. They
hoped to achieve:

> . . .the effect of gliding tones by tuning the
> 2nd and 3rd Solovox one-third of a half-tone
> above the 2nd, which I would operate by exten-
> sions of keys from a Duo-art piano to the 3 Solo-
> voxs, the whole being played by a Duo-art roll
> that I would cut muself. The question is whether
> these closer intervals (if the paper roll on the
> Duo-art is cut very legato, with very slight over-
> lapping of tones) would give me the impression
> of gliding tones, would be an ideal medium for
> my *Free Music,* which latter (if I may be par-
> doned for saying so) is the *only complete modern
> music* I know of. Many truly progressive modern
> experiments have been tried, but only in the Free
> Music are *all these elements of modernity united.*[76]

Although not technically perfect, the experiment was
not a failure, for "it showed us that we were headed in the
right direction; that a useful approximation of a gliding
sound — a controllable gliding sound, that's to say —
could be had by overlapping pitches a third of a half-tone

apart. The real trouble was that the Solovoxes did not have identical tone quality. This broke up the glide. But we were encouraged to go on."[77] Grainger was getting close to his machine.

Closely examining the latest technical advances of Dr. Earle L. Kent of the Conn Corporation and the recent electronic achievements of several organ builders, most notably, the Hammond Instrument Company, the two men began to experiment with available means such as organ pipes and harmonium reeds. By overlapping adjacent pitches, they obtained rough but controlled gliding sounds.

In March of 1950, Cross and Grainger achieved a victory over the elusive gliding tones by drawing lines on a sound track of a movie film. "Although the movie film idea was potentially a powerful one, it was discarded because it interposed too many steps between the composer and hearing the music — such as developing the film . . . And we had snared the elusive glides by then."[78]

Drawing ideas from their previous work, their machines became more electronic than mechanical. Originally, they had used suction provided by a modified vacuum cleaner but now Cross replaced vacuum tubes with transistors. In addition, graphs, inked onto a roll of clear plastic, regulated pitch and dynamics. The graph would pass beneath photocells which would control the frequency produced by a transistor oscillator. Each note had a pitch control and dynamics control graph and were regulated independently. One could hear the note being formed as the graph was painted on the plastic sheet, and it could be easily erased or modified. The composer could go from one pitch to another by means of an effortless, frictionless leap or by way of a controlled glide. But, best of all, the machine did not require a staff of engineers in order to function. By the early 1950's a crude performing machine was achieved which could produce four voices with the possible addition of three more.

Grainger and Cross continued to refine their machine. "It was tragic that Mr. Grainger became seriously ill," Cross states, "and died just when all the major technical problems of the free music machine had been overcome."[79]

Love and Pain

Since the early 1950's, Grainger had suffered difficulties with his urinary tract and visits to doctors came at more frequent intervals. By the spring of 1952 it was apparent that Cyril Scott's black strap molasses was not effective. In August, after an appearance at the University of Kansas, Grainger cancelled his pending American engagements and sailed for Denmark. Although his home in White Plains was close to a number of superb medical facilities, Grainger chose to return to the Scandinavian countries for treatment and selected Cai Holten, Karen's brother, for his doctor. On August 17 a prostate operation was advised. The following day Grainger performed a private concert for the nurses of the Kommune Hospital in Aarhaus; two days later he underwent the prescribed surgery. During his convalescence, he was notified that Roger Quilter had died and two weeks later, Karen Holten succumbed to a respiratory ailment.

The deaths of two of his oldest friends were added burdens to his recovery. The Frankfurt Group which had met and defeated so many opponents was now being attacked by the cruelest of enemies — old age. His deteriorating circle of friends gave Grainger a renewed impetus to finish his experiments and put his papers into acceptable order. On October 17, he arrived back in New York and spent several days resting at the White Plains hospital. Violating his own program of rest and study, he re-

turned to the concert stage in Poughkeepsie, October 28th
and, against his doctor's advice, followed with an October 31 performance of the Grieg Concerto as part of an
evening of Norwegian music in Carnegie Hall. In spite
of the pain the performance cost him, Grainger was im-
mensely pleased that the concert was sold out and that a
considerable sum was raised for the Norwegian-American
Welfare Institute.

By January of 1954, Grainger's health had weakened to
such an extent that he was again forced to cancel his few
scheduled appearances. Ralph Vaughan Williams called
on him during an American visit and Grainger seemed
pleased at the reunion. The photo of Vaughan William's
eyes, promised earlier, was added to his collection. After
two visits to the White Plains emergency ward, Grainger
accepted the advice of his local physician and left for
Minnesota's Mayo Clinic. By April he was well enough to
fulfill a single conducting engagement at the Ohio Intercollegiate Band Festival. Two first performances were
recorded on that date: *Bell Piece* for tuneful percussion
and wind choir, and *Let's Dance Gay in Green Meadow,*
set for band and "Dedicated to the 1954 Intercollegiate
Band Festival." Except for the opening number, the
program consisted entirely of Grainger's music. It was
May 13th before Grainger appeared publicly again; in all,
only five or six scattered performances were delivered
that year.

In the spring, Grainger received the coveted St. Olaf
Order Medal for his many years of friendship and support
of the Norwegian people. In his letter of thanks to Ambassador Wilhelm Morgenstierne, he stated his indebtedness to Grieg who "together with Wagner initiated the
modern [French] school [of composition]."[80] Percy related that he had once been at a meeting of composers
discussing Debussy and Franck at which Maurice Ravel
declared that it was Grieg who had exerted the greatest

influence on the movement, but he had never been given
the proper credit. It was almost impossible for Grainger
to receive laudatory acknowledgment without extending
credit to those he felt had helped him.

In July he returned to the Mayo Clinic for further tests
and examinations. He seemed to accept his illnesses and
seldom complained, although he was disturbed that his
age was hindering his work. He did not find all the dis-
comforts of aging morose for he observed that "I too am
getting very deaf, and hear the most delightful incon-
gruous nonsense when people talk."[81] As a result of his
limited appearances, Grainger's concert income was almost negligible; so he shrewdly booked an appearance at
the Rochester, Minnesota Music Festival from July 23-25,
then entered the Mayo Clinic the following day. After his
return to White Plains, he and Burnett Cross continued
work on the free music machine.

With the days of the great concert tours behind them,
Percy and Ella sailed to Australia (September, 1955). Only
two engagements were fulfilled that year, and for the
following season he managed to complete only two short
tours. Guest conducting with the Goldman Band in July
rounded off his 1956 season. But Grainger did not consider
himself finished with public appearances. When Bernard
Heinze of the Australian Broadcasting System suggested
he give a six-day Grainger Festival during the next season
or so, Grainger considered accepting. It was not to be accomplished.

From January until May of 1957, Percy and Ella vaca-
tioned in England and met with Dom Anselm Hughes
concerning future publications of their *English Gothic
Music*. During side trips to Copenhagen and Hamburg,
Grainger received radium treatments and frequent in-
jections for the constant pain he was now experiencing.
In spite of his condition, he was still able to record the
Grieg concerto on February 25 with Per Drier and the

Aarhaus Municipal Orchestra. It was 1962 before it was released on the Vanguard label.

Since his brief army career as a bandsman, Grainger had wanted to enroll in the band training program at Kneller Hall, England. His superior at Ft. Hamilton had been a graduate of the famous school and Grainger was impressed with his training. He was finally able to arrange a visit in 1957 — but not as a recruit. He was greeted as a celebrity and invited to conduct the band and pose for photographs with the musicians and their director, Major Pope.

Ella purchased a special cane for him during this trip, which he found to be "very helpful [to] develop foot-slide technique." It was becoming increasingly "hard to get to sleep," and by June, he found it difficult to "control my speech." He became frightened when he found himself "talking nonsense at times."[82] On July 3, the anniversary of his mother's birthday, he noted in his diary: "Beloved mother would have been 95 today. I have felt the tragic influence of her death more in this year, 1957, than in any other." But amid the formidable problems of health, Grainger was able to participate in a recording of his *Children's March* with Richard Franko Goldman. One year earlier Frederick Fennell and the Eastman Wind Ensemble had recorded *Lincolnshire Posy;* Grainger felt that this was the definitive performance. These were his first pieces for band to be recorded.

In February of 1958 Grainger attempted to resume limited appearances. In these concerts the emphasis was on his music and his solo performances were usually limited to the Grieg Concerto. A performance of his piece for "concerted improvisation," *Random Round,* received his approval: "At Cincinnati I heard for the first time a properly worked out performance of my *Random Round* in the dished up version for 6 pianists at two pianos. Six elderly ladies, all with immense back sides, romped away

at terrific speed and quite note perfect."[83] The occasion
was a joint offering of two-piano music by the Keyboard
Club and the German Club of the University of Cincinnati.
(Grainger had tried it out with Dennis Blood who had
consented only after Percy agreed to have his piano tuned.)

Because the bulk of Grainger's music for bands was
unpublished, it was necessary that he supply scores and
parts to each band, orchestra, and chorus he conducted.
Often he would rewrite parts to accommodate a particular
organization. Always aware of the time it took to prepare
the manuscripts, he would cut and paste parts from one
arrangement to satisfy another. Often an instrumental
part was a collage of color, directions, and mismatched
note sizes. It was his ability as a rehearsal conductor which
turned impossible situations into memorable performances.
The Grainger charm and commitment continued to win.

In March, 1958, a return to the Mayo Clinic was necessary although Grainger was discharged in a few days.
A trip to England was planned for April, for he had many
details to attend concerning his Australian museum project. The Jubilee celebration of the Folk Song Society scheduled for that summer was also a part of his itinerary. As
had so often been the case, tickets were purchased under
his christened name, George Grainger, even though it
was a futile attempt for the exuberant Grainger to ever
travel inconspicuously.

Wherever they traveled, the Graingers found themselves
in the company of interesting people and musical events.
Nashdom Abbey and Dom Hughes was a regular stop, as
were the parties of Eugene Goossens and continental
avant garde musical productions. In 1957 he had been
impressed by a performance of *Wozzeck*, and in January,
1958, he attended Samuel Barber's new opera *Vanessa*, as
well as the New York Philharmonic's performances of We-
bern's *Six Orchestral Pieces* and the *Rite of Spring;*
"First time I heard it [*Rite of Spring*], glorious," he re-

marked. In November he would approve of Stockhausen's electronic music but would question how new it really was, noting in his diary: "Columbia U. McMillan Theatre Karlheinz Stockhausen 'New (?) Electronic Music' good."[84]

Several concerts of Grainger's compositions, with the composer conducting, prefaced a three-month visit to England where he deposited discs and photostats of his English folk song collection with the British Institute of Recorded Sound. Further X-ray treatments dictated their return to America and Grainger, age 77, prepared his will. To coincide with his master plan Grainger carefully structured his Will to assure the completion of his museum project. Sufficient funds were set aside to cover the cost of duplicating his drawings, paintings, musical and literary manuscripts, and his correspondence. The duplicates were to be deposited with the Library of Congress, with all original material destined for the Melbourne museum. The final and most curious addition to his archive was to be his own skeleton.

Although his declining physical condition predicted even fewer appearances, he finished a new arrangement of Liszt's *Hungarian Rhapsody* for piano and band, which he performed on December 17 at Wisconsin State Teachers College-River Falls. Future performances of the work did not materialize.

Grainger's final public appearance occurred at Dartmouth College on April 29, 1960. To open the Third Annual Dartmouth Festival of Music, he lectured on "The Influence of Folksong on Art Music." After his morning lecture, Grainger appeared, without fanfare, as guest conductor with the Dartmouth College Band in a performance of *The Power of Rome and The Christian Heart*. For this, his final appearance, Grainger was not the center of attention. His part of the three-day festival was merely a warmup for subsequent concerts of the music of Dallapiccola, Stravinsky, Mozart, and Beethoven; lectures on electronic music by Milton Babbitt and on Wagner by Friedelind Wagner were given as well. Grainger, the man who envisioned his lasting fame to be that of an Australian composer and an innovator in free music, was not included in any additional events at the Festival. A small note on the program reminded the audience of "an Exhibit of Autograph Manuscripts, facsimilies, publications, and portraits of Mendelssohn, Chopin, Schumann, Spohr, Wolf, Ives, and Grainger is on display in Baker Library."

In March, 1960, Ella took over her husband's correspondence and that year his uniquely informative Christmas letters were absent. On February 20, 1961, at the age of 78, he died of cancer. Contrary to the terms of his Will,* his body was flown to Australia and buried next to those of his parents in the family plot in Adelaide. This was his first airplane ride, and, obviously, his last as well. He had always avoided air travel for, as he so succinctly wrote: "I don't care to ride in anything that does not back up."

> Somewhat recently, my almost life-long friend and well-known fellow composer, Percy Grainger, died, leaving his widow to mourn his loss. Wishing to have some news of him, I asked M. to contact him while she herself was at night on the astral plane. And there sure enough she found him, together with his widow, surrounded by a group of friends, some of whom had already passed over and some others who had not. I was with M. at the time, and Grainger, looking years younger and full of *joie de vivre,* immediately came forward to greet us with his characteristic warmth, told us how glad he was to be free and not to have to go back to earth-life, and said what wonderful music-making there was where he now found himself.
>
> Actually, during that earth-life, his attitude towards the question of survival had been a

---

*A copy of his Will is contained in the Appendix.

strange one. A few years before his death, the
subject having cropped up, I remember his saying: "I don't entirely disbelieve in an after-life,
but I'm simply not interested in it." Well, it
obviously interests him now; and I was amused
when M. told me he had turned to her and said:
"Cyril is always right" — though "always" was
indeed an overstatement![85]

— Cyril Scott

Notes

[1]Grainger, "Round Letter to Kin and Friends," Jan. 18, 1943.
[2]Letter to Cyril Scott from Grainger, Aug. 3, 1942.
[3]*Ibid.*
[4]Grainger, "Round Letter ..." Jan. 18, 1943.
[5]*Ibid.*
[6]Grainger, "Round Letter ..." Feb. 17, 1947.
[7]Letter to Eugene Goossens from Grainger, 1942.
[8]Grainger, "To Bandmaster," prefacing *Lads of Wamphray* (Carl Fischer, 1940).
[9]Letter to Ella Grainger from Percy Grainger, 1943.
[10]Letter to Cyril Scott from Grainger, Aug. 3, 1942.
[11]Grainger, "Round Letter ..." Jan. 18, 1943.
[12]Letter to Cyril Scott from Grainger, Aug. 3, 1942.
[13]Letter to Ellen Bull from Grainger, Jan. 3, 1941.
[14]Letter to Cyril Scott from Grainger, Sept. 20, 1941.
[15]Cyril Scott, "Percy Grainger: The Music and the Man," *The Musical Quarterly*, II (1916), 430.
[16]Grainger, "English-Speaking Leadership in Tone-Art" (8-page type-script, Oct. 21, 1943).
[17]*Ibid.*
[18]Grainger, "Round Letter ..." Sept. 3, 1943.
[19]*Ibid*, Sept. 26, 1944.
[20]Grainger, "Round Letter ..." Feb. 26, 1944.
[21]Grainger, personal Daybook entry, March, 1942.
[22]Letter to Ella Grainger from Percy Grainger, 1944.
[23]Grainger, "Round Letter ..." Feb. 26, 1944.
[24]Letter to Cyril Scott from Grainger, 1945.
[25]Letter to The Chancellor, University of Melbourne, from Grainger, Aug. 24, 1938.
[26]Grainger, personal Daybook entry dated Apr. 27, 1945.

[27]*Ibid.*, Apr. 20, 1945.

[28]*Ibid.*, Apr. 28, 1945.

[29]*Ibid.*

[30]Grainger, "Round Letter..." May 21, 1947.

[31]University of Kansas, Summer Music Camp, 1953.

[32]Grainger, "Round Letter..." 1946.

[33]*Ibid.*, Feb. 17, 1947.

[34]*Ibid.*

[35]Letter to Grainger from Henry Cowell, Nov. 2, 1947.

[36]Grainger, "Round Letter..." Aug. 23, 1946.

[37]Letter to Storm Bull from Grainger, July 20, 1947.

[38]Grainger, "Round Letter..." Jan. 13, 1948.

[39]*Ibid.*

[40]*Ibid.*

[41]*Ibid.*, 1947.

[42]*Ibid.*, June 8-11, 1949.

[43]Letter to Cyril Scott from Grainger, Nov. 19, 1947.

[44]Letter to G. Schirmer from Grainger, Jan. 12, 1948.

[45]*Ibid.*

[46]Letter to Grainger from Nathan Broder, Jan. 20, 1948.

[47]Letter to Grainger from Oscar Sonneck, June 3, 1920.

[48]Letter to Cyril Scott from Grainger, Feb. 29, 1949.

[49]*Ibid.*

[50]Letter to Warner Hawkins from Grainger, White Plains, New York, Mar. 1, 1949.

[51]Letter from Grainger to Cyril James, Vice Chancellor, McGill University, Montreal, April 24, 1945.

[52]*Australian Musical News*, May 1, 1956.

[53]Letter to Roger Quilter from Grainger, Apr. 14, 1952.

[54]Letter to Grainger from Delius' widow, July 12, 1952.

[55]Grainger, "Round Letter..." April 5-26, 1951.

[56]*Ibid.*

[57]*Ibid.*

[58]*Ibid.*

[59]*Ibid.*

[60]*Ibid.*

[61]*Ibid.*

[62]Letter to Roger Quilter from Grainger, Apr. 14, 1952.

[63]*Ibid.*

[64]*The New York Globe*, Sept. 17, 1921.

[65]*Ibid.*

[66]*Australia Musical News*, Oct. 1, 1924, p. 17

[67]*Ibid.*, p. 18.

[68]*Ibid.*

[69]*Ibid.*, p. 17.

[70]Grainger, unpublished typescript of lecture notes.

[71]*Ibid.*

[72]Grainger, notes on revised sketch of Free Music.

[73]"Theremin, Leon," *Baker's Biographical Dictionary of Musicians* (5th ed. revised; New York: G. Schirmer, 1965), p. 1637.

[74]Letter to author from Burnett Cross, July 17, 1965.

[75]Grainger, unpublished typescript, "*Free Music* ideas," a series of notes dated Feb. 21, 1943.

[76]Letter to Hammond Instrument Co. from Grainger, May 10, 1948.
[77]Letter to the author from Burnett Cross, Aug. 10, 1972.
[78]*Ibid.*
[79]*Ibid.*, July 17, 1965.
[80]Letter to Wilhelm Morgenstierne, 1954.
[81]Letter to Elsie Bristow from Grainger, July 17, 1955.
[82]Grainger, "Round Letter . . ." Mar, 25, 1958.
[83]*Ibid.*
[84]Grainger, personal Daybook entry, November, 1958.
[85]Cyril Scott, "Out-of-the-Body Reunions at Night," *Prediction*, XXXII/3
(March 1966), 14-16.

Introductory Note to the Appendixes

There are three main divisions to the Appendices. Section A (Parts 1 and 2) is a catalogue of all original compositions and arrangements listed alphabetically. Abbreviations used are BFMS for *British Folk Music Settings*, DFMS for *Danish Folk Music Settings*, and EGM *for English Gothic Music.* "Room-music" was a designation used by Grainger to describe chamber music. As an English language purist, he substituted the word "room" for the French-Latin root, "chamber." "Large Room Music," therefore, was an ensemble of from eight to twenty-three instruments or voices, each of which was treated soloistically. "Small Room Music" referred to combinations of less than eight, although this division was not always strict.

"Elastic scoring" was a term Grainger used to describe a type of orchestration he conceived during the early 1930's:

> It consists of so arranging the "cues" in the orchestral
> parts that the piece may be played by any combination
> of instruments from 2 or 3 to 100 or so . . .*

It was admittedly a commercial endeavor and a technique which did not receive wide public acceptance although Grainger's intrinsic cleverness did not go unnoticed. Elastic scoring was a type of *Gebrauchsmusik*, for it also was Grainger's desire to make his music more available to amateur groups with unusual instrumentation.

> The governing principle of "elastic scoring" is that
> good tonal balance be maintained at all times, and to
> this end almost any combination of instruments may
> be used. . . It is intended to encourage music-lovers
> of all kinds to play together in groups, large or small,
> and to promote a more hospitable attitude towards
> inexperienced music-makers.**

"Tuneful percussion" refers to percussion instruments with definite pitch and includes those commonly referred to as keyboard percussion. Grainger includes in this catagory: "All percussion instruments with clear intonation and therefore capable of playing tunes."

The original appearance of two number 41's (*The Three Ravens* and *Bold William Taylor*) in BFMS is probably a result of the publishers assigning the number without knowledge that the composer had already assigned it to an existing manuscript. *Bold William Taylor* has recently been changed to No. 43.

The earlier duplication of No. 18 (*There Was A Pig Went Out to Dig* and *Knight and Shepherd's Daughter*) may have resulted from a similar misunderstanding or from simple confusion when Grainger moved to the United States, changed publishers, and, shortly thereafter, entered the U.S. Army.

As regards the two No. 9's in the DFMS, both titled *Jutish Medley*, the 1931 version (two pianos, six hands) was extracted by the publisher from Grainger's earlier elastic scoring. This was the publisher's attempt to capture a public which had become fascinated by the era's multiple piano craze.

After 1916, G. Schirmer was Grainger's primary agent with Schott & Co. having exclusive control of the British market. No attempt is made to chronologically separate which of the two firms may have actually released material a few weeks prior to the other.

Section B contains reprints of lists of piano rolls and recordings made by Grainger as well as recordings of his works.

Section C is a selection of Grainger's writings, none of which have been published before. They deal with his concern for his place in history and bare a portion of his thoughts which were known to but a few close friends.

The most comprehensive compilation of Grainger material exists in the Grainger museum in Melbourne, Australia. This collection (to date) is almost unavailable because of a lack of organization and access to the public. The Library of Congress has the largest available collection which includes copies of many important items that are in Australia. Other important locations of Grainger material include Lincoln Center, National Library of Scotland, National Library of Ireland, the British Museum, the Sibley Library (at the Eastman School of Music), and his home in White Plains, New York.

The Percy Grainger Library Society, which has its headquarters at 7 Cromwell Place, White Plains, New York, is developing a clearing center for inquiries.***

°A Talk with Grainger," in *The Musical Courier* CI/24 (Dec. 13, 1930), 7.

°°Percy Aldridge Grainger, "To Conductors" ("Foreword") to *Jutish Medley* ("elastic scoring" version).

°°°For a discussion of source and bibliographical problems in Grainger studies, see David S. Josephson, "Percy Grainger: *Country Gardens* and Other Curses," *Current Musicology*, No. 15 (1973), 56-63.

117. Rufford Park Poachers

phonographed & noted by Percy Grainger.

(sung in F) Rather slow

sung by Mr Joseph Taylor, Brigg, 4. 8. 06.

(1) They — say that forty gallant poachers, they was in a mess. They'd often been attracted when the number it was less. Chorus So Poacher bold, as I unfold, keep up your gallant heart, & think about those poachers bold, that night in Rufford Park.

(2) A buck or doe, believe it so, a pheasant or a hare, was sent on earth for every one quite equal for to snare. Chorus So Poacher bold, as I unfold, keep up your gallant heart, & think about those poachers bold, that night in Rufford Park

(3) The keepers they began the fight
with stones & with their flails;
but when the poachers, they started to fight
they quickly turned their tails.

(The next verse tells of a head-keeper named Roberts being killed)

see 115, 116, 118, 119.

Appendix A
Catalogue of Compositions

Original Compositions and Folk Song Settings

After Word (1910-1911). Mixed unison chorus, brass. MS sketch.
Agincourt Song (1907). Mixed chorus. MS sketch.
Anchor Song (1915). Kipling Setting No. 6. Baritone, 4-part men's chorus. Schott & Co., 1923.
Arrival Platform Humlet (1908-1916).
   1. Viola solo. G. Schirmer, 1916.
   2. Piano. G. Schirmer, 1916.
   3. 2 pianos, 4 hands. G. Schirmer, 1916.
   4. Resnophone. MS.
   5. See *In a Nutshell Suite.*
As Sally Sat A' Weeping (1908-1909). 2 pianos. G. Schirmer, 1924.
At Twilight (1900-1909). Tenor, mixed chorus. Schott & Co., 1913.
Australian Up-Country Song (1928).
   1. Mixed chorus. G. Schirmer, 1930.
   2. Arr. G.C. Bainum. Band. G. Schirmer, 1970.
Ballad of the Bolivar (1901). Kipling Setting (unnumbered). Men's chorus and orchestra with augmented wind section (4 A clarinets, 4 English horns, 8 oboes) and 16 banjos. MS.
Ballad of the Clampherdown (1899). Kipling Setting.
   1. Voice and piano. MS sketches.
   2. Voice (baritone) and orchestra. MS sketches.
The Beaches of Lukannon (1898-1941). Kipling Setting No. 20. Mixed chorus, 9 strings. Schott & Co., 1958.
Bold William Taylor (1908).
   1. BFMS No. 41.* Voice, 2 clarinets, harmonium, 6 strings. Second version for violin (voice) and piano. MS. Available on rental from Schott & Co.
   2. Voice, piano. MS, 1955.
The Bridegroom Grat (1902). Contralto, 2 violas, 3 cellos. MS sketch.
The Bride's Tragedy (1908-1913). Chorus, orchestra. Schott & Co., 1914.
Brigg Fair (1906). BFMS No. 7. Tenor, mixed chorus. Schott & Co., 1911.
"The Brisk Young Sailor." See *Lincolnshire Posy* (4th movement).
The British Waterside (or *The Jolly Sailor*). BFMS No. 26. Voice, piano. G. Schirmer, 1921.

*recently renumbered as BFMS No. 43. See introduction to the appendix.

British Folk Music Settings. The series includes the following works: (1) *Molly on the Shore;* (2) *Sussex Mummer's Christmas Carol;* (3) *Shepherd's Hey;* (4) *Shepherd's Hey;* (5) *Irish Tune from County Derry;* (6) *Irish Tune from County Derry:* (7) *Brigg Fair;* (8) *I'm 17 Come Sunday;* (9) *Marching Tune;* (10) *Died for Love;* (11) *Six Dukes Went a Fishin';* (12) *Green Bushes;* (13) *Sir Eglamore;* (14) *Lord Maxwell's Goodnight;* (15) *Irish Tune from County Derry;* (16) *Shepherd's Hey;* (17) *The Sussex Mummer's Christmas Carol;* (18) *There Was a Pig Went Out to Dig;* (18) *Knight and Shepherd's Daughter;* (19) *Molly on the Shore;* (20) *Irish Tune from County Derry;* (21) *Shepherd's Hey;* (22) *Country Gardens;* (23) *Molly on the Shore;* (24) *The Sprig of Thyme;* (25) *Green Bushes;* (26) *British Waterside (The Jolly Sailor);* (27) *The Pretty Maid Milkin' Her Cow;* (28) *Scotch Strathspey and Reel;* (29) *Irish Tune from County Derry;* (30) *Ye Banks and Braes O' Bonnie Doon;* (31) *Ye Banks and Braes O' Bonnie Doon;* (32) *Ye Banks and Braes O' Bonnie Doon;* (33) *The Lost Lady Found;* (34) *Lincolnshire Posy;* (35) *Lincolnshire Posy;* (36) *The Duke of Marlborough, Fanfare;* (37) *Scotch Strathspey and Reel;* (38) *The Merry King;* (39) *The Merry King;* (40) *Lisbon (Dublin Bay);* (41) *Bold William Taylor;* (41) *The Three Ravens;* (42) *Lord Maxwell's Goodnight.* Unnumbered settings: *Creepin' Jane; Mary Thompson; Hard-Hearted Barb'ra (H)ellen.* See entries for the individual works.

Bush Music (1900). MS sketch.

Charging Irishrey. See *Train Music.*

Children's March: Over the Hills and Far Away (1916-1918).
  1. Military band. G. Schirmer, 1919.
  2. 2 pianos, 4 hands. G. Schirmer, 1920.
  3. Arr. by A. Schmid. Theater orchestra. G. Schirmer, 1928.
  4. Piano. G. Schirmer, 1918.
  5. Transc. by Barnes. Organ. G. Schirmer, 1927.
  6. Revised by Frank Erickson. Band. G. Schirmer, 1971.

Colleen Dhas (or *The Valley Lay Smiling*) (1904). Room-music. MS.

Colonial Song (1905-1912).
  1. 2 voices, harp, orchestra. Schott & Co., 1913.
  2. Military band. C. Fischer, 1921.
  3. Violin, cello, piano. Schott & Co., 1913.
  4. Theater orchestra. G. Schirmer, 1928.
  5. Small orchestra. Galaxy, 1928.
  6. Piano. Allan & Co., 1921.
  7. Piano. Schott & Co., 1921.
  8. Piano. G. Schirmer, 1921.
  9. Transc. by Orvis Ross. Organ. Galaxy, 1948.

Country Gardens (1918).
  1. Sketch for 2 whistlers and instruments, 1908.

2. BFMS No. 22. Piano (3 versions — original, easy, and 2 pianos, 4 hands). G. Schirmer, 1919.

3. Arr. Adolf Schmid. Domestic orchestra. Galaxy, 1925; Schott & Co., 1925; G. Schirmer, 1925.

4. Arr. Tom Clark. Military band. G. Schirmer, 1931.

5. 2 pianos, 4 hands. Schott & Co., 1932; G. Schirmer, 1932.

6. 2 pianos, 8 hands. Schott & Co., 1937; G. Schirmer, 1937.

7. Arr. Pietro Deiro. Accordian. G. Schirmer, 1934.

8. 1 piano, 4 hands. Schott & Co., 1937; G. Schirmer, 1937.

9. Arr. Walter Bergmann. Descant and treble recorders. Schott & Co., 1964.

Creepin' Jane (1920-1921). BFMS (unnumbered). Voice, piano. MS, 1921.

The Crew of the Long Serpent (1898).

1. Orchestra. MS, 1898.

2. Piano duet. MS, 1940.

Danish Folk Music Settings. The following works are included in this series: (1) *Lord Peter's Stable Boy;* (2) *The Power of Love;* (3) *Rammer;* (4) *The Power of Love;* (5) *Husband and Wife;* (6) *Jerusalems Skumager (Shoemaker from Jerusalem);* (7) *Lord Peter's Stable Boy;* (8) *Jutish Medley;* (9) *Jutish Medley;* (9) *Jutish Medley;* (10) *The Nightingale and the Two Sisters;* (11) *The Old Woman at the Christening;* (12) *Under a Bridge* (Under en Bro); unnumbered setting *The Maiden and the Frog* (Jomfruen og Froen). See entries for the individual works.

Danish Suite. See *Suite on Danish Folk Songs.*

Danny Deever (1903, 1922-1924). Kipling Setting No. 12. Men's double chorus (optional baritone solo), orchestra. Schott & Co., 1924.

David of the White Rock (1954). Trad. Welsh song. Schott & Co., 1963.

Death Song for Hjalmar Thuren (1917). MS sketch.

Dedication (1901). Kipling Setting No. 1. Male voice, piano. Schott & Co., 1912.

Died for Love (1906-1907).

1. Voice, piano. Schott & Co., 1912.

2. BFMS No. 10. Female voice, clarinet, flute, bassoon. Schott & Co., 1912.

3. Voice, violin, viola, cello. Schott & Co., 1912.

4. Voice, flute, viola, cello. Schott & Co., 1912.

Dollar and a Half a Day (1908-1909). Sea Chanty Setting No. 2. Men's voices. G. Schirmer, 1922; Schott & Co., 1923.

Drei Klavierstücke (1897). MS.

Dublin Bay (or *Lisbon*) (1906).

1. BFMS No. 40. Woodwind quintet. MS, 1931.

2. Saxophone choir. MS, 1943.

3. 3 recorders. MS, 1947.

4. See *Lincolnshire Posy* (1st movement).
The Duke of Marlborough (1939). BFMS No. 36. Brass choir. Schott & Co., 1949.
Early One Morning (1901).
1. Mezzo, 4-part male voices or 3-part alto voices. MS, 1901.
2. Solovoxes, reed organ. MS, 1950.
3. Orchestra. MS, 1950.
4. Various combinations, including theremin. MS, 1939-1940.
Eastern Intermezzo (1898-1899).
1. Piano. G. Schirmer, 1922.
2. 2 pianos, 4 hands. G. Schirmer, 1922.
3. Percussion ensemble (20 players). MS, 1933.
4. See *Youthful Suite* (2nd movement).
Echo Song (1945).
1. Chamber orchestra. MS, 1945.
2. Chamber band. MS, 1945.
English Dance (1901-1909).
1. Orchestra. G. Schirmer, 1929.
2. 2 pianos, 6 hands. Schott & Co., 1937.
3. Room-music. MS, 1952.
English Waltz (1899-1945).
1. 2 pianos, 4 hands. Schott & Co., 1947.
2. See *Youthful Suite* (1st movement).
Evan Banks (1898). Voice, piano. MS.
The Fall of the Stone (1901-1904). Kipling Setting No. 16. Mixed chorus, 2 violas, 3 cellos, contrabass, 2 horns, 2 bassoons. Schott & Co., 1924.
Faring-Song (or *A Song of Sweden*) (1904-1905). Voices, instruments. MS sketch.
Faroe Island Dance* (1954). Band. G. Schirmer, 1969.
Father and Daughter (1908-1909). 5 narrators, chorus, orchestra. Schott & Co., 1912.
The First Chanty (1899-1903). Kipling Setting (unnumbered). Voice, piano. MS sketch, 1903.
Fisher's Boarding House (1899). Kipling Setting (unnumbered). Orchestra. MS, 1899.
Free Music.
1. String quartet. MS, 1935.
2. No. 1. 4 theremins. Graph score, 1935.
3. No. 2. 6 theremins. Graph score, 1935-1936.
Gamelon Anklung (1935). Tuneful percussion. MS.
Ganges Pilot (1899). Kipling Setting (unnumbered). Baritone, piano. MS, 1899.
Gay but Wistful (1912-1916).
1. Piano. G. Schirmer, 1916.

*publisher name change from *Let's Dance Gay in Green Meadow*.

2. Two pianos, 4 hands. G. Schirmer, 1916.

3. See *In a Nutshell Suite*.

The Gipsy's Wedding Day (1906). 4 voices. MS.

Green Bushes (1905-1906).
   1. Orchestra. MS.
   2. BFMS No. 12. 22 solo players: flute, oboe, clarinet, bassoon, double bassoon, soprano saxophone, baritone saxophone, trumpet, 2 horns, 3 violins, 2 violas, 2 cellos, string bass, reed organ, piano, and 2 percussion. B. Schott's Söhne, 1931.
   3. BFMS No. 25. 2 pianos, 6 hands. G. Schirmer, 1937.

Gumsucker's March (1911-1914).
   1. Piano, band. MS, 1942.
   2. Piano. G. Schirmer, 1916.
   3. 2 pianos. G. Schirmer, 1916.
   4. See *In a Nutshell Suite*.

Handel in the Strand (1911-1912).
   1. Violin, cello, piano. Schott & Co., 1912.
   2. Strings, piano. Schott & Co., 1912.
   3. Orchestra. MS, 1949.
   4. Large room-music. MS, 1952.
   5. Piano. Schott & Co., 1930; G. Schirmer, 1930.
   6. Arr. R.F. Goldman. Band. Galaxy, 1962.
   7. 2 pianos, 4 hands. Schott & Co., 1947.

Hard-Hearted Barb'ra (H)ellen (1946). BFMS (unnumbered). Voice, piano. MS, 1946.

"Harkstow Grange" (1937). See *Lincolnshire Posy* (2nd movement).

Harvest Hymn (1905-1932).
   1. Orchestra, elastic scoring. G. Schirmer, 1940.
   2. Piano. G. Schirmer, 1940.
   3. Piano, 4 hands. G. Schirmer, 1940.
   4. Violin, piano. Allan & Co., 1940.
   5. 2 pianos, 8 hands. MS.
   6. Chorus. G. Schirmer, 1940.

Hermundur Illi (1905-1911). 2 pianos, 4 hands. G. Schirmer, 1924.

Hill Song Nr. 1 (1901-1902).
   1. 21 winds. MS, 1902.
   2. 2 pianos, 4 hands. G. Schirmer, 1922.
   3. Chamber orchestra. Universal Edition, 1924.
   4. Arr. R. Stevenson. Piano. MS.

Hill Song Nr. 2 (1907).
   1. 24 winds. Leeds, 1950.
   2. 2 pianos, 4 hands. G. Schirmer, 1922.

The Hunt is Up (1901). Male chorus, orchestra. MS sketch.

The Hunter in His Career (1904-1929).
   1. Old English Popular Music No. 3. Piano. G. Schirmer, 1930.
   2. Double men's chorus, orchestra. G. Schirmer, 1930; Schott & Co., 1930.

Hunting Song of the Seeonee Pack (1899-1922). Kipling Setting No. 8. 4-part men's chorus. Schott & Co., 1922.

Husband and Wife. DFMS No. 5. 2 voices 2 guitars, cellos, kettle drum. MS, 923.

I'm Seventeen Come Sunday (1905-1912). BFMS No. 8. Chorus, brass band. Schott & Co., 1915.

The Immovable Do (1933-1939).
  1. Mixed chorus. G. Schirmer, 1941.
  2. Organ. G. Schirmer, 1941.
  3. Orchestra. G. Schirmer, 1942.
  4. Band. G. Schirmer, 1941.
  5. Piano. G. Schirmer, 1940.
  6. Saxophone choir. MS, 1939.

In a Nutshell Suite. Movements: Arrival Platform Humlet; Gay but Wistful; Pastoral; The Gumsucker's March.
  1. Piano. G. Schirmer, 1916.
  2. Piano, orchestra. G. Schirmer, 1916.
  3. 2 pianos, 4 hands. G. Schirmer, 1916.

In Bristol Town (1906).
  1. Violin, organ. MS, 1947.
  2. Voice, room-music. MS, 1906.
  3. Piano, 6 hands. MS.

In Dahomey (1903-1909). Piano. MS.

The Inuit (1902). Kipling Setting No. 5. Mixed chorus. Schott & Co., 1912.

Irish Tune from County Derry (1902).
  1. Mixed chorus. G. Schirmer, 1927.
  2. Chamber orchestra. MS, 1949.
  3. Large room-music. MS, 1952.
  4. BFMS No. 5. 6-part mixed chorus. Schott & Co., 1912.
  5. BFMS No. 6. Piano. Schott & Co., 1939.
  6. BFMS No. 15. String orchestra, 2 horns ad lib. Schott & Co., 1913.
  7. BFMS No. 20. Military band. C. Fischer, 1918.
  8. BFMS No. 29. Wordless chorus, elastic scoring. G. Schirmer, 1931.

Jerusalems Skumager. See *The Shoemaker from Jerusalem.*

The Jolly Sailor. See *The British Waterside.*

Jungle Book Cycle. Includes the following songs: *(1) The Fall of the Stone; (2) Morning Song in the Jungle; (3) Night Song in the Jungle; (4) The Inuit; (5) The Beaches of Lukannon; (6) Red Dog; (7) The Peora Hunt; (8) Hunting Song of the Seeonee Pack; (9) Tiger, Tiger; (10) The Only Son; (11) Mowgli's Song Against People.* For complete information, see the individual entries for each song.

Jutish Medley (1923-1929).
  1. DFMS No. 8. Piano. G. Schirmer, 1931.

2. DFMS No. 9. Elastic scoring. G. Schirmer, 1930.

3. DFMS No. 9. 2 pianos, 6 hands. G. Schirmer, 1931.

4. See *Suite on Danish Folk Songs* (4th movement).

The Keel Row (1901). Whistlers, chorus, orchestra. MS sketch.

Kipling Settings. The following works are included in this series: (1) *Dedication;* (2) *We Have Fed Our Seas;* (3) *Morning Song in the Jungle;* (4) *Tiger, Tiger;* (5) *The Inuit;* (6) *Anchor Song;* (7) *The Widow's Party;* (8) *Hunting Song of the Seeonee Pack;* (9) *The Running of Shindand;* (10) *The Men of the Sea;* (11) *The Love Song of Har Dyal;* (12) *Danny Deever;* (13) *Soldier, Soldier;* (14) *The Peora Hunt;* (15) *Mowgli's Song;* (16) *The Fall of the Stone;* (17) *Night Song in the Jungle;*(18) *Recessional;* (19) *Red Dog;* (20) *The Beaches of Lukannon;* (21) *The Only Son;* (22) *The Sea Wife;* unnumbered settings include *The Ballad of Bolivar, The First Chanty, Fisher's Boarding House, Ganges Pilot, The Merchantmen, Merciful Town, A Northern Ballad, The Rhyme of the Three Sealers, Ride with an Idle Whip, There Were Three Friends, To Wolcott Balestier, We Were Dreamers, The Young British Soldier,* and *Ballad of the Clampherdown.* See entries for the individual works.

Kleine Variationen-Form (1898). Small orchestra. MS sketch.

Knight and Shepherd's Daughter (1918). BFMS No. 18. Piano. G. Schirmer, 1918.

The Lads of Wamphray (1904).

1. Band. C. Fischer, 1941.

2. 2 pianos, 6 hands. MS (incomplete).

3. Male chorus, orchestra. G. Schirmer, 1925.

Land of the Dead (1902). Voice, strings. MS sketch for *We Have Fed Our Seas.*

Let's Dance Gay in Green Meadow (1943).

1. Piano, 4 hands. Faber, 1967.

2. See *Faroe Island Dance.*

Lincolnshire Posy (1937). Movements: (1) Dublin Bay; (2) Harkstow Grange; (3) Rufford Park Poachers; (4) The Brisk Young Sailor; (5) Lord Melbourne; (6) The Lost Lady Found.

1. BFMS No. 34. Military band. Schott & Co., 1940.

2. BFMS No. 35. 2 pianos. Schott & Co., 1940.

Lisbon (or *Dublin Bay*) (1931). BFMS No. 40. Woodwind quintet. Schott & Co., 1972.

The Lonely Desert Man (1949).

1. 3 voices (or 3 instruments), with room-music accompaniment. MS, 1954.

2. Piano, 4 hands. MS, 1954.

Lord Maxwell's Goodnight (1904-1912).

1. BFMS No. 42. Tenor, 4 strings. MS, 1904.

2. BFMS No. 14. Baritone, small orchestra. MS, 1912; revised, 1947.

"Lord Melbourne" (1909-1912). See *Lincolnshire Posy* (5th movement).

Lord Peter's Stable Boy. (1922-1927).
    1. DFMS No. 1. Elastic scoring. G. Schirmer, 1930.
    2. DFMS No. 7. Voices, room-music. MS sketch, 1923.
    3. See *Suite on Danish Folk Songs* (2nd movement).

The Lost Lady Found (1910).
    1. Voice(s), piano. MS, 1940.
    2. BFMS No. 33. Mixed chorus and small room-music (3 horns, 2 trumpets, strings, percussion). Schott & Co., 1950 (out of print, available on rental).
    3. See *Lincolnshire Posy*, 4th movement.

The Love Song of Har Dyal (1901).
    1. Kipling Setting No. 11. High voice, piano. Schott & Co., 1923.
    2. Women's chorus, room-music. MS, 1957-1958.

Love Verses from "The Song of Solomon" (1899-1900).
    1. 4 solo voices, mixed chorus, chamber orchestra. Schott & Co., 1931.
    2. 4 solo voices, piano. Schott & Co., 1931; G. Schirmer, 1931.

Lullaby from "Tribute to Foster" (1915). Piano. Schott & Co., 1917; G. Schirmer, 1917.

The Maiden and the Frog. DFMS (unnumbered). Cello, piano. MS.

Marching Song of Democracy (1901-1917).
    1. Mixed chorus, orchestra. Universal Edition, 1916.
    2. Voice, piano. G. Schirmer, 1916; Universal Edition, 1916.
    3. Band, optional mixed chorus. MS, 1948.

Marching Tune (1905). BFMS No. 9. Mixed chorus, brass choir (3 cornets, 4 horns, tuba). Schott & Co., 1911.

Mary Thomson (n.d.) BFMS (unnumbered). Mixed chorus or mixed quartet. MS.

The Men of the Sea (1899). Kipling Setting No. 10. Voice, piano. Schott & Co., 1923.

The Merchantmen. Kipling Setting (unnumbered). Male voices, whistlers, strings, bassoon, 4 horns, contrabassoon. MS, 1902-1903; revised, 1909-1911.

Merciful Town (*ca.* 1899). Kipling Setting (unnumbered). Voice, piano. MS sketch.

The Merry King (1905-1906).
    1. Chorus. MS sketch, 1905.
    2. BFMS No. 38. Piano. G. Schirmer, 1939.
    3. BFMS No. 39. 3 clarinets, flute, bass clarinet, baritone saxophone, contrabassoon, horn, trumpet, piano. MS, 1939.
    4. Strings and Piano. MS, 1939.

Merry Wedding (1912-1915).
    1. Mixed chorus, piano. Oliver Ditson, 1916.
    2. 9 solo voices, mixed chorus, orchestra. Oliver Ditson, 1915

Mock Morris (1910).
1. Piano. Schott & Co., 1912.
2. 2 pianos, MS, 1910.
3. Orchestra. MS, 1914.
4. Violin, piano. Schott & Co., 1914; G. Schirmer, 1914.
5. Arr. Langey. Theater orchestra. G. Schirmer, 1911.
6. String orchestra. Schott & Co., 1911; G. Schirmer, 1915.
7. Brass band. Schott & Co., 1937.
8. Stokowski recording. MS, 1950.
9. Large room-music. MS, 1952.

Molly on the Shore (1907).
1. BFMS No. 1. String quartet. Schott & Co., 1911.
2. BFMS No. 19. Piano. G. Schirmer, 1918.
3. BFMS No. 23. Military band. C. Fischer, 1921.
4. Arr. Langey. Theater orchestra. Schott & Co., 1914; G. Schirmer, 1914.
5. Violin, piano. Schott & Co.; G. Schirmer, 1914.
6. Arr. Kreisler. Violin, piano. C. Fischer, 1924.
7. Voice, guitar, strings. Schott & Co.
8. 2 pianos, 4 hands. Schott & Co., 1948.

Morning Song in the Jungle (1905). Kipling Setting No. 3. Mixed chorus. Schott & Co., 1912.

Mowgli's Song Against People (1903). Kipling Setting No. 15. Mixed chorus, violin, 2 violas, 3 cellos, contrabass, oboe, horn, piano. Schott & Co., 1924.

My Love's in Germany (1903). Mixed chorus. MS sketch.

My Robin Is to the Greenwood Gone (1912).
1. Old English Popular Music No. 2. Flute, English horn, strings. Schott & Co., 1912.
2. Piano. Schott & Co., 1912.
3. Violin, cello, piano. Schott & Co., 1912.

Near Woodstock Town (or *Thou Gracious Power*) (1903). Mixed chorus. MS, 1942.

Night Song in the Jungle (1898). Kipling Setting No. 17. 4-part men's chorus. Schott & Co., 1925.

"Nightingale" and "The Two Sisters" (1923-1930).
1. DFMS No. 10. Elastic scoring. G. Schirmer, 1931.
2. See *Suite on Danish Folk Songs* (3rd movement).
3. 2 pianos, 4 hands. MS, 1940.

Norse Dirge (1899).
1. Orchestra. MS sketch, 1899.
2. See *Youthful Suite* (4th movement).

A Northern Ballad (1898-1899). Kipling Setting (unnumbered). Voice, piano. MS sketch.

"Northern March." See *Youthful Suite* (3rd movement).

Norwegian Idyll (1910). MS sketch, 1910.

O' Mistress Mine (1903). Mixed chorus. MS sketch, 1903.

Old English Popular Music. The following works are included in this series: (1) *Willow, Willow;* (2) *My Robin Is to the Greenwood Gone;* (3) *The Hunter in His Career.* See entries for the individual works.

The Old Woman at the Christening (1925). DFMS No. 11. Voices, piano, reed organ. MS.

One More Day, My John (1915). Sea Chanty Setting No. 1. Piano. G. Schirmer; Schott; Universal, 1916.

The Only Son (1945-1947). Kipling Setting No. 21. Soprano, tenor, optional chorus, 2 violins, viola, 2 cellos, contrabass. Schott & Co., 1958.

Orchestra Piece (1899). MS.

Pastoral (1907-1916).
1. Piano. G. Schirmer, 1916.
2. 2 pianos, 4 hands. G. Schirmer, 1916.
3. See *In a Nutshell Suite.*

Peace (1898). Piano. MS.

The Peora Hunt (1906). Kipling Setting No. 14. Mixed chorus, Schott & Co., 1924.

Piano Concerto (1896). 2 pianos. MS.

The Power of Love (1922).
1. DFMS No. 2. Elastic scoring. G. Schirmer, 1950.
2. DFMS No. 4. Voice(s), room-music. MS.
3. See *Suite on Danish Folk Songs* (1st movement).

Power of Rome and the Christian Heart (1918-1933).
1. Orchestra, organ. MS, 1933.
2. Band, organ. Mills, 1953.

The Pretty Maid Milkin' Her Cow (1920). BFMS No. 27. Voice, piano. G. Schirmer, 1921.

Pritteling, Pratteling, Pretty Poll Parrot.
1. 2 pianos. MS, 1911.
2. Sketch for guitar. MS.

The Rainbow. English folk tune. Recorder. MS.

Rammer and Goldcastle (Rammerlil og Guldborg). DFMS No. 3. Chorus. MS.

Random Round (1912-1914).
1. Voices, guitars, mandolins. MS, 1913.
2. 2 pianos, 12 hands. MS, 1943.
3. Mallet percussion. MS, 1946.
4. 3 voices, 10 instruments. MS, 1957.

Recessional (1905-1929). Kipling Setting No. 18. Mixed chorus. Schott & Co., 1930.

Red Dog (1941). Kipling Setting No. 19. 4-part men's chorus. Schott & Co., 1958.

A Reiver's Neck-Verse (1908). Voice, piano. Schott & Co., 1911.

The Rhyme of the Three Sealers (1900-1901). Kipling Setting (unnumbered). 4-part men's and boys' chorus. MS.

Ride with an Idle Whip (1899). Kipling Setting (unnumbered).
Voice, piano. MS.
The Rival Brothers (1905-1931). Voices, room-music. MS, 1940.
Rufford Park Poachers.
  1. Recorder. MS.
  2. See *Lincolnshire Posy* (3rd movement).
The Running of Shindand (1901-1904).
  1. Kipling Setting No. 9. Men's chorus. Schott & Co., 1922.
  2. Cello ensemble. MS, 1946.
"Rustic Dance" (1899). See *Youthful Suite* (5th movement).

The Saga of King Olaf (1899). Voice, piano. MS sketches.
Sailor's Chanty (1901). Men's chorus. MS sketch.
Sailor's Song.
  1. Tuneful percussion. MS, 1954.
  2. Piano (original and simplified versions). MS.
Saxon Twiplay (1898). Piano. MS.
La Scandinavie (Scandinavian Suite). Fingering by Herman Sandby. Movements: (1) Swedish Air and Dance; (2) Song of Vermeland; (3) Norwegian Polka; (4) Danish Melody; (5) Air and Finale of Norwegian Dance. Cello, piano. MS, 1902; B. Schotts Söhne, n.d.
Scotch Strathspey and Reel (1901-1911).
  1. BFMS No. 28. 4 male voices, 16 instruments (piccolo ad lib, flute, oboe, clarinet, bassoon, harmonium, xylophone, 2 guitars, 8 strings). B. Schotts Söhne, 1924.
  2. BFMS No. 37. Piano. G. Schirmer, 1937.
Scottish Folksongs. Songs: (1) O Gin I Were Where Gowrie Rins; (2) Will Ye Gang to the Highlands, Lizzie Lindsay; (3) Moninghean Dhu. Piano. MS, 1954.
Scottish Folksongs from "Songs of the North" (1900). The following songs are included: (1) Willie's Gone to Melville Castle; (2) Weaving Song; (3) Skye Boat Song; (4) This Is No My Plaid; (5) Turn Ye to Me; (6) Drowned; (7) Fair Young Mary; (8) Leezie Lindsa; (9) The Women Are a Gane Wud; (10) My Faithful Fond One; (11) Bonnie George Campbell; (12) O'er the Moor; (13) O Gin I Were Where Gowrie Rins (chorus and solo); (14) My Dark-Haired Maid. Voice, piano. MS.
Sea Chanty Settings. The following works are included in this series: (1) *One More Day, My John;* (2) *Dollar and a Half a Day;* (3) *Shallow Brown;* plus the unnumbered settings, *Shenandoah* and *Stormy.* See entries for the individual works.
Sea Song.
  1. MS sketch, 1907.
  2. 4 strings, organ. MS, 1946.
  3. Arr. Alan Stout. String quintet (1922). MS, 1970.
  4. Arr. Alan Stout. Eight strings (1907). MS, 1970.

The Sea Wife (1905). Kipling Setting No. 22. Chorus, brass (alternative accompaniments: 7 strings; brass and strings; piano duet; piano). Schott & Co., 1948.

The Secret of the Sea (1898). Voice, piano. MS.

Sekar Gadung. Tuneful percussion. MS sketch, 1933.

Shallow Brown (1910). Sea Chanty Setting No. 3. Solo voice, piano (alternate versions: unison chorus and piano; orchestra; voice, bassoon, 2 horns, euphonium, flute, harmonium, piano, 7 strings, 4 mandolins, 2 ukeleles, 4 guitars). G. Schirmer, 1927.

Shenandoah (1906). Sea Chanty Setting (unnumbered). 6-part male voices. MS, 1907.

Shepherd's Hey (1908-1913).
1. BFMS No. 3. Flute, clarinet, horn, concertino, 8 strings. Schott & Co., 1911.
2. BFMS No. 4. Piano (two versions — original, easy). Schott & Co., 1911.
3. BFMS No. 16. Orchestra. Schott & Co., 1913.
4. BFMS No. 21. Military band. C. Fischer, 1918.
5. 2 pianos. Schott & Co., 1948.
6. Stokowsky recording. MS, 1949.
7. Brass band. Schott & Co., 1937.
8. Arr. Langey. Theater orchestra. G. Schirmer, 1922.
9. Arr. Bonsor. Recorders, piano. Schott & Co., 1964.

The Shoemaker from Jerusalem (or *Jerusalems Skumager*) (1929). DFMS No. 6. Piano, cello, flute, trumpet, violin, viola, contrabass. MS.

Sir Eglamore (1904).
1. BFMS No. 13. Double mixed chorus, band. MS, 1912.
2. Double mixed chorus, orchestra. Schott & Co., 1912.

Six Dukes Went A' Fishin' (1905-1912).
1. BFMS No. 11. Voice, piano. Schott & Co., 1912.
2. 4 voices, flute. MS, 1910.
3. Recorder. MS.

Soldier, Soldier (1898-1908).
1. Kipling Setting No. 13. 6 single voices, mixed chorus. Schott & Co., 1925.
2. Voice, piano. MS, 1899.

Song (1903). Men's voices, strings. MS sketches, 1905.

A Song of Autumn (1899). Voice, piano. Schott & Co., 1923.

A Song of Sweden. See *Faring-Song.*

A Song of Vermland (c. 1904). Mixed chorus. Vincent Music, n.d.

Spoon River (1919-1922).
1. Band. MS, 1941.
2. Arr. G.C. Bainum. Band. G. Schirmer, 1967.
3. Elastic scoring. G. Schirmer, 1932.
4. Piano. G. Schirmer, 1922.
5. Orchestra. G. Schirmer, 1930.

6. 2 pianos, 4 hands. G. Schirmer, 1932.

The Sprig of Thyme (1907-1920).
1. BFMS No. 24. Voice, piano. G. Schirmer, 1920.
2. Recorder. MS.

Stalt Vesselil (1951). Voice, strings, bassoon, saxophone. MS sketch.

Stormy (1906). Sea Chanty Setting (unnumbered). 4-part male voices. MS, 1907.

Suite on Danish Folk Songs (1922-1930). Movements: (1) The Power of Love; (2) Lord Peter's Stable Boy: (3) Nightingale and the Two Sisters; (4) Jutish Medley. Orchestra, elastic scoring. G. Schirmer, 1930.

The Sussex Mummer's Christmas Carol (1905-1915).
1. BFMS No. 2. Piano. Schott & Co., 1911.
2. BFMS No. 17. Violin (cello), piano. Schott & Co., 1916.
3. Arr. R.F. Goldman. Band. Galaxy, 1965.

Thanksgiving Song.
1. String quartet. MS sketches, 1927.
2. 6 solo voices, orchestra. MS, 1945.

Theme and Variations (1898). String quartet. MS.

There Was a Pig Went Out to Dig (1905-1910). BFMS No. 18. 4-part women's chorus. Schott & Co., 1915.

There Were Three Friends. Kipling Setting (unnumbered). Orchestra. MS sketch, 1899.

Thora von Rimol. Voice, piano. MS sketch, 1898.

Thou Gracious Power (or *Near Woodstock Town*) (1903-1952). Mixed chorus. MS.

The Three Ravens (1902). BFMS No. 41. Baritone, mixed chorus, 5 clarinets (optional flute and 4 clarinets). Schott & Co., 1950.

Tiger, Tiger (1905).
1. Kipling Setting No. 4. Men's chorus, optional tenor solo. Schott & Co., 1912.
2. Cello ensemble. MS, 1946.

To a Nordic Princess (1927-1928).
1. Orchestra. G. Schirmer, 1930.
2. Piano. Schott & Co., 1929; G. Schirmer, 1929.
3. Arr. L. Farnam (as "Bridal Song"). Organ. G. Schirmer, 1930.

To Wolcott Balestier (1901). Kipling Setting (unnumbered). Chorus, organ. MS sketches, 1901.

Train Music (or *Charging Irishrey*).
1. Orchestra. MS sketch, 1901, 1907.
2. Piano, simplified version. MS.

Tribute to Foster (1913-1916). Orchestra, soloist, mixed chorus, musical glasses, piano. G. Schirmer, 1931; Oxford University Press, 1934.

The Twa Corbies (1903). Male voice, strings or piano. G. Schirmer, 1924.

Two Welsh Fighting Songs (1904). The songs include (1) March of the Men of Harlech and (2) The Camp. Double mixed chorus, drums. Winthrop Rogers, 1922.

Under en Bro (or *Under a Bridge*) (1945-1946). DFMS No. 12. Mezzo-soprano, baritone, flute. trumpet, piano, tuneful percussion. MS.

The Valley Lay Smiling. See *Colleen Dhas.*

Walking Tune (1905).
1. Woodwind quintet. Schott & Co., 1912.
2. Piano. Schott & Co., 1912.
3. Symphonic Winds. MS, 1940.
4. Piano, 4 hands. MS, 1905.

The Warriors (1913-1916).
1. Orchestra, 3 pianos. B. Schott's Söhne, 1926.
2. 2 pianos, 6 hands. B. Schott's Söhne, 1923.

We Be Three Poor Mariners (1901).
1. Tenor, male chorus, piano. MS sketch.
2. Chorus. MS sketch.
3. Baritone, male chorus, instrumental ensemble. MS sketch.

We Have Fed Our Seas (1900-1911). Kipling Setting No. 2. Mixed chorus, brass choir, strings ad lib. Schott & Co., 1912.

We Were Dreamers.
1. Kipling Setting (unnumbered). Chorus. MS sketches, 1899.
2. Kipling Setting (unnumbered). Orchestra. MS sketch, 1899.

When the World Was Young (1910-1911). 2 pianos. MS sketch.

Who Built de Ark? Solo voice, 3 male voices, guitar. MS sketch, 1911.

The Widow's Party (1906).
1. Voice, piano. MS, 1906.
2. Kipling Setting No. 7. Men's chorus, orchestra. Schott & Co., 1923.
3. Piano duet. MS, 1939.

Willow, Willow (1902-1911).
1. Old English Popular Music No. 1. Voice, piano. Schott & Co., 1912.
2. Voice, guitar, strings. Schott & Co., 1912.
3. Male chorus. MS, 1960.

The Wraith of Odin (1903).
1. Double chorus, orchestra. MS, 1903.
2. 2 pianos. MS, 1922.

Ye Banks and Braes O' Bonnie Doon (1901).
1. BFMS No. 30. Men's chorus, whistlers. Schott & Co., 1936.
2. BFMS No. 31. School or amateur orchestra (elastic scoring). Schott & Co., 1937.
3. BFMS No. 32. Military band or wind choirs. G. Schirmer, 1949.
4. BFMS No. 33. Mixed chorus, small room-music (3 horns, 2 trumpets, strings, percussion). Schott & Co., 1950 (out of print, available on rental).

The Young British Soldier (1899). Kipling Setting (unnumbered).
Voice, piano. MS.

Youthful Rapture (1901). Cello, piano or room-music. Schott &
Co., 1930.

Youthful Suite. Movements include: (1) English Waltz; (2) Eastern
Intermezzo; (3) Northern March; (4) Norse Dirge; (5) Rustic
Dance. Orchestra. Schott & Co., 1950.

Zanzibar Boat Song (1902). Piano, 6 hands. Schott & Co., 1923.

Arrangements of Other Composers' Music

Addinsell, Richard.
  1. *Festival.* 2 pianos, 4 hands. MS, 1954.
  2. *Warsaw Concerto.* 2 pianos. Chappell, 1946.
African Folk Tune. *Binu Adami.* MS sketch.
Alford, Kenneth. *Bridge on the River Kwai — Marches.* Piano,
  6 hands. MS, *ca.* 1959.
Anonymous.
  1. *Ad cantum laetitiae.* EGM. Voices with winds or strings.
  MS sketch, n.d.
  2. *Alleluia psallat.* EGM.
    a. 3 unmixed voices or 6 mixed voices with winds or strings. G.
    Schirmer, 1943.
    b. Saxophone trio. MS.
    c. Clarinet trio. MS.
    d. Brass trio. MS.
    e. Recorder trio. MS.
  3. *Angelus ad virginem.* EGM.
    a. EGM. 3 or 6 unmixed voices with winds or strings. G.
    Schirmer, 1943; New ed., 1952.
    b. EGM. Brass trio. MS, 1942.
    c. EGM. Saxophone trio. MS, 1942.
    d. EGM. Augmented combinations of 3 or 6 brass instruments.
    MS, 1942.
    e. EGM. Augmented combinations of 3 or 6 saxophones.
    MS, 1942.
    f. EGM. Recorder trio. MS, 1942.
    g. Piano. MS, 1937.
    h. EGM. Band. MS.

i. Chosen Gems for Winds. Chamber combinations. MS, 1942.
j. Chosen Gems for Winds. Band. MS.
k. Chosen Gems for Winds. Saxophone choir. MS.
l. Chosen Gems for Winds. Clarinet choir. MS.
m. Chosen Gems for Winds. Brass choir.
4. *Beata viscera.* EGM.
a. 3 mixed or unmixed voices with winds or strings. G. Schirmer, 1943.
b. Woodwind choir and horns. MS, 1942.
c. Wind trio. MS, 1942.
d. Clarinet trio. MS, 1942.
e. Any combination of 3 or 6 clarinets. MS, 1942.
f. Saxophone trio. MS, 1942.
g. Any combination of 3 or 6 saxophones. MS, 1942.
h. Recorder trio. MS, 1947.
5. *Credo.* EGM. 3 or 6 single unmixed voices with an optional accompaniment of winds or strings. MS, 1939.
6. *Edi beo thu.* EGM. 2 mixed or unmixed voices with winds or strings. MS, 1939.
7. *Foweles in the frith.* EGM. 2 unmixed voices. MS, 1933.
8. *Fulget coelestis curia.* EGM. 3 or 6 mixed voices with winds or strings. MS, 1936.
9. *Hac in anni janua.* EGM. 3-part chorus. MS, 1939.
10. *Jubilemus omnes una.* EGM. Double unison chorus. MS.
11. *Marionette Douce.* EGM. 4 mixed voices (single or chorus) with strings or winds. G. Schirmer, 1950.
12. *Princesse of Youth.* EGM. 6 mixed voices with keyboard acc. MS, 1937.
13. *Pro beati pauli - O praeclara patriae.* EGM. 4 celli or string orchestra. MS, 1939.
14. *Puellare Gremium.* EGM. 3 or 6 unmixed voices with strings or winds. G. Schirmer, 1950.
15. *Worcester sanctus.* EGM.
a. 3 or 6 mixed voices (in C). MS, 1939.
b. 3 or 6 mixed voices with string acc. or string sextet (in E$\flat$). MS, 1939.

Bach, J.S.
1. *"Air" from Overture No. 3, D Major.* Piano. G. Schirmer, 1923.
2. *Blithe Bells* (Sheep May Safely Graze).
a. Piano. Schott & Co., 1931.
b. Band, tuneful percussion. MS, 1931.
c. 2 pianos, 4 hands. G. Schirmer, 1932.
d. Orchestra, elastic scoring. G. Schirmer, 1932.
3. *Brandenburg Concerto No. 3.*
a. Piano. MS.
b. Strings, piano. MS.

4. *Fugue in A Minor* (Bk. I, Well-Tempered-Clavier).
   a. Piano, MS.
   b. 2 pianos, 8 hands. Schott & Co., 1930.
5. *Fugue No. 1, C Major* (Bk. II, W.T.C.). 2 harmoniums. MS, 1927.
6. *Fugue in D♯ Minor.* (Bk. II, W.T.C.). 2 pianos. MS, 1928.
7. *Fugue* (No. 4, Bk. 1, W.T.C.). Soprano, alto, 2 tenors, baritone and bass saxophones. MS, 1943.
8. *Fugue No. 9 in E Major* (Bk. II, W.T.C.).
   a. Piano. MS.
   b. 2 pianos, 8 hands. MS, 1950.
   c. 4 pianos ("octave study"). MS, 1928.
9. *March* (Notebook for Anna Magdalena Bach).
   a. Band. MS, 1946.
   b. 6 saxophones. MS, 1946.
   c. Clarinet choir. MS, 1946.
   d. Brass choir. MS, 1946.
   e. Wind choir. MS, 1946.
10. *O Mensch, bewein dein Sünde gross.*
   a. Band. MS, 1937; revised, 1942.
   b. Brass choir. MSS, 1937 & 1942.
11. *Prelude and Fugue* (Bk. I, W.T.C.).
   a. Chosen Gems for Winds. Saxophone choir.
   b. Chosen Gems for Winds. Band.
12. *Prelude and Fugue, D Major* (Bk. II, W.T.C.). String quartet. MS, 1927.
13. *Prelude and Fugue* (No. 5, Bk. II, W.T.C.). Soprano, alto, tenor and baritone saxophones. MS, 1943.
14. *Sehet was die Liebe tut* (from Cantata No. 85). Band. MS, 1937.
15. *Toccata in F* (organ). 3 pianos (or multiples of 3). G. Schirmer, 1940.

Bird, George. *Melody*. Harmonized. MS, 1945.

Brahms, Johannes.
   1. *Cradle Song*, Op. 49, No. 4. Free Settings of Favorite Melodies No. 1. Piano. G. Schirmer, 1923.
   2. *Paganini Variations No. 12* (simplified). Piano. MS, 1957.

Byrd, William. *The Carman's Whistle*. Piano. MS, 1947.

Cabezon, Antonio de. *Prelude in the Dorian Mode.*
   1. 4 saxophones. MS, 1943.
   2. Wind band. MS, 1941.
   3. Chosen Gems for Strings. 2 violas, 2 cellos. MS, 1957.

Chinese Folk Tune. *Beautiful Fresh Flower.* (Harmonized by Joseph Yasser.) Piano. Schott & Co., 1967.

Chosen Gems for Strings. The series includes the following works: *Prelude in the Dorian Mode*, Antonio de Cabezón; *Negro*

Lullaby, Natalie Curtis-Burlin; *A l'heure que je vous,* Josquin Despréz; *La bernardina,* Josquin Despréz; *Le jour s'endort,* Guillaume Dufay; *The Four Note Pavan,* Alfonso Ferrabosco; *O schönes Weib,* Heinrich Finck; *Nenciozza mia,* Jean Jappart; *5-Part Fantasy, No. 1,* John Jenkins; *6-Part Fantasy and Air, No. 1,* William Lawes; *Ballade No. 17,* Guillaume de Machaut; *Rondeau No. 14,* Guillaume de Machaut; *Paesabase, The Moorish King,* Diego Pisador; *Anima mea Liquefacta est,* Lionel Power; *Love Song,* Herman Sandby; *The Quiet Brook,* Alessandro Scarlatti; *Harraytre amours,* Johannes Stokem. See entries for individual composers.

Chosen Gems for Winds. The series includes the following works: *Royal Fanfare,* Josquin Despréz; *La bernardina,* Josquin Despréz; *Prelude in the Dorian Mode,* Antonio de Cabezón; *Prelude and Fugue V* (Bk. II, W.T.C.), J.S. Bach; *March* (notebook for Anna Magdalena Bach); *O salutaris hostia,* Adrian Willaert; *Ballade No. 17,* Guillaume de Machaut; *Angelus ad virginem,* anonymous; *The Four Note Pavan,* Alfonso Ferrabosco; *Six Part Fantasy and Air, No. 1,* William Lawes; *The Quiet Brook,* Alessandro Scarlatti. See entries for individual composers.

Curtis-Burlin, Natalie.
 1. *Lullaby* (Negro folk song). Chosen Gems for Strings. Mixed voices and strings. MS, 1934.
 2. *Sangre de Cristo* (Lenten chant). Orchestrated. MS, 1925.
 3. *Matachina Dance.* Orchestrated. MS, 1925.

Debussy, Claude.
 1. *Bruyères* (Heather Bells). Wind ensemble. MS, 1918.
 2. *Pagodas.* Tuneful percussion, harmonium. MS, 1928.

Delius, Frederick.
 1. *Dance Rhapsody.* 2 pianos. Universal Edition, 1923.
 2. *Hassan, Dance Movement for.* MS sketches, 1923.
 3. *The Song of the High Hills.* 2 pianos. MS, 1923.

Despréz, Josquin.
 1. *A l'heure que je vous.* Chosen Gems for Strings.
    a. String quartet. MS, 1934.
    b. String ensemble. MS, 1939.
 2. *La bernardina.*
    a. Chosen Gems for Strings. String trio. MS, 1934.
    b. Brass trio. MS, 1943.
    c. Clarinet trio. MS, 1943.
    d. Band. MS, 1953.
    e. Wind ensemble. MS, 1953.
    f. Chosen Gems for Winds. Brass ensemble.
 3. *Royal Fanfare.* Brass quintet. MS, 1937.

Dolmetsch Collection of English Consorts. Works in this series include: *The Four Note Pavan,* Alfonso Ferrabosco; *Five Part Fantasy, No. 1,* John Jenkins; *Six Part Fantasy and Air, No. 1,*

William Lawes. See entries for individual composers.

Dowland, John. *Now, O Now, I Needs Must Part* (Bell Piece).
1. Tuneful percussion, band, optional voice. MS, 1948.
2. Piano, optional voice. Schott & Co., 1937.
3. Free Settings of Favorite Melodies No. 5. Piano (easy version). G. Schirmer, 1937.
4. Free Settings of Favorite Melodies No. 6. Piano (concert version). G. Schirmer, 1937.

Dufay, Guillaume. *Le jour s'endort*. Chosen Gems for Strings. Mezzo-soprano, violin, viola (cello), and cello. MS.

Dunstable, John
1. *O rosa bella*. EGM. 4 or 6 mixed voices. Schott & Co., 1963.
2. *Regina coeli*. EGM. MS sketch.
3. *Veni sancte spiritus*. EGM. 4-part single or mixed voices with ad lib organ/harmonium, ad lib tuneful percussion. MS, 1939.

Elgar, Edward. *Nimrod Variation* (Enigma variations). Piano. MS, 1953.

English Gothic Music. Works in this series include: *Ad cantum laetitiae*, anon.; *Alleluia psallat*, anon.; *Angelus ad virginem*, anon.; *Beata viscera*, anon.; *Credo*, anon.; *Edi beo thu*, anon.; *Foweles in the frith*, anon.; *Fulget coelestis curia*, anon.; *Hac in anni janua*, anon.; *Jubilemus omnes una*, anon.; *Marionette Douce*, anon.; *O rosa bella*, John Dunstable; *Princess of Youth*, anon.; *Pro beati pauli - O praeclara patriae*, anon.; *Puellare Gremium*, anon.; *Regina coeli*, John Dunstable; *Sanctus*, Lionel Power; *Veni sancte spiritus*, John Dunstable; *Worcester sanctus*, anon. See entries for individual composers or "Anonymous" entries.

Fauré, Gabriel-Urbain.
1. *Après un rêve*. Free Settings of Favorite Melodies No. 7. Piano. G. Schirmer, 1939.
2. *Quartet*, Op. 45. 2 pianos, 4 hands. MS.
3. *Nell*, Op. 18, No. 1. Free Settings of Favorite Melodies No. 3. Piano. G. Schirmer, 1925.
4. *Tuscan Serenade*, Op. 3, No. 2. Band. MS, 1937.

Ferrabosco, Alfonso. *The Four Note Pavan*.
1. Winds. MS, 1940.
2. Brass quintet. MS, 1940.
3. Saxophone quintet. MS, 1940.
4. Wind quintet. MS, 1940.
5. Chosen Gems for Strings. Dolmetsch Collection of English Consorts. 2 violins, 2 violas, 2 celli. G. Schirmer, 1944.
6. Chosen Gems for Winds. Band. MS, 1940.
7. Chosen Gems for Winds. Brass choir.
8. Chosen Gems for Winds. Saxophone choir or quintet.
9. Chosen Gems for Winds. Woodwind choir.

Finck, Heinrich. *O schönes Weib.* Tenor, violin, viola, cello. MS, 1934, 1940.

Franck, Cesar. *Chorale No. 2* (organ). Band. MS, 1942.

Free Settings of Favorite Melodies. Works in this series include: (1) *Cradle Song,* Johannes Brahms; (2) *Hornpipe from the Water Music,* George F. Handel; (3) *Nell,* Gabriel Fauré; (4) *The Rose Bearer, Ramble on the Love Duet from Der Rosenkavalier,* Richard Strauss; (5) *Now, o now I needs must part,* John Dowland; (6) *Now, o now I needs must part,* John Dowland; (7) *Après un rêve,* Gabriel Fauré, (8) Tchaikovsky *B-flat minor Piano Concerto* (opening).

Gardiner, H. Balfour.
1. *English Dance.* 2 pianos. MS, 1925.
2. *Flowing Melody.* MS sketch, 1947.
3. *Joyful Homecoming.* MS sketches, 1946.
4. *Prelude* (de profundis). Piano. G. Schirmer, 1905.
5. *Gardineriana Rhapsody.* Piano, small orchestra. MS, 1947.

Gershwin, George.
1. *Embraceable You.* Piano solo and piano duet. MS, 1951.
2. *Love Walked In.* Piano. Gershwin Publ. Co., 1946.
3. *The Man I Love.* Piano. New World Music Corp., 1944.
4. *Porgy and Bess* (fantasy on). 2 pianos. Gershwin Publ. Co., 1951.
5. *Oh Lord, I'm On My Way.* 2 pianos. MS sketches, 1950.

Goossens, Eugene. *Folktune.* Band. MS, 1942.

Grainger, Ella.
1. *Farewell to an Atoll.*
   a. Voice, piano. MS, 1944.
   b. Mixed chorus, orchestra. MS, 1944-45.
2. *Love at First Sight.* Chorus. G. Schirmer, 1946 [2 versions].
3. *To Echo.* Voice, 7 instruments. MS, 1945.
4. *Crying for the Moon.* Voice, tuneful percussion. MS, 1946.
5. *Honey-Pot Bee.* Mezzo-soprano, room music (5 strings, harp, piano, harmonium, vibraharp). MS, 1948.
6. *Playing On Heart-Strings.* Alto solo, tenor solo, mixed chorus or women's chorus. MS, 1950.
7. *The Mermaid.* Mezzo-soprano, soprano saxophone. MS, ca. 1948.
8. *Heartless.* Mezzo-soprano, mixed chorus, room-music ad lib. MS, 1947-1948.

Grieg, Edvard.
1. *Album for Male Voices.* Chorus. Peters, 1925.
2. *Four Psalms,* Op. 74. Baritone, mixed chorus. Peters, 1925; Peters, 1953.
3. *Knut Luråsens Halling II.* 2 pianos. MS, 1921.
4. *Norwegian Bridal Procession.* Piano. Schott & Co., 1920; Presser, 1920.

5. *Piano Concerto,* Op. 16.
   a. Piano. G. Schirmer, 1945.
   b. 2 pianos. Peters, 1920; G. Schirmer, 1920.
6. *Symphony in E Minor.* Orchestra. MS sketch (based on Op. 7), 1944
7. *Three Lyric Pieces.* Orchestra. MS, 1898.

Handel, George F. *Hornpipe from the Water Music.* Free Settings of Favorite Melodies No. 2. Piano. G. Schirmer, 1923; Schott & Co., 1923; Allan & Co., 1926.

Jappart, J. *Nenciozza for Strings.* Chosen Gems for Strings. Strings. MS, 1934.

Jenkins, John. *Fantasy in D, No. 1* (Five Part Fantasy, No. 1).
   1. Brass quintet. MS, 1937.
   2. Wind quintet. MS, 1937.
   3. Saxophone quintet. MS, 1937.
   4. Clarinet quintet. MS, 1937.
   5. Band (optional brass or reed band). MS, 1937.
   6. Chosen Gems for Strings. Dolmetsch Collection of English Consorts. 2 violins, 2 violas, 2 cellos. G. Schirmer, 1944.

Lawes, William. *Fantasy and Air, No. 1* (Six Part).
   1. Piano. MS, 1932.
   2. 2 pianos. MS, 1932.
   3. Band. MS, 1937
   4. Strings. MS, 1937.
   5. Wind choir. MS, 1944.
   6. Brass choir. MS, 1944.
   7. Clarinet choir. MS, 1937.
   8. Saxophone choir. MS, 1944.
   9. Chosen Gems for String. Dolmetsch Collection of English Consorts. 2 violins, 2 violas, 2 cellos. G. Schirmer, 1944.
   10. Chosen Gems for Winds. Saxophone sextet or choir.
   11. Chosen Gems for Winds. Clarinet sextet or choir.
   12. Chosen Gems for Winds. Combined saxophone and clarinet choirs.
   13. Chosen Gems for Winds. Woodwind choir (reed band).

Le Jeune, Claude. *Pretty Swallow* (La bel' aronde).
   1. Saxophone choir. MS, 1942.
   2. Clarinet choir. MS, 1942.
   3. Brass choir. MS, 1942.
   4. Wind choir. MS, 1942.
   5. 6 mixed voices. MS, 1932.

Lineva, Eugenie E.
   1. *The Flowers that Bloomed in the Field.* Mixed chorus. MS, 1934.
   2. *Kindling Wood.* Vocal trio or 3-part chorus. MS, 1934.

Liszt, Franz. *Hungarian Fantasy.* Piano, band. MS, 1959.

Machaut, Guillaume de.
  1. *Ballade, No. 17.*
     a. Mixed voices. MS, 1934.
     b. Band. MS, 1942.
     c. Brass trio. MS, 1940.
     d. Saxophone trio. MS, 1942.
     e. Chosen Gems for Strings. Strings. MS, 1939.
     f. Chosen Gems for Winds. Wind group.
     g. Chosen Gems for Winds. Band.
     h.· Chosen Gems for Winds. Saxophone choir.
     i. Chosen Gems for Winds. Brass choir.
  2. *Rondeau No. 14.* Chosen Gems for Strings. Strings. MS, 1939.
Mohr, Halsey K. *Liberty Bell.* (Arr. G.F. Briegel). Band. MS additions.

Olsen, Sparre.
  1. *Mountain Norway.* Mixed chorus, piano. MS, 1934.
  2. *When Yuletide Comes.* Saxophone trio. MS, 1943.

Parker, Kath. *Down Longford Way.* Elastic scoring. Boosey & Hawkes, 1936.

Pisador, Diego. *Paesabase, The Moorish King.* Chosen Gems for Strings. Baritone voice, violin, viola, cello. MS.
Power, Lionel.
  1. *Anima mea liquefacta est.* Chosen Gems for Strings. Mezzo-soprano, violin, viola, cello (viola). MS.
  2. *Sanctus.* EGM. 3 mixed voices (alto, tenor, bass) or 3 single men's voices or 3-part men's chorus with strings or winds. G. Schirmer, 1950.
Purcell, Henry. *Four Part Fantasy, No. 8.* Strings, harmonium. MS.

Rachmaninoff, Sergei. *Piano Concerto, No. 2* (last movement). Piano. G. Schirmer, 1946.
Ravel, Maurice. *La vallée des cloches.* Tuneful percussion. MS, 1944.

Sandby, Herman.
  1. *Chant* (Solemn Chant) (The Page's Song).
     a. Room-music. MS, 1900.
     b. Violin, cello, harmonium, piano. MS.
  2. *Elverhøj.* Song sketch. MS, 1937.
  3. *Love Song.* Chosen Gems for Strings. Strings and Harmonium. MS, 1939.
  4. *Two Pieces for Celli.* MS, 1899.
  5. *Two Pieces for Piano.* MS, 1901.
Scarlatti, Alessandro. *The Quiet Brook.*
  1. Chosen Gems for Strings. String quartet. G. Schirmer, 1930.
  2. Chosen Gems for Winds. Clarinet quintet or clarinet choir. MS, 1942.

Schumann, Robert. *Piano Concerto* (first movement). Piano.
G. Schirmer, 1947.

Scott, Cyril.
1. *Handelian Rhapsody.* Piano. Elkin & Co., 1909.
2. *Solemn Dance.* 7 strings, harmonium, piano, percussion.
MS, 1933.

Stanford, C. Villiers. *Four Irish Dances.* Movements: (1) A March-
Jig (Macguire's Kick); (2) A Slow Dance; (3) The Leprechaun's
Dance; (4) A Reel. Piano. J. Fischer & Bros., 1916.

Stokem, Johannes. *Harraytre amours.* String trio. MS, 1934.

Strauss, Richard. *The Rose Bearer, Ramble on the Love Duet*
from *Der Rosenkavalier.* Free Settings of Favorite Melodies No. 4.
Piano. Fürstner, 1925; G. Schirmer, 1928.

Tchaikovsky, Peter I.
1. *Flower Waltz.* Piano. Schott & Co., 1916.
2. *B-flat Minor Piano Concerto* (opening). Piano. Free Settings
of Favorite Melodies No. 8. G. Schirmer, 1943.

Willaert, Adrian. *O salutaris hostia.*
1. Room-music, 2 voices. MS, 1941.
2. Brass choir, 2 voices. MS, 1935, 1941.
3. Brass choir, 2 clarinets. MS.
4. Chosen Gems for Winds. Brass choir, 2 clarinets or 2
voices. 1941.

Appendix B
Recordings

The three articles reprinted in Appendix B are from *Recorded
Sound,* Vol. 45-46 (January-April 1972). Used by permission.

The recorded works of Percy Grainger

ERIC HUGHES

This list of recordings of Grainger's music attempts to include all important commercially published discs, but some omissions are made in the case of frequently encountered works. Also included are non-commercial discs (e.g. BBC and BBC Transcription) and tapes in the collection of the British Institute of Recorded Sound. All disc recordings are 33 rpm save those marked † (78 rpm) and ‡ (45 rpm) following the maker's catalogue number. Stereo recordings are indicated by (s) following the catalogue number.

The abbreviation Gramo is used for records issued by the Gramophone Company (HMV)

ARRIVAL PLATFORM HUMLET   *vla. unacc.*
W. Forbes. Decca M 540†
BLITHE BELLS (ramble on Bach's 'Sheep may safely graze')
P. Grainger (pf). Columbia 68006D†, in set M 166
BBC Concert Orch.—T. Lovett. BIRS tape M4353W.
BOLD WILLIAM TAYLOR (folksong arr.)
P. Pears (t) & V. Tunnard (pf). Argo RG 439: ZRG 5439 (s)
J. Shirley-Quirk (b) & English Chamber Orch.—B. Britten. Decca SXL 6410 (s); London CS 6632 (s)

BOLD WILLIAM TAYLOR, cont'd.
P. Pears (t) & V. Tunnard (pf). BBC Transcription 114881
J. Mitchinson (t) & W. Parry (pf). BBC Transcription 126829
P. Pears (t) & V. Tunnard (pf). BIRS tape P66W
BRIGG FAIR   *T. & unacc. cho.*
N. Stone & Oriana Madrigal Society—G. Kennedy Scott. Gramo E 473†
English Singers. Roycroft 160†

BRIGG-FAIR. cont'd.
  I. Partridge & Elizabethan Singers—L. Halsey. Argo
    RG 496: ZRG 5496 (s)
  P. Pears & Elizabethan Singers—L. Halsey. BBC
    Transcription 117407
  P. Pears & Ambrosian Singers—B. Britten. BBC
    Transcription 120724
(THE) BRITISH WATERSIDE (folksong arr.)   1921
  J. Mitchinson (t) & W. Parry (pf). BBC Transcription
    126829 BIRS tape T121W
  P. Pears (t) & V. Tunnard (pf). BIRS tape T121W
COLONIAL SONG   2 voices & small orch.   1928
  A. Atwater (s), L. O. Sanchez (t) & orch.—P. Grainger.
    Columbia 2066M†
  Victor Sym. Orch. Victor 36035†
  Eastman Rochester Pops—F. Fennell. Mercury
    MMA 11108: AMS 16060 (s): MG 50219: SR 90219 (s);
    Wing 14060; 18060 (s); World Record Club T 895:
    ST 895 (s): tape T 895
  P. Grainger (pf). Everest [Archives of Piano Music]
    913:X913 (s), recorded from a piano roll
  BBC Chorus & BBC Concert Orchestra—B. Priestman.
    BIRS tape M4354W
COUNTRY GARDENS   pf. or orch. or band   1918
  P. Grainger (pf). Columbia A606†
  P. Grainger (pf). Columbia D1664†: 2072M†: 154M†
  P. Grainger (pf) USA broadcast in 'The Magic key
    of RCA' Hollywood, 12 Jan. 1936 BIRS tape
    M4432W
  P. Grainger (pf), USA broadcast in 'Royal Gelatine
    hour', USA. 28 Jan. 1937 BIRS tape M4432R
  M. Hambourg (pf). Gramo B4437†
  P. Grainger (pf). Decca 24159†, in set A586
  C. Dixon (pf). Columbia DB1713†
  E. List (pf). Vanguard VRS 1072
  H. Wells (pf). Educo 3012
  P. Grainger (pf). BBC 31589; Everest [Archives of
    Piano Music] 913:X913 (s), recorded from a piano roll
  J. Ogdon (pf). BBC Transcription 117408
  Minneapolis Symphony Orchestra—E. Ormandy.
    Gramo DA1400†, Victor 1666†
  Rochester Pops—M. Gould. Columbia AL49: set
    A1912‡; Coronet KLL 004; Philips NBE 11054‡;
    409519BE‡: SFB 175‡
  Orch.—Levin. Silatone 7†; Mercury MG25047
  Orchestra—Stokowski. Victor LM1238: set WDM
    1663‡
  Hamburg Philharmonia Orch.—H. J. Walther. Music
    Sound Books 78113†
  Eastman-Rochester Pops—F. Fennell. Mercury MMA
    11108: AMS 16060 (s): MG 50219: SR 90219 (s): Wing
    14060; 18060(s); World Record Club T 895: ST 895
    (s): tape T895, Mercury; XEP 9065‡ SEX 15015‡
    (s)
  Orch.—C. Dragon. Capitol P 8466: SP 8466 (s):
    FAP 4–8466‡: SFP 4–8466‡ (s)
  Boston Pops—A. Fiedler. RCA INTS 1035 (s)
  Royal Marines Band—V. Dunn. Gramo CLP 1607:
    CSD 1469 (s)
DANCE FROM THE FAROE ISLANDS
  B. Britten & J. Ogdon (pf duet). BBC Transcription
    117405
  Cornell Wind Ensemble—Stith. Cornell University
    WE 8 (s)

DANISH FOLKSONG SUITE
  P. Grainger & Aarhus Municipal Orch.—Drier. Van-
    guard VRS 1098 [public performance, Aarhus 25
    February 1957]
  P. Grainger & T. Best (pfs) & Orch.—B. Cameron.
    BIRS tape M801W
DANNY DEEVER (Kipling)
  B. Drake (b) & Elizabethan Singers—L. Halsey. BBC
    Transcription 117406
(THE) DUKE OF MARLBOROUGH FANFARE
  Mbrs. English Chamber Orch.—B. Britten. Decca
    SXL 6410 (s); London CS 6632 (s)
  Coldstream Guards' Band—T. Sharpe. BBC Tran-
    scription 126829
EARLY ONE MORNING
  Orch.—L. Stokowski. Victor LM 1238: WDM 1663‡
EASTERN INTERMEZZO
  P. Grainger (pf). BBC 31255 from a piano roll
ENGLISH DANCE   orch. & org.
  BBC Concert Orch.—V. Tausky. BBC Transc   ion
    126831
FATHER AND DAUGHTER (folksong arr.)
  BBC Chorus & BBC Concert Orch.—T. Lovett. BIRS
    tape M4349R
FOSTER LULLABY
  J. Ogdon (pf). BBC Transcription 117408
GREEN BUSHES   orch.   1906
  BBC Concert Orch.—T. Lovett. BIRS tape M4355R
HANDEL IN THE STRAND   pf. & Orch. or orch   1930
  New Light Sym. Orch.—M. Sargent. Gramo C2002†
  Queen's Hall Orch.—H. Wood. Decca K767†: 25609†
  Boyd Neel String Orch. Decca K1216†; London
    T5229†: 40357†
  P. Grainger (pf) & orch.—Stokowski. Victor LM 1238:
    set WDM 1663‡: ERA 124‡; Gramo 7ER 5046‡
  E. Lush (pf) & Philharmonia Orch.—W. Braithwaite.
    Columbia DX1660†: SCD2173‡: RL3042
  Eastman Rochester Pops—F. Fennell. Mercury MMA
    11108: AMS16060 (s):MR50219: SR 90219 (s); Wing
    14060: 18060 (s); World Record Club T895: ST895 (s):
    tape T895; Mercury XEP 9065; SEX15015 (s)
  E. List (pf). Vanguard VRS1072
  University of Illinois Concert Band — M. Hindsley
    Illinois University 32
HARD-HEARTED BARB'RA ELLEN (folksong arr.)
  P. Pears (t) & V. Tunnard (pf) BIRS tape P66W
HILL SONG No. 1   1922
  P. Hamburger & L. Fuchsova (pfs). BBC Transcription
    126831
HILL SONG No. 2   1922
  Eastman Wind Ens.—F. Fennell. Mercury MMA
    11131: AMS 16078 (s): MG 50221: SR 90221 (s):
    MG 50388: SR 90388 (s)
  Westpoint Academy Band — P. Frainger rehearsal
    c. 1950 BIRS TAPE M4432W
(THE) HUNTER IN HIS CAREER (folksong arr.)
  P. Grainger (pf). broadcast USA 'Royal Gelatine
    hour, 28 Jan. 1937 BIRS tape M4432R
(THE) IMMOVABLE DO
  Eastman-Rochester Pops—F. Fennell. Mercury MMA
    11108: AMS 16060 (s): MG 50219: SR 90219 (s);
    Wing 14060 (s); World Record Club T895: ST895 (s):
    tape T895; Mercury XEP 9065‡: SEX 15015‡ (s)

I'M SEVENTEEN COME SUNDAY (folksong arr.) *1915*
Ambrosian Singers & English Chamber Orch.—B.
Britten. Decca SXL6410 (s); London CS 6632 (s)

IN A NUTSHELL, SUITE   *orch. & pf.*   *1916*
...No. 1, The arrival platform Humlet
C. Aronowitz (viola). BBC Transcription 117408
W. Forbes (vla) Decca M 540†
...No. 2, Gay but wistful
Vienna Tonkünstler Orch.—S. Robinson. BBC 18428
P. Grainger (pf). BBC 31255 *from a piano roll*
...No. 4, Gum-suckers' March
P. Grainger (pf). Columbia A 3381†
P. Grainger (pf). Columbia 7147M†
P. Grainger (pf). BBC 31255 *from a piano roll*
L. Fuchsova & P. Hamburger (pfs). BBC Transcription
126832

ÍRISH TUNE FROM COUNTY DERRY
(LONDONDERRY AIR) *1911*
P. Grainger (pf). Decca 24158†, in set A586
C. Dixon. Columbia DB1735†
E. List. Vanguard VRS 1072
P. Grainger (pf). Everest [Archives of Piano Music]
913: X913 (s), *recorded from a piano roll*
Boyd Neel String Orch. Decca M596†
L. Heward String Orch. Columbia DX1174†
Hallé Orch.—J. Barbirolli. Gramo C3819†
Liverpool Phil. Orch.—M. Sargent. Columbia
DX1584†: RL3042
Kasschau's Solo Choir—P. Grainger. Columbia
7111M†
Elizabethan Singers—L. Halsey. BBC Transcription
117407
Carnegie Pops Orch.—O'Connell. Columbia 7628M†:
ML 2176
New Sym. Orch.—M. Sargent. Gramo B2913†
Minneapolis Symphony Orch.—Ormandy. Gramo
DB2685†; Victor 8734†
New State Sym. Orch. Decca F 3104†
Philadelphia String Sinfonietta—F. Sevitzky. Victor
4186†
Band—M. Gould. Columbia 4516M†, in set MM743:
ML2029
Orchestra—L. Stokowski. Victor LM 1238: set WDM
166‡: ERA 124‡, Gramo 7ER 5046‡
Sydney Symphony Str. Orch.—Beck. Diaphon DPM 1
Philharmonia Orch.—W. Braithwaite. Columbia DX
1660†: SCD 2173‡
Hallé Orch.—J. Barbirolli. Pye CEC 32022‡
Eastman-Rochester Pops—F. Fennell. Mercury MMA
11108: AMS 16060 (s): MG 50219: SR 90219 (s);
Wing 14060: 18060 (s); World Record Club T895:
ST 895 (s); tape T895; Mercury XEP 9077‡: SEX
15021‡ (s)
ABC Sydney Sym. Orch.—E. Goossens. Gramo
DB 9792†
Hamburg Philharmonia Orch.—H. J. Walther. Music
Sound Books 78023†: 60041
Rochester Pops—M. Gould. Columbia AL 49: set
A1912‡; Coronet KLL004
Philharmonia Orch.—G. Weldon. Columbia SED
5547‡; Gramo 7P 394‡
Sinfonia of London—R. Irving. Gramo CLP 1225:
QCLP 12053: CSD 1262 (s): CSDQ 6258 (s); Capitol
G 7178: SG 7178 (s); Gramo tape SCT 1525 (s)

IRISH TUNE FROM COUNTY DERRY cont'd.
Hollywood Bowl—F. Slatkin, Capitol tape ZF 95 (s)
Sydney Symphony Orch.—J. Hopkins. [Australian]
World Record Club S4433 (s)

JUTISH MEDLEY (folksong arr.)
P. Grainger (pf). Columbia 50129D†
Orchestra—B. Cameron. Decca A1002†
E. List (pf). Vanguard VRS1072
...No. 5, Lord Peter's stable-boy
P. Grainger (pf) & R. Leopold (harmonium). Columbia
163M†

KNIGHT AND SHEPHERD'S DAUGHTER
R. Paul (pf). Onslo FH1

LADS OF WAMFHREY   *band   1905, revised 1937 8*
Goldman Band—Goldman. Decca DL8931: DL78931
(s)

LET'S GO GAY IN GREEN MEADOW   *2 pfs.*
V. Tunnard & B. Britten, Decca SXL 6410 (s), London
CS 6632 (s)

LINCOLNSHIRE POSY   *military band*
Eastman Wind Ens.—F. Fennell. Mercury MMA
11034: AMS 16023 (s): MG 50173: SR 90173 (s):
XEP 9059‡: SEX 15010‡ (s)
Illinois University Concert Band—Hindsley. Illinois
University 34
Coldstream Guards' Band—T. Sharpe. BBC Tran-
scription 126830

LISBON (folksong arr.) *fl., ob., cl., hn & bsn.*
Mbrs. English Chamber Orch.—B. Britten. Decca
SXL 6410 (s); London CS 6632 (s)
Interlocken Arts Wind Quintet. Mark 28486 (s)

LORD MAXWELL'S GOODNIGHT
P. Pears (t) & English Chamber Orch.—B. Britten.
Decca SXL 6410 (s); London CS 6632 (s)

LOST LADY FOUND (folksong arr.)
Ambrosian Singers & English Chamber Orch.—
B. Britten. Decca SXL 6410 (s); London CS 6632 (s)
Louis Halsey Singers—L. Halsey. BBC 33249
Elizabethan Singers—L. Halsey. BBC Transcription
117407

MOCK MORRIS   *1910*
P. Grainger (pf). Gramo 05558*†: D353*†
E. List (pf). Vanguard VRS 1072
Orch.—H. Wood. Columbia LX200†: 7338M†
Queen's Hall Orch.—H. Wood. Decca K767†: 25609†
Philharmonia Orch.—W. Braithwaite. Columbia DB
2572†: RL 3042
Boyd Neel Str. Orch. Decca K 1215†
Hallé Orch.—J. Barbirolli. Pye CEC 32022‡
Eastman-Rochester Pops—F. Fennell. Mercury MMA
11108: AMS 16060 (s): MG 50219: SR 90219 (s):
MG50340: SH 90340 (s); Wing 14060: 18060 (s).
World Record Club T 895: ST 895 (s): tape T 895;
Mercury XEP 9077‡: SEX 15021‡ (s)
Sydney Symphony Str. Orch.—Beck. Diaphon DPM 1
Orchestra—Stokowski. Victor LM1238; set WDM
1663†: ERA 124‡, Gramo 7ER 5046‡
Rochester Pops—M. Gould. Columbia AL 49: set
A 1912‡; Coronet KLL 004
Philharmonia Orch.—G. Weldon. Columbia SX 1436:
SCX 3446 (s); Gramo SXLP 30123 (s)
Sydney Symphony Orch.—J. Hopkins [Australian]
World Record Club S 4433 (s)

MOCK MORRIS cont'd.
Aldeburgh Festival String Ensemble. BBC Transcription 117406
MOLLY ON THE SHORE   *orig. str. qtt.*   *1907*
P. Grainger (pf). Columbia A6145*†
P. Grainger (pf). Columbia 2057 M†
P. Grainger (pf). Decca 24158†, in set A 586
E. List (pf). Vanguard VRS 1072
P. Grainger (pf). Everest [Archives of Piano Music] 913: X913 (s) *recorded from a piano roll*
Boyd Neel Str. Orch. Decca K1215†
Philharmonia Orch.—W. Braithwaite. Columbia DB 2572†: RL 3042
New Mayfair Str. Orch.—W. Goehr. Columbia B 8976†
Prisca String Quartet. Polydor 10541†
Decca Little Sym. Orch.—Mendoza. Decca 23119†, in set A 90: DL5211
Carnegie Pops Orch.—C. O'Connell. Columbia 7628M†: ML 2176
Minneapolis Sym. Orch.—E. Ormandy. Gramo DB 2685†; Victor 8734†
Philadelphia Str. Sinfonietta—F. Sevitzky. Victor 11560†
Covent Garden Opera Orch.—L. Collingwood. Gramo B2641†; Victor 4165†
Orchestra—H. J. Wood. Columbia LX 200†: 7338 M†
Orchestra—L. Stokowski. Victor LM 1238: set WDM 1663‡: ERA 124‡; Gramo 7ER 5046‡
Hamburg Philharmonia Orch.—H. J. Walther. Music Sound Books 78113†
American Art String Quartet. Victor LBC 1086
Rochester Pops—M. Gould. Columbia AL49: set A 1912‡; Coronet KLL 004; Philips NBE 11054‡: 409519 BE‡: S313432F‡: SBF175‡
Hallé Orch—Barbirolli. Pye CEC 32032‡
Eastman-Rochester Pops—F. Fennell. Mercury MMA 11108: AMS 16060 (s): MR 50219: SR 90219 (s): MG50294: SR90294 (s); Wing 14060: 18060; World Record Club T895 (s): tape T895; Mercury XEP 9077‡; SEX 15021‡
Aldeburgh Festival String Ensemble. BBC Transcription 117406
BBC Concert Orch.—V. Tausky. BBC Transcription 115214
MORNING SONG IN THE JUNGLE (Kipling)   *cho.*   *1898*
Elizabethan Singers—L. Halsey. BBC Transcription 117406
(2) MUSICAL RELICS OF MY MOTHER (folksong arr.) *2 pfs. 1924*
L. Fuchsova & P. Hamburger. BIRS tape M4354R
MY ROBIN IS TO THE GREENWOOD GONE
           fl., cor anglais & str.
Eastman-Rochester Pops—F. Fennell. Mercury MMA 11108: AMS 16060 (s): MG 50219: SR 90219 (s): Wing 14060: 18060; World Record Club T895: ST895 (s): tape T895; Mercury XEP 9077‡: SEX 15021‡ (s)
Mbrs. English Chamber Orchestra—B. Britten. Decca SXL 6410 (s); London CS6632 (s)
Sydney Symphony Orch.—J. Hopkins. [Australian] World Record Club S4433 (s)
E. List (pf). Vanguard VRS 1072
NIGHT SONG IN THE JUNGLE   *male cho.*
BBC Chorus—P. Gellhorn. BIRS tape M2066W

ONE MORE DAY, MY JOHN
P. Grainger (pf). Columbia A 6128*†
P. Grainger (pf). Columbia 7150 M†
P. Grainger (pf). Decca 24159†, in set A586
OVER THE HILLS AND FAR AWAY (Children's March) *1918*
E. List. Vanguard VRS 1072
P. Grainger (pf). BBC 31253; *recorded from a Duo-Art piano roll*
Victor Sym. Orch. Victor 36035†
Rochester Pops—M. Gould. Columbia AL 49: set A1912‡; Coronet KLL 004
P. Grainger (pf) & Goldman Band. Decca DL8633: DL78633 (s)
Eastman Rochester Pops—F. Fennell. Mercury MMA 11108: AMS 16060 (s); MG 50219: SR 90219 (s): MG 50325
Coldstream Guards' Band—T. Sharpe. BBC Transcription 126824
Band — H. Legge. Boosey & Hawkes BH1
POEMS FROM THE 'JUNGLE BOOKS' by Rudyard Kipling
BBC Chorus—R. Sinton. BIRS tape 031R
(THE) POWER OF LOVE
A. Atwater (s), R. Leopold (pf) & P. Grainger (harmonium), etc. Columbia 7147M†
(THE) POWER OF ROME AND THE CHRISTIAN HEART
University of Illinois Concert Band — M. Hindsley Illinois University 10
(THE) PRETTY MAID MILKIN' HER COW   *1921*
P. Pears (t) & B. Britten (pf). Decca SXL6410 (s); London CS 6632 (s)
P. Pears (t) & B. Britten (pf). BBC Transcription 126829
J. Mitchinson (t) & W. Parry (pf). BBC Transcription 126829
P. Pears (t) & V. Tunnard (pf). BIRS tape P66W
RAMBLE ON LOVE (on themes from *Der Rosenkavalier*)
P. Grainger (pf). Columbia 1898D†: 2137M†: DB28†
P. Grainger (pf). Vanguard VRS 1098
SCOTCH STRATHSPEY AND REEL
Grainger Singers & Players—Kasschau [P. Grainger & R. Leopold, guitars]. Columbia 7104M†
Ambrosian Singers & English Chamber Orch.—B. Britten. Decca SXL 6410 (s); London CS 6632 (s)
SHALLOW BROWN   *cho.*   *1927*
J. Shirley-Quirk (b) & English Chamber Orch.—B. Britten. Decca SXL 6410 (s); London CS 6632 (s)
B. Drake (b) & Elizabethan Singers—L. Halsey. BBC Transcription 117407
J. Shirley-Quirk (b), Ambrosian Singers & English Chamber Orch.—B. Britten. BBC Transcription 120726
SHEPHERD'S HEY
P. Grainger (pf). Gramo 5581*†: E147*†
P. Grainger (pf). Columbia A6060*†
P. Grainger (pf). Columbia 154M†: 2072M†: D1664†
C. Dixon (pf). Columbia DB1713†
M. Hambourg (pf). Gramo B3172†
L. Pouishnoff (pf). Columbia 4829†
O. Gabrilovitch (pf). Victor 1095†: Gramo DA 717†; LM 2824: VIC1210
E. List (pf). Vanguard VRS 1072
P. Grainger (pf). Everest [Archives of Piano Music] 913: X913 (s), *recorded from a piano roll*
J. Ogdon (pf). BBC Transcription 117408
Royal Artillery Band—Geary. Decca F7657†

SHEPHERD'S HEY, cont'd.

Covent Garden Opera Orch.—L. Collingwood. Gramo B 2641†; Victor 4165†

Minneapolis Symphony Orch.—E. Ormandy. Gramo DA1400†; Victor 1666†

Columbia Sym. Orch.—P. Grainger. Columbia 163M†

Welsh Guards Band. Regal Zonophone MR3100†

Morton Gould Band. Columbia 4516M†, in set MM 743: ML2029

Orchestra—L. Stokowski. Victor LM1238: set WDM 1663‡

Hamburg Philharmonia—H. J. Walther. Music Sound Books 71113†

Rochester Pops Orch.—M. Gould. Columbia AL49: set A1912‡; Coronet KLL 004; Philips NBE 11054‡: 409 519 BE‡

New Symphony Orch.—A. Collins. Decca LW5297; Ace of Clubs ACL 108

Irish Guards' Band—C. H. Jaeger. Gramo CLP 1076: HCLP 104: tape HTC 611; Encore ENC 107; Victor LM 2020

Massed Bands—H. Mortimer. Decca DFE 6614‡: STO 127 (s)‡

G.U.S. Band—H. Mortimer. Columbia SX1621, SCX 3512 (s)

Hallé Orch.—J. Barbirolli. Pye CEC 32022‡

Eastman-Rochester Pops—F. Fennell. Mercury MMA 11108: AMS 16060 (s): MG50219: SR 90219 (s): MG50340: SR90340 (s); Wing 14060: 18060 (s); World Record Club T895: ST 895 (s), tape T895; Mercury XEP 9065‡: SEX16015‡ (s)

English Chamber Orch.—B. Britten. Decca SXL 6410 (s); London CS6632 (s)

English Chamber Orchestra—B. Britten. BBC Transcription 120720

SIX DUKES WENT A'FISHING (folksong arr.)

P. Pears (t) & B. Britten (pf). Gramo DA 2032†: 7P268‡: 7EP7071‡

P. Pears (t) & B. Britten (pf). BBC Transcription 117408

J. Mitchinson (t) & W. Parry (pf). BBC Transcription 126829

SONG OF THE DEAD (Kipling)   *cho. & band*

BBC Chorus & Coldstream Guards' Band—T. Sharpe. BIRS tape M4355W

SPOON RIVER   *1919–29*

P. Grainger (pf). Columbia A3685*†

E. List (pf). Vanguard VRS 1072

P. Grainger (pf). Everest [Archive of Piano Music] 913:X913 (s) *recorded from a piano roll*

Rochester Pops—M. Gould. Columbia AL 49: set A1912‡; Coronet KLL 004

Eastman-Rochester Pops—F. Fennell. Mercury MMA 11108: AMS 16060 (s): MG 50219: SR 90219 (s): Wing 14060: 18060 (s); World Record Club T895: ST895 (s): tape T895

(THE) SPRIG OF THYME   *1921*

J. Vyvyan (s) & E. Lush (pf). Decca LXT 2797; London LL806; Eclipse ECS 589 (s)

P. Pears (t) & B. Britten (pf). Decca SXL 6410 (s); London CS6632 (s)

J. Mitchinson (t) & W. Parry (pf). BBC Transcription 126829

SUSSEX MUMMERS' CHRISTMAS CAROL   *1905–11*

W. Forbes (viola) & E. de Chaulieu (pf). Decca M540†

E. List (pf). Vanguard VRS 1072

P. Grainger (pf). Everest [Archives of Piano Music] 913:X913 (s) *recorded from a piano roll*

E. Rubach (pf). BBC Transcription 126830

—ARR. Band—Goldman

Maryland University Symphonic Band—Ostling. Coronet S 1411 (s)

THERE WAS A PIG WENT OUT TO DIG (Anon. & Grainger)   *female cho.*

Ambrosian Singers—B. Britten. Decca SXL6410 (s); London CS6632 (s)

TO A NORDIC PRINCESS. Bridal song. *orch. & org. 1928*

BBC Concert Orchestra—T. Lovett. BIRS tape M4352W

TRIBUTE TO STEPHEN FOSTER *5 solo voices, cho. & orch.*   *1931*

BBC Chorus & BBC Concert Orch.—T. Lovett [P. Challis, pf]. BIRS tape M4352R

(THE) TWA CORBIES (Scott)   *1924*

B. Drake (b) & Aldeburgh Festival String Ensemble. BBC Transcription 117406

(AN) UP-COUNTRY SONG   *1930*

Elizabethan Singers—L. Halsey. BBC Transcription 117406

VERMELAND—Swedish folk song set by YCREPREGNIARG

BBC Chorus—J. Poole. BIRS tape M4353R

WALKING TUNE   *fl., ob., cl., horn & bsn.*

Philadelphia Wind Quintet. Columbia ML 5984: MS 6584 (s)

P. Grainger (pf). BBC 31255 *from a piano roll*

(THE) WARRIORS

BBC Concert Orch.—V. Tausky. BBC Transcription 126832

WILLOW, WILLOW   *B., str. & guitar*

P. Pears (t) & mbrs. English Chamber Orch.— B. Britten. Decca SXL 6410 (s); London CS6632 (s)

YOUTHFUL RAPTURE *vlc., vln., harmonium & pf. 1930*

B. Harrison (vlc) & Orch.—M. Sargent. Gramo C1929†

YOUTHFUL SUITE

Sydney Symphony Orch.—J. Hopkins. [Australian] World Record Club S4433 (s)

ZANZIBAR BOAT SONG   *pf.—6 hands*

J. Ogdon, B. Britten, & V. Tunnard. BBC Transcription 117408

ARRANGEMENTS

ANON. 13TH CENTURY. Beata Viscera *3vv.*

Trapp Family Choir—F. Wasner. Brunswick LAT 8038; Decca DL 9489

BRAHMS: Cradle Song

P. Grainger (pf). Columbia A3685*†

P. Grainger (pf). Columbia 2057M†

GERSHWIN: Love walked in

E. Rubach (pf). BBC Transcription 126830

HANDEL: Water Music—Hornpipe

P. Grainger (pf). Columbia 30010D*†

E. Rubach (pf). BBC Transcription 126830

JENKINS: Fantasy in five parts No. 1

London Studio Strings—M. Dods. BIRS tape M4356R

SCOTT: Symphonic dance No. 1, D minor

C. Scott & P. Grainger (pf duet) *from piano roll* Klavier KS102

STANFORD: Irish dances, Op. 89
No. 1 March jig
    P. Grainger (pf). Gramo 5569*
    P. Grainger (pf). *from piano roll* BBC 31253

No. 3, Leprachaun's dance & No. 4, Reel
    P. Grainger (pf.) *from a piano roll* Everest (Archives of piano music') 909 : X909 (s)
(7) Lincolnshire Folksongs, collected by Grainger, ARRANGED Phyllis Tate: in Gramo CLP 3640 : CSD 3640 (s)

Records of Percy Grainger as an interpreter

A. F. R. LAWRENCE

The Gramophone Company

Acoustic recordings; matrix numbers are shown on the left and catalogue numbers in bold type
probably recorded 16 May 1908: recordist William C. Gaisberg

8393e	**5569**	not doubled 10″ STANFORD, arr. GRAINGER Irish Dance No. 1 (March Jig—McGuire's Kick)
8394e	**5570**	not doubled 10″ GRIEG Concerto in A minor: 1st movement, Cadenza
2467f	**05503**	not doubled 12″ LISZT Hungarian Rhapsody No. 12 (abridged)

14 July 1914

Ak-18043e	**5581 E 147**	10″ GRAINGER Shepherd's Hey
Al-8033f	**05558 D 353**	12″ GRAINGER Mock Morris Dance
Al-8034f	**05554 D 353**	12″ DEBUSSY Toccata in C sharp minor

NOTE: The reverse of E 147 is not by Grainger

*

The Columbia (The United States) Graphophone (later Phonograph) Company 1917–1931

The recordings are listed by matrix number under the date they were made. The official practice was that, should a recording need to be remade, either at the original session or at a later date, the original matrix number would be used followed by a 'take' or 'dash' number indicating the specific wax. With the advent of electrical recording in March 1925, this practice was changed to the extent that in America no electrical recording was given an old acoustic process matrix number, even for a repeat of the same work. In two cases in the electrical group a new number was assigned when an older number should have been used. These have been noted.

In the acoustic process group the first two digits indicate size, thus 77, 79, 80 and 81 indicate 10″; while 49 and 98 indicate 12″.

In the electrical process group 144, 145, 147 and 150 indicate 10″; while 98 indicates 12″.

Following the list of matrix numbers by sessions is a list showing which matrices were used to make the double-sided records. These double-sided numbers are the basic catalogue number as assigned in the United States. No list is included of sets arranged in automatic sequence.

ACOUSTIC recordings

28 August 1917

77294–1	STANFORD, arr. GRAINGER Irish Dance No. 1 (March Jig—McGuire's Kick)	Rejected
–2		OK but later Rejected
77295–1	Irish Tune from County Derry	OK but later Rejected
–2	Idem	Rejected

29 August 1917

49243–1	LISZT Hungarian Rhapsody No. 2 Pt. 1	Unpublished
–2	Idem	Unpublished
–3	Idem	on A 6000

1 September 1917

77303–1	GRAINGER The Gum Sucker's March (Australian March) (Grainger, piano, with The Band of The 15th Coast Artillery)	Rejected
–2		OK but later Rejected
–3		Rejected

19 September 1917

49248–1	LISZT Hungarian Rhapsody No. 2, Pt. 2	Unpublished
–2	Idem	on A 6000
49249–1	GRIEG Norwegian Bridal Procession (Although Rejected in the United States, this plate was used for one side of L 1386 in Great Britain)	Rejected

31 October 1917

77294–3	STANFORD, arr. GRAINGER Irish Dance No. 1 (March Jig—McGuire's Kick)	Rejected
–4		Rejected
–5	Idem	OK but later Rejected
77295–3	(Arr.) GRAINGER Irish Tune from County Derry	Rejected
–4		Rejected
–5	Idem	OK but later Rejected

3 December 1917

49281–1	CHOPIN Valse in A flat, Op. 42	on A 6027

2 January 1918

49295–1	(Arr.) GRAINGER Paraphrase on Tchaikovsky's Flower Waltz	Unpublished
–2		Unpublished
–3	Idem	Unpublished
–4	Idem	Unpublished
–5	Idem	on A 6192
49296–1	CHOPIN Polonaise in A flat, Op. 53	Unpublished
–2	Idem	on A 6027

3 January 1918

77605–1	GRAINGER One more day, my John and Shepherd's Hey	OK but later Rejected OK but later Rejected
–2	Idem	

5 January 1918

77611–1	GRIEG To Spring	OK but later Rejected
–2	Idem	OK but later Rejected
–3	Idem	Rejected

7 June 1918

49441–1	CHOPIN Prelude in A flat, Op. 28 No. 17	Unpublished
–2	Idem	on A 6060
49442–1	GRAINGER Country Gardens and Shepherd's Hey	on A 6060

17 December 1918

49561–1	LISZT Hungarian Fantasy, Pt. 1	Unpublished
–2	(Grainger, piano, with [Columbia	Unpublished
–3	Symphony] Orchestra, probably directed by Charles A. Prince)	on A 6115
49562–1	LISZT Hungarian Fantasy, Pt. 2	Unpublished
–2	(See data on 49561)	Unpublished
–3	Idem	on A 6115

16 June 1919

49638–1	DEBUSSY Toccata in C sharp minor *(Pour le piano)*	*Rejected*

17 June 1919

49639–1	SCHARWENKA Polish Dance in E flat, Op. 3, No. 1	*on A 6128*
49640–1	GRIEG To Spring *and* GRAINGER One more day, my John	*on A 6128*

10 February 1920

49748–1	GRAINGER Molly on the Shore	*Rejected*
–2	*Idem*	*on A 614d*
49749–1	BRAHMS Waltz in A flat *and*	*Reject52*
–2	DETT Juba Dance (Southern Negro Dance)	*on A 6145*
49750–1	LISZT Hungarian Rhapsody No. 12, Pt. 1	*Rejected*
–2	*Idem*	*on A 6161*
49751–1	LISZT Hungarian Rhapsody No. 12, Pt. 2	*Rejected*
–2	*Idem*	*on A6161*

5 February 1921

49921–1	GRIEG Wedding Day at Troldhaugen	*on A 6191*

7 February 1921

79715–1	Turkey in the straw (Cowboy's and old	*Rejected*
–2	fiddler's breakdown, *arr.* David W.	*Rejected*
–3	Guion)	*on A 3381*
79716–1	GRAINGER The Gum Sucker's March (*or*	*Rejected*
–2	Australian born in the Sate of Victoria)	*Rejected*

8 February 1921

79716–3	GRAINGER The Gum Sucker's March	*on A 3381*

18 February 1921

49932–1	SCHUBERT, *arr.* TAUSIG Marche Militaire	*Rejected*
49933–1	GRIEG Norwegian Bridal Procession	*Rejected*
–2	*Idem*	*on A 6217*

26 November 1921

49999–1	LISZT Liebestraum No. 3	*on A 6217*

29 November 1921

98000–1	LISZT Polonaise in E major, Pt. 1	*Rejected*
–2	*Idem*	*on A 6205*
–3	*Idem*	*Rejected*
98001–1	LISZT Polonaise in E major, Pt. 2	*Rejected*
–2	*Idem*	*Rejected*
–3	*Idem*	*on A 6205*

2 August 1922

80487–1	BRAHMS *arr.* GRAINGER Cradle Song	*Rejected*
–2	*Idem*	*Rejected*
–3	*Idem*	*on A 3685*
80488–1	Spoon River, American folk dance	*Rejected*
–2	(Collected by Edgar Lee Masters	*Rejected*
–3	and *arr.* Grainger)	*on A 3685*
80489–1	GRAINGER Eastern Intermezzo *and*	*Rejected*
–2	HANDEL *Water Music*—Hornpipe	*Rejected*

3 August 1922

80489–3	GRAINGER Eastern Intermezzo *and* HANDEL *Water Music*—Hornpipe	*Rejected*
80490–1	CHOPIN Etude in A flat (unidentified)	*Rejected*
–2	*Idem*	*Rejected*
–3	*Idem*	*Rejected*
98033–1	LISZT Rakoczy March (Hungarian *OK but never issued*	
–2	Rhapsody No. 15)	*Rejected*
–3	*Idem*	*Rejected*

4 August 1922

98033–1	LISZT Rakoczy March (Hungarian Rhapsody No. 15)	*Rejected*

7 August 1922

98034–1	DEBUSSY Jardins sous la pluie *(Estampes)*	*Rejected*
–2	*Idem*	*Rejected*

8 August 1922

98034–3	DEBUSSY Jardins sous la pluie *(Estampes)*	*Rejected*
98035–1	STANFORD, *arr.* GRAINGER Irish dance	*Rejected*
–2	No. 4, Reel	*Rejected*
–3	*Idem*	*Rejected*
98036–1	GRAINGER Colonial song (The Composer's	*Rejected*
–2	impressions of his birthland, Australia)	*Rejected*

29 October 1923

81298–1	MACDOWELL To a water lily	*on 30006D*
–2	*Idem*	*Rejected*
–3	*Idem*	*Rejected*
81299–1	GLUCK, *arr.* BRAHMS Gavotte	*Rejected*
–2	*Idem*	*on 33001D*

31 October 1923

81323–1	DEBUSSY Golliwogg's cake walk	*Rejected*
–2	(*Children's Corner*)	*Rejected*
–3	*Idem*	*on 33001D*
81324–1	SINDING Rustle of Spring	*Rejected*
–2	*Idem*	*Rejected*
–3	*Idem*	*on 30006D*
–4	*Idem*	*Rejected*

25 February 1924

81582–1	CHOPIN Scherzo in B flat minor, Op. 31, Pt. 1	*Rejected*
–2	*Idem*	*Rejected*
–3	*Idem*	*Rejected*
–4	*Idem*	*on 30019D*
81583–1	CHOPIN Scherzo in B flat minor, Op. 31, Pt. 2	*Rejected*
–2	*Idem*	*Rejected*
–3	*Idem*	*on 30019D*
–4	*Idem*	*Rejected*

27 February 1924

81587–1	SCHUMANN *arr.* GRAINGER Warum?	*on 30010D*
–2	*Idem*	*Rejected*
–3	*Idem*	*Rejected*
–4	*Idem*	*Rejected*

28 February 1924

81588–1	HANDEL *arr.* GRAINGER *Water Music*—	*Rejected*
–2	Hornpipe	*Rejected*
–3	*Idem*	*Rejected*
–4	*Idem*	*on 30010D*

ELECTRIC recordings

9 May 1925

W98171–1	(*Arr.*) GRAINGER Irish tune from	*Rejected*
–2	County Derry (Kasschau's Solo Choir,	*Rejected*
–3	conducted by Percy Grainger)	*on 7111M*

19 May 1925

W98175–1	GRAINGER Scotch Strathspey and Reel, Pt. 1	*Rejected*
–2	The Grainger Singers and Players,	*OK (2nd choice)*
–3	conducted by Frank Kasschau	*on 7104M*
	(Guitars by Percy Grainger and Ralph Leopold)	
W98176–1	GRAINGER Scotch Strathspey and Reel, Pt. 2	*Rejected*
–2	(See data for W98175)	*OK (2nd choice)*
–3	*Idem*	*on 7104M*

10 June 1925

W98177–1	CHOPIN Sonata in B minor, Op. 58,	*OK (2nd choice)*
–2	Allegro maestoso, Pt. 1	*on 67158D*
–3	*Idem*	*Rejected*
W98178–1	CHOPIN Sonata in B minor, Op. 58,	*on 67158D*
–2	Allegro maestoso, Pt. 2	*Rejected*
–3	*Idem*	*Rejected*
W98179–1	CHOPIN Sonata in B minor, Op. 58,	*on 67159D*
–2	Allegro maestoso, Pt. 3 *and* Scherzo	*Rejected*
–3	*Idem*	*OK (2nd choice)*

11 June 1925

W98180–1	CHOPIN Sonata in B minor, Op. 58,	*on 67150D*
–2	3rd movement, Pt. 1	*Rejected*
–3	*Idem*	*Rejected*
W98181–1	CHOPIN Sonata in B minor, Op. 58,	*on 67160D*
–2	3rd movement, Largo Pt. 2 *and* Presto	*Rejected*
–3	Pt. 1	*Rejected*
W98182–1	CHOPIN Sonata in B minor, Op. 58,	*on 67160D*
–2	3rd movement, Presto Pt. 2	*Rejected*
–3	*Idem*	*Rejected*

30 January 1926

W98217–1	BRAHMS Sonata in F minor, Op. 5,	*OK (2nd choice)*
–2	Allegro Maestoso, Pt. 1	*on 67183D*
W98218–1	BRAHMS Sonata in F minor, Op. 5,	*OK (2nd choice)*
–2	Allegro Maestoso, Pt. 2	*on 67183D*
W98219–1	BRAHMS Sonata in F minor, Op. 5,	*on 67184D*
–2	Andante, Pt. 1	*Rejected*
W98220–1	BRAHMS Sonata in F minor, Op. 5,	*OK (2nd choice)*
–2	Andante, Pt. 2	*on 67184D*

2 February 1926

W98221–1	BRAHMS Sonata in F minor, Op. 5,	*on 67185D*
–2	Scherzo	*Rejected*
–3	*Idem*	*OK (2nd choice)*
W98222–1	BRAHMS Sonata in F minor, Op. 5,	*OK (2nd choice)*
–2	Intermezzo	*on 67185D*
W98223–1	BRAHMS Sonata in F minor, Op. 5,	*on 67186D*
–2	Finale, Pt. 1	*OK (2nd choice)*
W98224–1	BRAHMS Sonata in F minor, Op. 5,	*Rejected*
–2	Finale, Pt. 2	*OK (2nd choice)*
–3	*Idem*	*on 67186D*

31 March 1926
W98245-1 CHOPIN Etude, Op. 25 No.12 *and*   on 7109M†
   -2   BRAHMS Waltz in A flat   *OK(2nd choice)*
W98246-1 DEBUSSY Clair de lune *(Suite bergamasque)* on 7124M
   -2   *Idem*   *Rejected*
W98247-1 LISZT Liebestraum No. 3   *Rejected*
   -2   *Idem*   *Rejected*
NOTE: Contrary to the usual practice, when this selection was remade at a later date (see W98357) the first matrix number (W98247) was not used.

W98248-1 DEBUSSY Toccata in C sharp minor   *Rejected*
   -2   *(Pour le piano)*   on 7124M
1 April 1926
W98249-1 CHOPIN Prelude in A flat, Op. 28, No. 17 on 7109M†
   -2   *Idem*   *Rejected*
W98250-1 SCHUMANN Romance in F sharp   *Rejected*
   -2   *Idem*   *Rejected*
NOTE: Contrary to the usual practice, when this selection was remade at a later date (see W98543) the first matrix number (W98250) was not used.

W98251-1 Sheep and Goats Walkin' to the Pasture   on 7134M
   -2   (arr. David W. Guion) *and*   *Rejected*
        BACH Partita No. 1—Gigue
W98252-1 GRIEG Norwegian Peasant Dance   *Rejected*
   -2   *Idem*   *Rejected*
24 May 1927
W144204-1 GRAINGER Shepherd's Hey   *Rejected*
   -2   *Idem*   *OK (2nd choice)*
   -3   *Idem*   on 154M
W144205-1 GRAINGER Country Gardens   *OK (2nd choice)*
   -2   *Idem*   on 154M
   -3   *Idem*   *Rejected*
W144206-1 BRAHMS *arr.* GRAINGER Cradle Song   *Rejected*
   -2   *Idem*   *Rejected*
25 May 1927
W144206-3 BRAHMS *arr.* GRAINGER Cradle Song   *Rejected*
1 June 1927
W98353-1 SCHUMANN Sonata in G minor, Op. 22,   *Rejected*
   -2   Pt. 1   *OK (2nd choice)*
   -3   *Idem*   on 67509D
W98354-1 SCHUMANN Sonata in G minor, Op. 22,   *Rejected*
   -2   Pt. 2   *OK (2nd choice)*
   -3   *Idem*   on 67509D
W98355-1 SCHUMANN Sonata in G minor, Op. 22,   *Rejected*
   -2   Pt. 3   on 67510D
   -3   *Idem*   *OK (2nd choice)*
W98356-1 SCHUMANN Sonata in G minor, Op. 22,   *Rejected*
   -2   Pt. 4   *OK (2nd choice)*
   -3   *Idem*   on 67510D
W98357-1 LISZT Liebestraum No. 3   *Rejected*
   -2   *Idem*   *OK (2nd choice)*
   -3   *Idem*   *Rejected*
   -4   *Idem*   on 7134M
NOTE: An earlier attempt to record this composition had been on W98247.

W98358-1 GRIEG To Spring *and* GRAINGER One more   *Rejected*
   -2   day, my John (Sailor's sea-chanty)   *Rejected*
   -3   *Idem*   *Rejected*
W98359-1 GRIEG Wedding Day at Troldhaugen   *Rejected*
   -2   *Idem*   *Rejected*
W144246-1 GRAINGER Molly on the shore   *Rejected*
   -2   *Idem*   *Rejected*
   -3   *Idem*   on 2057M
15 June 1927
W98358-4 GRIEG To Spring *and* GRAINGER one more   *Rejected*
   -5   day, my John (Sailor's sea-chanty)   on 7150M
W98359-3 GRIEG Wedding day at Troldhaugen *OK (2nd choice)*
   -4   *Idem*   on 7150M
   -5   *Idem*   *Rejected*
W144206-4 BRAHMS *arr.* GRAINGER Cradle song *OK (2nd choice)*
   -5   *Idem*   on 2057M
   -6   *Idem*   *Rejected*
22 November 1927
W98410-1 GRAINGER The Power of love   *Rejected*
   -2   Anita Atwater (soprano) Ralph Leopold   *Rejected*
   -3   (Harmonium) etc.   *Rejected*
W98412-1 GRAINGER Gum Sucker's March   on 7147M
   -2   *Idem*   *Rejected*
   -3   *Idem*   *OK (2nd choice)*

† Dubbing on MJA 1968-2 (33 rpm)

W145228-1 Lord Peter's stable boy (Danish folk song   *Rejected*
   -2   collected by E. T. Kristensen and   *Rejected*
   -3   P. Grainger) P. Grainger (piano) and *Wax not used*
        R. Leopold (harmonium)
25 November 1927
W145237-1 GRAINGER Shepherd's hey   *Rejected*
   -2   The Columbia Symphony Orchestra   *Rejected*
   -3   conducted by Percy Grainger   *OK (2nd choice)*
   -4   *Idem*   on 163M
20 December 1927
W98410-4 GRAINGER The Power of love   *Rejected*
   -5   Anita Atwater (soprano), Ralph Leopold   *Rejected*
   -6   (piano) and Percy Grainger   on 7147M
        (harmonium) etc.
W145228-4 Lord Peter's stable boy (Danish folk song   *Rejected*
   -5   collected by E. T. Kristensen and *OK (2nd choice)*
   -6   P. Grainger) P. Grainger (piano) and   on 163M
        R. Leopold (harmonium)
22 December 1927
W145385-1 GRAINGER A Colonial song, Pt. 1   *OK (2nd choice)*
   -2   Anita Atwater (sop.), Luis Alberto   *Rejected*
   -3   Sanchez (tenor) with Orchestra   on 2066M
        cond. P. Grainger
W145386-1 GRAINGER A Colonial song, Pt. 2   *Rejected*
   -2   Anita Atwater (sop.), Luis Alberto   on 2066M
   -3   Sanchez (tenor) with Orchestra   *OK (2nd choice)*
        cond. Percy Grainger
28 May 1928
W98507-1 SCHUMANN Etudes symphoniques, Op. 13, Pt. 1 *Rejected*
   -    Theme; Var. 1; Etude 1; Var. 2;   *OK (2nd choice)*
   3   Etude 2   on 67506D
W98508-1 SCHUMANN Etudes symphoniques, Op. 13, on 67506D
   -2   Pt. 2, Etude 3; Var. 3; Etude 4;   *Rejected*
   -3   Var. 4; Etude 5; Var. 5; Etude 6 *OK (2nd choice)*
W98540-1 SCHUMANN Etudes symphoniques,   *OK (2nd choice)*
   -2   Pt. 3, Var. 6; Etude 7; Var. 7;   on 67507D
   -3   Etude 8; Etude 9   *Rejected*
W98541-1 SCHUMANN Etudes symphoniques,   *OK (2nd choice)*
   -2   Pt. 4, Var. 8; Etude 10; Var. 9;   on 67507D
   -3   Etude 11; Etude 12 part 1   *Rejected*
W98542-1 SCHUMANN Etudes symphoniques,   *Rejected*
   -2   Pt. 5, Etude 12 Pt. 2   on 67508D
   -3   *Idem*   *OK (2nd choice)*
W98543-1 SCHUMANN Romance in F sharp   *OK (2nd choice)*
   -2   *Idem*   *Rejected*
   -3   *Idem*   on 67508D
NOTE: *The gap between W98508 and W98540 consists of numbers assigned to another studio and does not include anything performed by Percy Grainger.*

9 October 1928
W98593-1 CHOPIN Sonata in B flat minor,   *Rejected*
   -2   Op. 35, Doppio movimento, Pt. 1   on 67603D†
   -3   *Idem*   *OK (2nd choice)*
W98594-1 CHOPIN Sonata in B flat minor,   on 67603D†
   -2   Op. 35, Doppio movimento, Pt. 2 *OK (2nd choice)*
        and Scherzo, Pt. 1   *Rejected*
W98595-1 CHOPIN Sonata in B flat minor,   *Rejected*
   -2   Op. 35, Scherzo, Pt. 2   on 67604D†
   -3   *Idem*   *OK (2nd choice)*
W98596-1 CHOPIN Sonata in B flat minor,   *Rejected*
   -2   Op. 35, Marche funebre, Pt. 1   on 67604D†
   -3   *Idem*   *OK (2nd choice)*
W98597-1 CHOPIN Sonata in B flat minor,   *Rejected*
   -2   Op. 35, Marche funebre, Pt. 2   on 67605D†
   -3   and Finale: Presto   *Rejected*
W98598-1 CHOPIN Etude, Op. 25, No. 10,   *Rejected*
   -2   B minor   *Rejected*
   -3   *Idem*   *OK (2nd choice)*
   -4   *Idem*   on 67605D†
21 January 1929
W98613-1 Jutish medley, Pt. 1, for piano solo *OK (2nd choice)*
   -2   Danish Folk Songs collected by   *Rejected*
   -3   Evald Tang Kristensen and   on 50129D
        P. Grainger
W98614-1 Jutish medley, Pt. 2, for piano solo *OK (2nd choice)*
   -2   Danish Folk Songs collected by   *Rejected*
   -3   Evald Tang Kristensen and   on 50129D
        P. Grainger
W147871-1 Ramble on love, Pt. 1   *OK (2nd choice)*
   -2   (On themes from *Der Rosen-*   on 1898D
   -3   *kavalier* by Richard Strauss)   *Rejected*

† Dubbing on MJA 1968-2 (33 rpm).

W147872-1	Ramble on love, Pt. 2			Rejected
-2	(On themes from *Der Rosen-*			OK (2nd choice)
-3	kavalier by Richard Strauss)			on 1898D
14 October 1930				
W150875-1	GRAINGER Handel in the Strand			Rejected
-2	*Idem*			Rejected
-3	*Idem*			Rejected
W150876-1	GRAINGER The Hunter in his career			Rejected
13 October 1931				
W98743-1	BACH *Toccata and Fugue in			on 68003D‡
-2	D minor, Pt. 1			Rejected
W98744-1	BACH *Toccata and Fugue in			Rejected
-2	D minor, Pt. 2			on 68003D‡
W98745-1	BACH, arr. LISZT Prelude and Fugue in			on 68004D‡
-2	A minor, Pt. 1			Rejected
W98746-1	BACH, arr. LISZT Prelude and Fugue in			on 68004D‡
-2	A minor, Pt. 2			Rejected
W98747-1	BACH arr. LISZT Prelude and Fugue in			Rejected
-2	A minor, Pt. 3 *and* Fantasia and			on 68005D‡
	Fugue in G minor, Pt. 1			
15 October 1931				
W98748-1	BACH, arr. LISZT Fantasia and Fugue			on 68005D‡
-2	in G minor, Pt. 2			Rejected
W98749-1	BACH, arr. LISZT Fantasia and Fugue in			Rejected
-2	G minor, Pt. 3			on 68006D‡
W98750-1	Blithe bells (A Free ramble by Percy			Rejected
-2	Grainger on Bach's aria 'Sheep			on 68006D
	may graze in safety')			

* On W98743 and W98744 Mr. Grainger uses 'alternately the Tausig and Busoni transcriptions', in a combination he himself has made.

ACOUSTIC RECORDINGS

Matrix of one side	Matrix of other side	Original Catalogue number	Reissue number	Great Britain
12"				
49243-3	49248-2	A6000		L1302
49281-1	49296-2	A6027		
49441-1	49442-1	A6060		
49561-3	49562-3	A6115		L1368
49639-1	49640-1	A6128		
49748-2	49749-2	A6145		
49750-2	49751-2	A6161		
49295-5	49921-1	A6192	7002M	
98000-2	98001-3	A6205	7003M	L1441
49933-2	49999-1	A6217		
10"				
79715-3	79716-3	A3381	2002M	
80487-3	80488-3	A3685	2000M	
81298-1	81324-2	30006D	2003M	
81587-1	81588-4	30010D	2004M	
81582-4	81583-3	30019D	2025M	
81299-2	81323-3	33001D	2001M	
			also 183M	

12" (Alternate couplings for Great Britain)

49249-1	49295-5	NOTE: 49249-1 issued only on	L1386
49296-2	49441-1		L1352

ELECTRIC RECORDINGS

Matrix of one side	Matrix of other side	Original Catalogue number	Great Britain
12"			
W98171-3	(Not Grainger)	7111M	
W98175-3	W98176-3	7104M	
W98177-2	W98178-1	67158Dzz in	L1695
W98179-1	W98180-1	67159DzzSet 32	L1696
W98181-1	W98182-1	67160Dzz	L1697
W98217-2	W98218-2	67183Dzz	L1954
W98219-1	W98220-2	67184Dzz in	L1955
W98221-1	W98222-1	67185DzzSet 37	L1956
W98223-1	W98224-3	67186Dzz	L1957
W98245-1	W98249-1	7109M	L1805
W98246-1	W98248-2	7124M	L1829
W98251-1	W98357-4	7134M	
W98353-3	W98354-3	67509Dzz in	
W98355-2	W98356-3	67510DzzSet 102	
W98358-5	W98359-4	7150M	
W98412-1	W98410-1	7147M	
W98507-3	W98508-1	67506Dzz in	
W98540-2	W98541-2	67507DzzSet 102	

‡ Dubbing on anonymous MVD 0887 (33 rpm).

Matrix of one side	Matrix of other side	Original Catalogue number	Great Britain
12"			
W98542-3	W98543-3	67507Dzz	
W98593-2	W98594-1	67603Dzz in	
W98595-2	W98596-2	67604DzzSet 116	
W98597-2	W98598-4	67605Dzz	
W98613-1	W98614-3	50129D	
W98743-1	W98744-2	68004Dzz in	
W98745-1	W98746-2	68005DzzSet 166	
W98747-2	W98748-1	68005Dzz	
W98749-2	W98750-2	68006Dzz	
10"			
W144204-3	W144205-2	154M	
W144246-3	W144206-2	2057M	D1664
W145237-4	W145228-6	163M	
W145385-3	W145386-2	2066M	DB28
W147871-3	W147872-3	1898D	

*

The Aeolian Company
'Pianola' Piano ['make' as printed on label]
Disc, 12" 78 rpm, issued by the Aeolian Co. Ltd., perhaps as a demonstration of the pianola; apparently electrical recording
[side] 1 ELGAR Salut d'amour
        J. H. Clapham (pianola) *taken from piano roll*
[side] 2 GRIEG To Spring
        Percy Grainger (pianola) *taken from piano roll*

*

Decca (U.S.A.)
Electric recordings; 78 rpm; 10".
(NOTE: The Decca system of matrix numbers is very individual but the data below is correct, in spite of the apparent anomalies in matrix order and date)

29 December 1944		
72665	GERSHWIN The Man I love	Unpublished
72666	GRIEG Theme from the Concerto in	Unpublished
	A minor, Op. 16 (*Arr.* Grainger)	
72607	GRAINGER Country Gardens *and*	Unpublished
	One more day, my John	
4 April 1945		
72806	ARNDT Nola	Unpublished
72807	SCOTT Lento	24160 in A 586
72813W	GERSHWIN The Man I love	Unpublished
72812W	COWELL The Aeolian harp *and*	Unpublished
	The Lilt of the reel	
73613	GERSHWIN The Man I love	Unpublished
13 April 1945		
72821W	(*Arr.* Grainger) Molly on the shore	24158 in A 586
11 June 1945		
72925	GRIEG Theme from the Concerto in	Unpublished
	A minor (*Arr.* Grainger)	
73156	GERSHWIN Love walked in	Unpublished
5 September 1945		
73071	GRAINGER Country Gardens *and*	24159 in A 586
	One more day, my John	
73059	DETT Joba Dance *and* Excerpt	24159 in A 586
	(Night) from Prelude	
24 September 1945		
W73059	SCOTT Danse nègre *and*	24160 in A 586
	HORN arr. SCOTT: Cherry Ripe	
W73055	STANFORD, arr. GRAINGER Irish	24158 in A 586
	Tune from County Derry	

The six 10" sides were numbered as indicated, and issued as Decca Album A 586 'PERCY GRAINGER—Favorite piano solos.'
Later Grainger made some (tape) recordings for American Decca with the Goldman Band, under the direction of Richard Franko Goldman. The only item to be identified is:
15 August 1957
103078 Arr. GRAINGER Over the hills and far   on DL 8633
        away (Children's march), Percy Grainger
        (piano) and the Goldman Band, cond.
        Richard Franko Goldman

RCA Victor
LM 1238 issued 1951
GRAINGER Country gardens
    Shepherd's hey
    Molly on the shore
    Mock morris
    Early one morning
    Handel in the strand
    Irish Tune from County Derry
Percy Grainger (piano) with Symphony Orchestra cond. Leopold Stokowski
It is not clear from the record labels and sleeve that Grainger himself takes part in any of the pieces other than Handel in the Strand
The following items from LM1238 were issued on a 45 in the USA on RCA Victor ERA 124 and in the UK on HMV 7ER5046
Molly on the shore; Handel in the Strand; Mock Morris; Irish tune from County Derry

Vanguard
One double-sided 12" mono LP was manufactured by Vanguard but for various reasons was not officially placed on sale; surviving copies seem to originate from stores in New York which received stock before the record was withdrawn
Recorded 25 February 1957 public performance in Denmark

VRS 1098A   GRIEG Concerto in A minor, Op. 16
    Percy Grainger, piano, with Aarhus Municipal Orchestra, cond. Per Drier

VRS 1098B   GRAINGER Country gardens
    Ramble on love (*arr. from Der Rosenkavalier* by Richard Strauss)
    Percy Grainger, piano
    Suite on Danish folk songs
    Percy Grainger, piano, with Aarhus Municipal Orchestra cond. Per Drier

INDEX TO COMPOSERS AND TITLES OF WORKS RECORDED BY GRAINGER ON COMMERCIAL RECORDS (EXCLUDING RECORDS MADE FROM PIANO ROLLS)

GRAMOPHONE RECORDS MADE FROM PIANO ROLLS PLAYED BY PERCY GRAINGER

Discs are mono 33 rpm unless otherwise stated

GRAINGER Eastern Intermezzo
— Gay but wistful *(in a nutshell)*
— Gum sucker's march *(In a nutshell)*
— Walking tune
  Above all on BBC 31255

— Colonial song
— Country gardens
— Irish tune from County Derry
— Molly on the shore
— Shepherd's hey
— Spoon river
— Sussex mummer's Christmas carol
  Above all on Everest ('Archives of piano music') 913: X913
  (stereo)
GRIEG Ballade, Op. 24, G minor. Klavier KS101 (stereo); Distinguished Recordings DR108
— Concerto, Op. 16, A minor. Klavier KS101 (stereo); BBC 31256
— Erotik, Op. 43, No. 5. Klavier KS101 (stereo)

— To spring, Op. 43, No. 6. Aeolian 'Pianola Piano' 2 (78 rpm); Klavier KS101 (stereo)
— Wedding day at Troldhaugen, Op. 65, No. 6. Klavier KS101 (stereo)
GRIEG, *arr.* GRAINGER Peer Gynt Suite No. 1. Distinguished Recordings DR108
LISZT Hungarian Rhapsody No. 12. BBC 31254; Klavier KS109 (stereo)
— Polonaise No. 2, E major. Klavier KS109 (stereo)
SCHUMANN Etudes symphoniques, Op. 13. Klavier KS109 (stereo)
— *Idem* Nos. 1–8 only. BBC 31255
— Romanze, Op. 28, No. 2, F sharp. Klavier KS109 (stereo)
— Sonata, Op. 22, G minor. Klavier KS105 (stereo)
SCOTT, *arr.* GRAINGER Symphonic dance No. 1. Klavier KS102 (stereo)
STANFORD Irish Dances Nos. 3 and 4. Everest ('Archives of piano music') 909: X909 (stereo)
STRAUSS, R. Till Eulenspiegel. Klavier KS102 (stereo)
TCHAIKOVSKY Romeo and Juliet. Klavier KS102 (stereo)

MISCELLANEOUS

Interview, with special reference to Cyril Scott, USA. BIRS tape 2112W
Broadcast interview, excerpt. BBC Transcription 126829
Interview, with John Amis. 1 July 1959. BBC LP27562
Talk about Grieg. 15 June 1959. BBC LP27558
In programme about Nellie Melba: 'Portrait of a prima donna'. 15 Dec. 1950. BBC LP27971–2
CBS interview 3 Aug. 1952. BIRS tape M4524W
Free Music experiments introduced by P. Grainger. 2 Nov. 1951. BIRS tape M4524W
Sea sketch fragments with solo voxes (12 takes) introduced by Burnett Cross. 10 Feb. 1950. BIRS tape M4524R
Experiment with Butterfly piano, introduced by P. Grainger. BIRS tape M4525W
Tests with three oscillators introduced by Burnett Cross. Nov.-Dec. 1952. BIRS tape M4525R
Blithe bells, rehearsal. BIRS tape M4526W
Gliding chords from reed box tone tool recorded on Mason G1 machine introduced by Burnett Cross. BIRS tape M4527W
Vocal experiments and Free music machine examples with slowing down by Grainger of folk music cylinders for analysis of time measures. BIRS M4528R
Gliding tones and Butterfly piano, introduced by P. Grainger. BIRS tape M4526R
Experiments with Reeds: Burnett Cross and Howard Cross. 29 Jan. 1951. BIRS tape M4528R
The Lonely desert man, rehearsal etc. (A series of experiments in recording various voices and instruments, solo and in combination, eventually arriving at some sort of synthesis by playing the recordings and superimposing another performance.) Percy and Ella Grainger, Mr. and Mrs. and Howard Cross, Burnett Cross, William Durrieu, (cello).
Various dates in August 1949. BIRS tape T449W
Vocal experiment,s with a number of voices; gliding tones. BIRS tape M4531W

Phonograph cylinders of folk music, sung by peasants, collected early in the century by Percy Grainger. Transferred to tape from unprocessed discs which Mr. Grainger presented to the Institute, with annotated manuscript scores, during his visits to the Institute in 1956/8. BIRS tapes 209–218W & R
Joseph Taylor was among the singers in this collection. At Percy Grainger's suggestion HMV made acoustic 78 rpm discs of him as follows in 1908 (catalogue numbers are shown in bold type):

Matrix
2518e Bold William Taylor **02148**
8747e Sprig o'thyme
8748e Died for love; Brigg Fair **3-2973**
8750e The White hare **3-2976**
8751e Lord Bateman **3-2972**
8752e Gypsy's wedding day; Rufford Park poacher
8753e Worcester city **8753e**
8754e Creeping Jane **3-2974**
8756e Murder of Maria Martin; Sprig o'thyme **3-2971**
These, with the following cylinders taken from the above-mentioned Grainger collection have appeared on Leader LEA4050 (33 rpm):
Joseph Taylor: Bold Nevison (cylinder 110);
  Landlord and tenant (cylinder 106)
Mr Thompson: Lord Bateman (cylinders 95–96)
Joseph Leaning: The Sheffield apprentice (cylinders 100/101/102);
  The Green bushes (cylinder 100)
George Gouldthorpe: Horkstow grange (cylinder 84)
George Wray: Lord Melbourne (cylinder 111)
Dean Robinson: Bold Robin Hood (cylinder 130);
  T'owd yowe wi'one horn (cylinder 131)

The Institute wishes to express its thanks to Mr. William Fitzwater for identifying and annotating the Free music and other experimental recordings listed above.

Recordings and Piano Rolls Made by Grainger

GERALD STONEHILL

Bach-Liszt. *Organ Fantasia & Fugue,* G minor 7161 & 7174, 1927.

Bizet-Grainger. *L'Arlésienne* Suite 524 & 525: D611 & D613, 1925.

Brahms-Grainger. *Cradle Song,* Op. 49, No. 4 6718: D1019, 1923.

Chopin. *Etude,* Op. Posth, No. 2, A flat 6548, 1921.

Debussy. *Toccata* (Pour le piano) 6409, 1921.

Delius. *Piano Concerto,* 1921 (2 rolls).

Delius-Grainger. *Brigg Fair* 7443, 1933 (for 2 pianos, with Ralph Leopold).

————. *North Country Sketches* 7190, 7191 & 7192, 1928 (for 2 pianos, with Ralph Leopold).

Dett. *Juba Dance* (*In the Bottoms*) 6339, 1920.

Faure-Grainger. *Nell* 6931, 1926.

Gardiner. *Humoresque* 6415, 1921.

Grainger. *Colonial Song* 5666, 1915.

————. *Country Gardens* 6149, 1919.

————. *Eastern Intermezzo* 6997, 1926.

————. *Idem* (for 6 hands — 4-hand roll) 1185, 1926.

————. *In a Nutshell.* Gay But Wistful 6072, 1919. Gum-sucker's March (*In a Nutshell*) 6059, 1919.

————. *Irish Tune from County Derry* 5679, 1915.

————. *Jutish Medley* (Danish Folk Music Settings No. 8) 7274, 1928.

————. *Lullaby* (*Tribute to Foster*) 5821, 1917.

————. *Molly on the Shore* 6284, 1920.

————. *Mock Morris* 5688, 1915.

————. *One More Day, My John* 6030, 1919.

————. *Over the Hills and Far Away* 6368, 1920 (with Lotte M. Hough).

————. *Idem* (second piano part only) 1184, 1920.

————. *A Reiver's Neck Verse* (song accompaniment for tenor or soprano), 1925.

————. *Shepherd's Hey* 5661, 1915.

————. *Spoon River* 6617, 1923.

————. *Sussex Mummer's Christmas Carol* 5712, 1915.

————. *Two Musical Relics of My Mother* (a) Hermund the Evil (Hermundi Illi, a Dorset tune), (b) As Sally Sat A-Weeping 6760, 1924 (with Rose Grainger).

————. *Walking Tune* 5735, 1916.

————. *The Warriors,* 1927 [Specially made for the 100th anniversary of Denton, Cottier & Daniels, Buffalo, N.Y.].

————. *Zanzibar Boat Song* 6824, 1925.

Grieg. *Ballade in G Minor*, Op. 24 7437, 1933.

_____. *Concerto in A Minor*, Op. 16 (with orchestral accompaniment adapted and added by Grainger) 6475, 6479 & 6485: D93, D95 & D97, 1921.

_____. *Erotik*, Op. 43, No. 5 6693, 1924.

_____. *6 Norwegian Folksongs*, Op. 66 (1. Cattle Call. 2. Love Song. 10. Wedding Song. 14. In Old Valley. 19. Gjerdine's Cradle Song. 16. Peasant Dance. 18. Wrapt in Thought I Wander) 7377, 1930.

_____. *To Spring*, Op. 43, No. 6 6206, 1920.

_____. *Wedding Day at Troldhaugen*, Op. 65, No. 6 7370, 1930.

Grieg-Grainger. *Peer Gynt Suite*, Op. 46, No. 1 (1. Morning 3. Anitra's dance 6522, 1922. 2. Ase's Death. 4. In the Hall of the Mountain King 6530, 1922).

Guion. *Sheep and Goat Walking to the Pasture* 7083, 1927.

_____. *Turkey in the Straw* 6444, 1921.

Handel-Grainger. *Hornpipe (Water Music)* 6754, 1924.

Liszt. *Hungarian Rhapsody* No. 12 6497, 1921.

_____. *Polonaise* No. 2 in E 6668, 1923.

Schumann. *Etudes Symphoniques*, Op. 13, 1925. Nos. 1-8 6859; Nos. 9-12 6868.

_____. *Romanze*, Op. 28, No. 2, F sharp 6384, 1920.

_____. *Sonata*, Op. 22, No. 2, G minor 7361, 7362 & 7363, 1930.

Scott. *Lento*, Op. 35, No. 1 (*2 Pierrot Pieces*) 7252, 1929.

_____. *Lotus Land*, Op. 47, No. 1 7217, 1929.

Scott-Grainger. *Symphonic Dance* No. 1 6514, 1922 (with Cyril Scott).

Stanford-Grainger. *Four Irish Dances* (1. March Jig 5838, 1918. 3. Leprechaun's Dance 6572: D287, 1922. 4. Reel 6117, 1919).

R. Strauss. *Till Eulenspiegels lustige Streiche*, Op. 28 7400, 1932 (arranged for two pianos; with R. Leopold).

Tchaikovsky. *Concerto*, Op. 23, No. 1, in B flat minor C1087-90, 1925 (solo part only).

_____. *Romeo & Juliet, Fantasy-Overture* 7351, 1930 (arranged for four hands; with R. Leopold).

Tchaikovsky-Grainger. *Nutcracker Suite*, Op. 71a, (a) March, (b) Dance of the Sugar Plum Fairy, (c) Russian Dance, (d) Trepak 6798, (e) Arab Dance, (f) Chinese Dance, (g) Dance of the Reed Flutes 6810, 1924, (h) Paraphrase on the Valse des Fleurs 6085, 1919.

Appendix C
Selected Writings by Percy Grainger

My Wretched Tone-Life

Let no-one read this book who dislikes hearing a man call himself an over-soul (genius); for that's what I'm going to do all the time. What do I mean by over-soul (genius)? I mean a man who feels himself more answerable for the sorrows & witless-nesses of the world than most men. A sweetly gifted, yet lesser, over-soul (genius) like Mendelssohn does not seem to have been overly churned-up by the griefs & unjust-nesses of life, while more gifted men — such as Bach, the writer of "The Saga of Grettir the Strong", Thurston Jonsson, Hogarth — are held in a cramp of rack-pain (agony) at the sorrows they see happening "under the sun". In my own case, every time I see a paper napkin I mourn for the woods that are being thoughtlessly wasted; every time I see a bit of wrought-ore (metal) I tremble for the men — the miners — who are losing their lives needlessly in the mines, just because the world has gone mad about wrought-ore (metal). If all people felt as I do they would never use a piece of wrought-ore (metal) without first wondering whether its useful-ness weighs up against the might-be-ness (possibility) of a man's death. Fancy an age in which men take their children to watch men & women do life-risking acts on the trapeze & in the lion-cage — an age in which prize-fighting & wrestling are law-hallowed (sanctioned) while nakedness & lewdness (such guilt-less mirth) are not!

We live in an art-rich age because of all the heart-breaking things that are happening all around us — young men needlessly killed in the wars, people dying before their time because of their silly eating-wonts & living-wonts, millions of tame-beasts (animals) murdered every day, countless love-stirs & art-stirs bootlessly squelched because of the mood of vie-ment (competition) & sin-search we live in. In such an age the only thing an art-man (artist) can do is to let out one everlasting grumble-shout (protest). And the sourer the grumble, the louder the shout, the greater the art-man (artist). That is why I feel myself to be an over-soul (genius); because ever since I was about 7 years old I have felt the cruel-hoods (cruelty) & mean-nesses of the world like a knife going through me. When I was about 7 (I know the age because my father left my

mother & me when I was about 7) I saw an etching in "The Illustrated London News", or some such weekly-paper, of some as-
good-as-naked Matabelle warriors charging a square of British
fight-for-pay-men (soldiers), with the British mowing the Mata-
beles down with Maxim-guns. I said to my father: "Isn't it a shame
to kill lovely, brave naked men like that?" (for at that time I was
making drawings of Greek shape-art-pieces (statues) & I deemed
nakedness a great goodness & clothes a proof-of-folly). My father
laughed & said: "You'll feel differently about these things as you
grow older." But I knew I never would & I said to myself that I
would never forgive my father for what he had said (for not mind-
ing the hero-mooded Matabelles being mowed down without their
having a chance, I mean). And I never have. And that is why my
tone-works (compositions) are full of hangings, drownings, murders, jailings, death-for-loves's-sake, knights mouldering in ditches,
the sad fates of young men killed before their time and grumble-
shouts (protests) against town-skill-th (civilization). (Hangings:
Dedication, The Reiver's Neck-Verse, Danny Deever. Drownings:
The Bride's Tragedy, The Sea Life. Murders: Father and Daughter,
The Rival Brothers. Jailings: The Running of Shindand. Death-
for-love's sake: Died for Love, Near Woodstock Town. The sad
fates of young men killed before their time: The Power of Rome
and the Christian Heart, The Widow's Party, Soldier, Soldier.
Knights mouldering in ditches: The Three Ravens, The Twa Cor-
bies. Grumble-shouts (protests) against town-skill-th (civilisation):
Kipling "Jungle-book". Cycle, Hill-songs I & II.)

Almost the only part of my tonery (music) that isn't doom-
mooded is that part dealing with the mankind-less world of the
hill, the sea, the sand-wastes (deserts).

And if it is true that art in our time is merely a grumble-shout
(protest) about the hinder-able (preventable) doom plays (tragedies) of an only half-pity-swayed world, what will art do in the
fair years to come, when all the wrongs are righted & most of the
sorrows are blunted (for example: If men can learn to live to be 100
years old & more, grief at their dying will be much softened by the
thought that they have lived to such a ripe age)? Art can come to
an end & stop smearing life with a tale of woe. But with life as it
is — an endless again-&-again-ness (repetition) of hinder-able
doom-plays (preventable tragedies) — I deem myself an over-soul
(genius) because I answer so sharply to life's rack-pains (agonies).

To some it will seem as if my stand-take-ment (attitude) as a foe
of war, cruel-hood (cruelty) & wastefulness is weakened (indeed,

utterly set at nought) by my having be-sung & be-praised fight-keen-th (bellicosity), cruel-hood-worship (sadism) & wreck-fain-th (destructiveness) in such tone-works (compositions) as *The Warriors, The Lads of Wamphray, The Ballad of the "Bolivar"*. And such works are true self-lay-bare-ments (self-revealments). For I am as cruel as I am kind, as merciless as I am sorrow-sharing. The wildly-happiest time-specks (moments) in my life have been whipping the naked bodies of women, or being whipped myself — I don't care which, as long as pain is given or taken. I am an un-cure-able (incurable) whip-worshipper. But I will deal with that side of my life in another book. An over-soul (genius) covers a lot of ground, & all we can ask of him is that he is evenly strong at both ends.

Remarks on Hill Song Nr. 1

I consider Hill-Song No. 1 by far the best of all my compositions. But the difficulties of conducting its highly irregular rhythms are almost prohibitive. At the time of composing Hill-Song No. 1 (1901-1902, aged 19-20) wildness and fierceness were the qualities in life and nature that I prized most & wished to express in music. These elements were paramount in my favorite literature — the Icelandic sagas. I was in love with the double-reeds (oboe, English horn, etc.) as the wildest & fiercest of musical tone-types. In 1900 I had heard a very harsh-toned rustic oboe (piffero) in Italy, some extremely nasal Egyptian double-reeds at the Paris Exhibition & bagpipes in the Scottish Highlands. I wished to weave these snarl-ing, nasal sounds (which I had heard only in single-line melody) into a polyphonic texture as complex as Bach's, as democratic as Australia (by "democratic", in a musical sense, I mean a practice of music in which each voice that makes up the harmonic weft enjoys equal importance & independence — as contrasted with "undemocratic" music consisting of a dominating melody sup-ported by subservient harmony.) In this way I wished to give mu-sical vent to feelings aroused by the soul-shaking hill-scapes I had recently seen on a three days tramp in Western Argyleshire. I was not in favor of program-music. I had no wish to portray tonally any actual scenes or even to record musically any impressions of nature. What I wanted to convey, in my Hill-Song, was *the nature of the hills themselves* — as if the hills themselves were telling of themselves through my music, rather than that I, an onlooker, were recording my "impressions" of the hills. (In this respect my purpose, in Hill-Song No. 1, differed radically from Delius's in his "Song of the High Hills". I asked him whether he, in that noblest of nature-music, had aimed at letting the hills speak of themselves, as it were, or whether, instead, his aim had been to record in music the impressions received by a man in viewing the face of nature. He said that the latter had been his intention. When Delius and I first met, in 1907, we felt a very close compositional affinity. Our chordal writing seemed to both of us almost identical in type. And this was not unnatural; for although, up to then, we had seen nothing of each other's work, our melodic & harmonic inheritances came from much the same sources: Bach, Wagner, Greig & folk-music. It was Delius who arranged for the first public performance of my larger compositions. His favorites among my works were my first & second Hill-Songs, which I played to him in 1907. He had always been devoted to the mountains of Norway. So it was no surprise to me to see that pinnacle of his muse, "The Song of the High Hills", emerge around 1911.)

The musical idiom of Hill-Song No. 1 derives much of its character from certain compositional experiments I had undertaken in 1898, 1899 & 1900 & from certain nationalistic attitudes that were natural to me as an Australian. As chief among these may be mentioned:

Wide-toned Scales

From my Australian standpoint I naturally wanted to make my music as island-like (British, Irish, Icelandic, Scandinavian) as possible, & as unlike the music of the European Continent as I could. Since I thought that close intervals (diatonic or chromatic) were characteristic of the European continent, while "gapped scales" (3-tone, 4-tone, 5-tone, 6-tone scales) were typical of Britain & the other North Sea islands, I strove to make my melodic intervals as wide as possible. Wishing to avoid half-tones (chromatic) as much as I could I embarked around 1898 on a study of the possibilities of whole-tone melody & harmony. In Hill-Song No. 1 the melodic results of these whole-tone studies may be seen in the C natural in bar 26 (Ex. 1), in the D natural in bar 42 (Ex. 2), in the top voice of bars 116-119 (Ex. 3), & in countless other places. The harmonic influence of these whole-tone studies is evident in bars 83-85 (Ex. 4), bars 88-91, bars 273-276 (Ex. 5), bars 322-324 (Ex. 6), bars 343-346 (Ex. 7) & throughout the whole work. The continual use of the "flat seventh (B flat in C major), as seen in bars 269-272 (Ex. 8), is another result of this predilection for wide intervals. (Here was an influence presumably drawn from Grieg; for I did not encounter English folksingers — whose art abounds, of course, in flat sevenths — until 2 years later.)

Irregular Rhythms

Studies in the rhythms of prose speech that I undertook in 1899 led to such irregular barrings as those in bars 69-74 of Love Verses from "The Song of Solomon" (Ex. 9), composed 1899-1900, which (as far as I know) was the first use of such irregular rhythms in modern times, though of course Claude Le Jeune (1528-1602), in his "non-metrical" pieces, used rhythms quite as irregular. (The "innoculation" of the European continent with my irregular rhythms is easily traceable. Cyril Scott, with my enthusiastic permission, adopted my irregular rhythms in his Piano Sonata, op. 66, written 1908. This finest of all modern piano sonatas was widely played in Central Europe by Alfred Hoehn soon after its appearance. By 1913 these irregular rhythms appear in Stravinsky's "Rite of Spring" & in other modernistic music of that period.) The rhythmic irregularities launched in Love Verses from "The Song of Solomon" were carried to much greater lengths in Hill-Song No. 1.

"Democratic" Polyphony

My Australian ideal of a many-voiced texture in which all, or most, of the tone-strands (voices, parts) enjoy an equality of prominence & importance led to such passages as bars 51-60 (Ex. 10) & bars 347-350 (Ex. 11).

Semi-discordant Triads

Around 1898 I adopted the practice of adding mild discords to triads & regarding the combinations thus arrived at as full concords — concords with which it would be suitable to close a composition or a section or phrase. Thus in 1899 I ended "Rustic Dance" (2nd movement of my "Youthful Suite") with the chord F, C, A, D, F (Ex. 12) & in 1901 ended "Willow Willow" with the chord E, B, G, D (Ex. 13). Hill-Song No. 1 also closes with the last-named chord (Ex. 14). In bar 328 (Ex. 15) is seen the addition of the second of the scale to a minor triad. Typical results of the adding of mild discords to triads may be seen in Ex. 16. (Debussy ended the first act of "Pelleas" with the Chord F sharp, C sharp, A sharp, D sharp, G sharp. But "Pelleas" did not reach my ears or those of the musical public until 1902. I saw the score of "Pelleas" during the summer of 1902, when Hill-Song No. 1 was virtually completed. However, there are a few bars in Hill-Song No. 1 that were composed after my contact with "Pelleas" & I think they show the influence of Debussy.) (bars 134-137, Ex. 20)

Triads in Conjunct Motion

As a form of "harmonic melodiousness" — in which all the component notes of the harmony move to the same degree in the same direction (as contrasted with normal harmonic procedures in which some, at least, of the component parts of the harmony move in contrary motion to the melody) — I introduced into my music, well before the turn of the century, passages of triads in conjunct motion. One of the earliest instances is in "Eastern Intermezzo" (4th movement of my "Youthful Suite") composed around 1898 (Ex. 17). Instances in Hill-Song No. 1 are bars 297-298 (Ex. 19) and bars 328-329 (Ex. 19).

Non-repetition of Themes

No thematic or melodious material is repeated in Hill-Song No. 1, except immediate repetition within a phrase, as in the case of bars 393-397. I view the repetition of themes as a redundancy — as if a speaker should continually repeat himself. I also consider the repetition of themes undemocratic — as if the themes were singled out for special consideration & the rest of the musical material deemed "unfit for quotation".

Non-architectural Form-procedures

As music does not stand complete at any one moment (as architecture does), but unfolds itself in time — like a ribbon rolled out on the floor — I consider a flowing unfoldment of musical form to be part of the very nature of music itself. Therefore, in such a work as Hill-Song No. 1, I eschew all architectural up-buildment & try to avoid arbitrary treatments of musical ideas & the stressing of sectional divisions. My aim is to let each phrase grow naturally out of what foreran it & to keep the music continually at a white heat of melodic & harmonic inventiveness — never slowed up by cerebral afterthoughts or formulas. In other words, I want the music, from first to last, to be *all theme* & never thematic treatment.

Large Chamber-music

Under the influence of Bach's Brandenburg Concertos & the chamber music arias & recitatives in Bach's Passions I developed the idea of "large chamber-music" around 1898. This included comparatively small combinations for voice & instruments such as "Willow Willow" for voice, guitar & 4 strings (sketched 1901) & larger scorings such as Hill-Song No. 1 for as many as 24 single instruments — none of the instruments to be played "massed" as the strings are in the symphonic orchestra & even in the chamber orchestra. The earliest of my pieces for large chamber-music were thus written 10 years before Vaughan Williams's "On Wenlook Edge" 9 or 10 years before the Chamber Symphonies of Schönberg & Shreker, 14 years before Schönberg's "Pierrot Lunaire" & 22 years before Stravinsky's "Story of a Soldier".

The balance of tone in the Hill-Song No. 1 score is totally different to the balance of tone in an orchestral score. In the orchestra the strongest families are the strings & the brass. In Hill-Song No. 1 the double-reeds & saxophones constitute the strongest group, the brass the next strongest & the strings & harmonium the weakest. This over-weight of nasal & reedy tone-color in Hill-Song No. 1 makes for intensity of tone rather than for volume of tone. This carries out the main intention of the composition: to sound wild and fierce rather than grand or forceful. The original (1902) scoring of Hill-Song No. 1 was for 2 small flutes, 6 oboes, 6 English horns, 6 bassoons & double-bassoon. The present scoring (for small flute, flute, 6 double-reeds, 2 saxophones, 3 brass, percussion, harmonium, piano & 6 strings) was undertaken in 1921-1922, the non-double-reed instruments being introduced to provide a foil to the double-reed tone. To ensure a wide range of tone-strength differentiation I applied to large chamber music what I would call Wagner's "organ registration type of scoring". That is to say: where waxing and waning tone-strengths are called for in one and the same tone-strand ("voice" or "part") they are attained not merely by changing dynamics in the instruments playing the total tone-strand, but also by adding extra instruments to the tone-strand where a loudening of the tone [is] desired [and] by withdrawing the extra instruments where a softening of tone is intended.

To the best of my knowledge all of the procedures enumerated above were complete innovations at the time that Hill-Song No. 1 was conceived and scored.

Percy Aldridge Grainger, September, 1949.

English-Speaking Leadership
in Tone-Art

It is clear-to-see that the snobbish, priggish view of the English "County Families" — that all "foreigners" & "foreign ways" are abysmally below them & inferior to themselves & their own ways — is utterly justified by the facts of life, by the course of the way & by cultural history. Anybody who knows anything of modern life, anywhere in the world (but especially in Germany, Russia & other countries supposed to be go-ahead) knows that every thought they think in those lands is just a pale echo of thoughts first thought in England, Ireland, Scotland, America, Australia, etc. Most European countries have taken over into their languages English words that express thoughts that began in the English speaking world & nowhere else — such words as flirt, malthusianism, strikes, lock-outs, trams, trains, jazz, sport, cooperative societies, 5 o'clock tea, sandwich, bar, cocktail, cowboy, gangster, pre-raphaelite, tank, submarine. And these words form the roots of their modern thinking. There is not a people, anywhere (worse luck), who nourish any other wish than to be like the British, the Americans, the Australians. They want to share our prosperity. And since our prosperity is the outcome of our daring & original thinking, these foreign peoples would like to share our thoughts & our ways. So they imitate us, in politics, in music, in clothes, in sport. There is no experiment in politics that can be tried, in any land, except by some refugee who has lived for years in an English-speaking country & absorbed (wittingly or unwittingly) its thoughts. Take Russia: Built on the thoughts of Marx, who lived for years in England, & carried out by Lenin (who lived for years in England) & Trotsky (who lived in New York). Take Germany: Naziism is simply Boy-Scout-ism, invented by Baden-Powell. Take India: its hopes & procedures lit by Keir-Hardies's tour to India (1902-1908?). When Ibsen or Bjornson want to show a progressive Norwegian on the stage they show someone who has just come home from Nebraska or the Dakotas. When my mother & I went to Germany in 1895 we got a *Dream-book* (explanations of dreams, intended for low-class people) which contained: Sieht man einen Kapitan im Traum: es bedeutet "Gute Nachricht aus Amerika. A German joke of that time: An Englishman is criticising the Germans because they eat horse-flesh. The German says "But the English eat horse-flesh too — Ross-biff (roast beef)." Always the English-speaking thing is the chic thing, the sought-after thing. Everything that the wars are won by (air force, tanks, submarines, radar, commandos) are invented or worked out by English-speaking minds. The Allies end the 1st world war with tanks; so the Germans begin the next war with tanks. And so it goes, all along the line. Teetotalism, votes for women, lack of discipline for children, wholesale divorces, trampdom & hobo-ism, filibustering, boycotting, abolition of slavery — all these & many more are lovely English-speaking inventions (let us get up and take a bow).

This English-speaking leadership is no new thing. Why is the first (& always the longest) hero-poem in a Germanic tongue written in England (Beowulf)? Why is the most famous French mediaeval hero-poem (The Song of Roland) signed with a Scandinavian name — Torolfus (Icelandic *Thorulf*, English Thor-wolf)? (For of course from the standpoint of this article, the Scandinavians, the Dutch, the Norman French, the Low-Germans are all one — the seat of racial superiority.) Why were the finest prose novels of all time written in Iceland (the sagas)? Why was protestantism started in England before the Norman conquest? Why did English innovations in war-technic (the yeoman boymen at Crecy — or was it Agincourt? The small mobil English sea-craft of the Spanish Armada fight. The invention of gunpowder.) so often change war methods? Why did Charlemaine pick Alcuin for his library? Why were Germany & Scandinavia christianised by English missionaries? Is not Bede's Church Histories one of the first, biggest & best? Why is there no sign of complicated harmony & polyphony having come from great Southern-European culture-centers such as Rome or Constantinople? Why did the greatest Norwegian composer (Grieg) come on his father's side from a Scotch family — his father & grandfather having been British Consuls in Bergen? Why does an Italian inventor (Marconi) & a Flemish Author (Maeterlinck) have to have English mothers, in order to be great? Is there any non-Nordic Historical Record that can compare with the Anglo-saxon Chronicle in length-of-years, scope, power & charm? Why does Ibsen (the greatest 19th century play-wright) have to have Scottish blood? For an answer to these questions read James MacKinnon Fowler's epoch-making "False Foundations of British History" (Melbourne, 1943).

In hunting Superiority to its lair I am (as hinted before) not sundering English superiority from general Northern, or Nordic, superiority. Just as the British are superior to the European Continent as a whole, so are Scandinavians superior to the British, the Dutch & the Germans; so are the Dutch superior to the Germans & the French; so are the North Germans superior to the Southern Germans & the Austrians; so are the Northern French (the French Belgians, the Walloons, the old Burgundians) superior to the Southern French, the Italians, etc. In the art of music this Northern superiority has always been as clear as mud. It is obvious that European harmony lay wallowing in the organum-rut (harmonies made of nothing but fourths & fifths) until it became enriched by the Scandinavian thirds (Saint Magnus Hymn, Orkney. Was it 11th cent?), the English sixths & thirds (Fowles in the Frith). When John Dunstable (died 1453) went to the Burgundian court he made European music a present of 2 new intervals to be used in harmony; they had the 4th & 5th, & he gave them the 6th & the 3rd. John Field, discovering or developing pedal-held (as distinct from finger-held) piano-sonorities opened the door to the piano's richest music — Chopin. The musical innovations of 13th & 14th century England, the early innovations of Northern France (Guillaume de Machaut, Dufay, Le Jeune), the vast musical developments of the Netherlanders (responsible, I guess, for about 80 per cent of the formulas & traditions we call "classical music") are hard to exaggerate. These Northern musical cultures make those of Italy & Spain (any period) look like kindergarten stuff. And the same holds good of Northern Germany, as against Southern Germany & Austria. "My darling Austrians" one hears our nit-wit Nordics say. Everything is done to belittle the Prussians & North Germans (as everything is always done to belittle superior races) while everything nice is said of the South Germans & Austrians (because everybody feels comfortable in the presence of *inferiority*). "They are so artistic." "They are so music-loving." What are the facts? That all Austrian composers (Haydn, Mozart, Mahler. Maybe Schubert is an exception) are just rut-hounds, chewing the cud of superior North-German music & inferior Italian music. Compare with them the towering figures of North-German music: Handel, Bach, Beethoven, Weber, Wagner, Schumann, Brahms — all of them bristling with size & spirituality. And of these, the *Saxon* composers (Handel, Bach, Wagner, Schumann) show a marked emotional superiority over the other North German composers except Brahms, who was a North Scandinavian. And not without good reason. The Saxons were *North Sea Dwellers*, until they were moved South & East by Charlemain (I know that the modern Saxons are deemed to be full of Wendish & other Slavic blood.

There is seemingly enough Northernness left in them to allow them to easily overtop the other Germans, in music). No one in his right senses could compare a Bavarian like Richard Strauss with Saxons like Bach & Wagner.

But there are heights & heights. Just as the North Germans are vastly superior to the South Germans & Austrians, so do British & Scandinavian composers tower above even the best North Germans. At their best, even Bach, Wagner & Brahms always sound faked, or else rough-sounding. Brahms's loveliest tone-thoughts are marred by tweediness or grittiness of tone. And Wagner's & Bach's greatest moments are soiled by fakery, artificiality & beauty parlor tactics. They sound face-lifted. Compare Siegfried Idyll or Prelude to 3rd Act of Meistersinger (or the Preludes to Tristan & Parsifal, if you like) with Greig's *The Last Spring* for Strings. Or pit the very best in German chamber music (say Brahms) against the first 5-part Fantasy for viola by John Jenkins. In such competition the German gems sound unclean, impure, clumsy — just as Goethe & Nietsche read clumsy, uncertain & unconcentrated beside Walt Whitman & the Icelandic Sagas.

You will have noticed that I have said nothing about Jews in this discussion of racial superiorities & inferiorities. Not that I think there is nothing to say about the relative powers of Jews & non-Jews. My own personal experience would lead me to say that Jews are intellectually lazy (once they have found a way to earn a living) & feeble generally. My greatest objection to Jews (in Nordic communities) is that they seem to lower prosperity & the standard of achievement. If a Jew conducts an orchestra it soon ceases to pay. If Jews get into an artistic field (such as the movies) it soon gets *dull & boring* beyond the dullness of the dryest & most old-maidish Christian. But I would be unable to go into the Jewish Composer question without a mass of information (as to the degree of Jewishness in Jewish composers) which I neither possess nor know how to acquire. If Delius, Bizet, Tchaikovsky, Ravel, Rachmaninoff, Stravinsky, Gershwin, Schoenberg are Jewish, or part-Jewish, composers I must say I have nothing to say against them. Delius assured me he had no Jewish blood, while his niece (Miss Kroenig) is sure he had. I can only say that Delius (who, actually, had no drop of *English* blood in him) seems to me to have all the superiority of an English composer & that Gershwin seems to me to have all the superiority of an American composer. So I will not try to determine how much blood counts, & how much environment counts, in the national superiorities & inferiorities I see in music.

Yet I guess that I ought to say (in passing) that a great many Jewish composers *do* seem to me especially copycattien in making convenient use of other men's musical ideas. (I shall have something to say of this in its bearings upon Grainger & Scott musical thoughts used by Gershwin & Gould in their music.) I must relate this of Delius — if he was a Jew: Delius used to call Cyril Scott "that little Liverpool Jew" & dwelt on the family name Meir used by Cyril as a young man, while announcing that Cyril copies his (Delius's) ideas. While I take it for granted that *all gifted men* copy one another's ideas to some extent (& thus take it for granted that Cyril copied some of Delius's ideas, here & there — tho I cannot think of cases) I must say I think this charge most unfounded. I think it more likely that Delius copied Cyril's ideas, as Delius certainly copied mine. It seems to me that the type of chords in Cyril Scott's *Solemn Dance* (piano) appear later in Delius works such as the 1st Cello & Piano Sonata. But it may be that Cyril, Delius & I had (each more or less on his own) worked out a typically English chord type that was well nigh identical in the 3 of us.

Having spoken loosely of English-speaking superiority & priority-of-ideas in general, down the ages, I wish to speak of its specific workings, under my nose, in my own time, in my own art.

When my mother & I went to Frankfurt, in 1895, I had been brought up almost wholly on German music. Certainly I was imbued with the overwhelming superiority of German music. I think I can say that I went to Frankfurt with expectations of German superiority all along the line — in life & in the arts. I know I was longing to see German Kriegspiel played by boys in the streets. But a more sissified lot of soft-paps than the boys I saw in Frankfurt I would never want to meet. As for musical talent at the Conservatorium, among the young Germans & other foreigners — it was just non-existent. When the English students arrived (or swung into my ken), that was another story. Cyril Scott was a delicious Mozart player (as was Ethel Liggins — later Leginska when she arrived a few years later) & Balfour Gardiner a fine rich-toned player of Schumann & such music. (I have related how my mother took to his playing & singled him out, the very first students concert she went to in Frankfurt.) It was plain to see that Ivan Knorr (the composition teacher) looked upon Cyril as his most promising pupil. And the English Leonard Borwick (a lovely pianist if there ever was one) had been the *only student* of the Conservatorium to play at the Museum's Gesellschaft Symphony Concerts while still a pupil. So I found no reason to believe the German dictum that the English were without musical talent.

I have often asserted that Greig (that British-backgrounded Norwegian) was the main harmonic influence on almost all modernist composers in all countries that came after him. In my Grieg article in *The Etude* (1943) I quoted what Delius had told me of talk between him & Ravel on that subject. So I am glad to note the following statement, said to have been made by Ravel in Norway in 1926: "I have never to this day written a work that was not influenced by Grieg." In my Grieg article (above mentioned) and in my transcription of Gershwin's "The Man I Love" I have listed a few indebtednesses of modern composers to Grieg. An imposing list might be made of the indebtedness of living modernist composers to American swing & jazz. But what I want to do in this brief draft is to list some of the indebtednesses of modernist composers to Cyril Scott & myself. In this draft I shall not go into the question of priority-of-ideas as between Scott & myself. It is too complicated. First of all: it seems to be as if I might never have been a modernist composer but for my contact with Cyril Scott. When he found me (around 1897?) I was writing in the style of Handel & seemed to know nothing of modern music. "Aren't you interested in writing modern music?" he said to me. "What do you mean by modern music?" I answered. He played me Grieg's Ballade & Tchaikovsky's Theme & Vars (both quite new to me). Then, his own modernist music was a fiery awakener of my own modernist powers. It is true that, as a boy of 11 or 12, in Australia, I had heard in my head my *Free Music,* made up of beatless lilts, gliding interval-less tones & non-harmonic voice-leadings. But this early tone-vision had no connection with the conservative composing I was doing in Frankfurt in the pre-Scott days. So (leaving the *Free Music* out of the question, as another branch of music altogether) one may say that I never would have become a modernist composer without Cyril Scott's influence. But my influence upon him, in a modernising sense, was soon to become equally great. My discordant diatonic harmonies (as in my Kipling Setting "The Beaches of Lukannon," 1898, ex. 1) were an influence. Still more so my irregularly-barred music (Train-Music, 1899. Song of Solomon, 1899-1900), which, after a few years, led Scott to ask my permission to take up this aspect into his own music, with results seen in his Piano Sonata, op. 66 & numberless other works. His extremely discordant harmonic style (which, I am convinced, led to Schoenberg's atonalism & Stravinsky's discordance) was, I think, evolved without influence from me. It, in turn, (together with Schoenberg's influence upon works such as "My Robin is to the Greenwood gone") influenced my discordance in "The Warriors" & the *Pastoral* in the Suite "In a Nutshell." In short, Scott's influence upon me, mine upon him, were very mutual & interwoven. So for the purpose of this article, I will consider the Scott-Grainger modernizing influence *as one unit,* without distinguishing between what he started & what I started.

In my early years (1889-1907) as a modernist I took it for granted that I, *as an Australian,* would be ahead of my European tone-fellows in original inventivity & experimentalism. When Jacques Blanche met me in Dieppe, the summer of 1902, & showed me Debussy's music for the 1st time, I said to him, of it: "That is only one of the trees — in my forest" (so he recorded, years later) — so much bigger than any European did I feel myself to be. For if I took it for granted that an Englishman was a super-European, I equally took it for granted that an Australian was a super-Englishman. And there was nothing lacking to bolster up this idea. All my fellow-composers took my titles, my formulas, my tone-moods. I wrote an *English Dance;* then Roger Quilter wrote 3 *English Dances* & Balfour Gardiner one *English Dance.* I wrote an *English Waltz;* then Cyril Scott did. I used "wordless syllables" in choral writing from 1898 on; pretty soon Vaughan Williams & Delius were using it (after meeting me & seeing my *Irish Tune* for chorus & *Brigg Fair* for tenor voice & chorus Delius changed from the "la la la" he had used in Appalachia, before meeting me, to the wordless vocalism he uses in *The Song of the High Hills*). I wrote *Hill-Songs* (1902-1907); very soon Bax had written a *Hill-Tune.* I used the title *Hill-Song,* then Delius wrote *The Song of the High Hills.* (It is true that, before me, Grieg had written *Hill-Taken, the Hill-Man's Song, Evening in the High Hills.* But I did't know of them when I wrote my Hillsongs. But that makes no difference; his were published first, & that is all I go by. He should have the credit for all this *Hill-Music.*)

Around 1898 or 1899 I got the idea (born of the solo-&-chamber numbers in Bach's Passions) of writing for *Large Chamber Music* rather than for the conventional orchestra (which later I never liked). This attitude led to works such as *Willow Willow* (voice, guitar, 4 strings, 1902-1911), *English Dance* (first sketched for large chamber music, 1899), *Scotch Strathspey & Reel* (4 mens voices & 16 instruments, 1901-1911), *Hill-Song I* (22 solo woodwinds, 1902) & scores more, all started at the turn of the century.

If these did not influence Vaughan Williams to write his "On Wenlock Edge & Schoenberg in his *Pierrot Lunaire* & Stravinsky in his *Story of a Soldier* I can only say that my experiments preceded theirs by several years. It is easy for a composer to say "I never heard of Grainger" or "I know nothing about his hillsongs" (any foreigner is apt to talk of an English-speaker that way), but all that (however sincerely meant by the foreigner) does not prove that he never came under the influence of my tone-thinking, directly or indirectly. Scott was always going to the continent & mixing with musicians & artists. The first thing he would do would be to talk of my remarkable works. Around 1908 Alfred Hoehn played Scott's epoch making Piano Sonata all over Germany, etc. In claims to priority the only thing I go by is the time when the idea was born, hatched, finished, published.

In dealing with the origins of American popular or semi-popular music the wish (in musical circles) is always to attribute as much as possible to the lower races (the Jews, the Negroes) or to the poorer peoples (such as the Irish) and to give as little credit as possible to the higher and more well-to-do peoples. Everyone wants to call "Shepherds Hey" an *Irish* dance. When I insist that it is *English* all the fun goes out of it for them. Everyone wants to pretend that American music owes a lot to Indian influence, to Negro influence. Anything rather than admit that it owes the greater part of its characteristics to the sources it is likely to have come from: White American influences & English folksong influences. A great deal of fuss is made of "typical Negro rhythms". But when these are examined they often turn out to be the syncopation natural to English language-rhythms in such words as "father, sister, never". These can be seen in such a typical English folksong as "The Rainbow", recorded phonographically by me from the singing of Mr. George R. Orton at Brigg, 1906 (ex. 2). It is obvious that when the Negroes took over the English tongue in America that they took with it the syncopated rhythms that have always accompanied it in English & English-American folksong. It is obvious from *Porgy & Bess* that Gershwin liked to deal in Negro color. It may be that he thought his rhythms & harmonics were strongly Negro-swayed. But I can only see that he was swayed by the characteristics of English folksong (which, thru English-American folk-channels, have swayed the whole music of America, White & Negro) & — that in his art-music influences he was mainly swayed by Grieg, Scott & Grainger. (I do not suggest that he always got these influences direct — for very few influences are taken direct by anybody.

What I mean is: the innovations of those 3 British & partly-British composers are the original sources whence most of the Gershwin formulas flowed).

Take that chord upon which so much of Gershwin's charm and originality rests: the dominant-seventh chord with a major third in the lower octave and a minor third in the higher octave (in C major the notes would be G, B natural, D, F, B flat). (For the purpose of this discussion I don't care whether the clash between the major & minor thirds is resolved or unresolved; for both Gershwin & I use it in both forms. The charm lies in the clash itself, not in whether it is resolved or not.) This chord I worked out early in my folk-song-harmonising career to tally the English folksong habit of singing a major third in the lower octave but a minor third in the higher octave of the melody. See ex. 3, "Lord Melbourne", sung by Mr. George Wray, 1906. Thus my chord was *consciously evolved* in order to provide a harmonic expression of a melodic habit common in English folksong. It is possible that Gershwin's use of my chord was worked out by him to tally a melodic characteristic of White American folksong, or a characteristic of American-Negro melody (influenced, of course, by White-American folksong habits). But it seems to me more probable that he got it from my music, directly or indirectly (if indirectly, I presume that his teacher, Joseph Schillinger, would have been capable of passing on such a formula). Versions of this major-minor dominant-seventh chord appear in exs. 9, 10. So it would appear that Gershwin's main harmonic stock-in-trade is an adjunct of English folksong, & used by me as a chord in art-music as early as 1902.

Morton Gould is a delightful Jewish-American composer whose originality & effectiveness cannot be gainsaid. But he, like most American quasi-popular art-music composers, has dipped not unfruitfully into the Scott-Grainger bucket. I think the charming *Pavanne* was one of his first hits. It begins with 4 bars in the bass that are identical with the first 2 bars of the Cello part of my "Molly on the Shore" (composed 1907, published 1911). (The Gould copyright is 1939.) The Gould & Grainger basses are seen in exs. 12 & 13. Later on, at Letter B, he has the accompaniment seen in ex. 14, which is identical with the accompaniment I use in bar 129 (see ex. 15) of my *Scotch Strathspey & Reel*, composed 1901-1911, published 1924. The second motive (Letter D) in the Gould Pavanne is strongly reminiscent of a passage in Cyril Scott's "The Jocund Dance", published in 1918. The two may be compared in exs. 16 & 17. In the case of Gould, he could hardly say that "he hadn't seen my scores" (not that I am suggesting he would want to say that; he writes praisingly to me about my music), as he has adopted my specifically "Blue-eyed English" (non-French, non-Latin, non-Greek) expression & tempo markings, as seen in his "American Concertette" No. 1, for piano & orchestra, which uses: "louden" "loudening", "soften", "quicken", "fading away", "slowing down to end", "hold back", "louder", "low strings", "crisp", etc. The Gavotte in this Concertette sounds as if it has a bowing acquaintance with my *Mock Morris*, especially the bass (see exs. 18 & 19). I am not suggesting that any of these similarities amount to plagiarism, but merely that the modern American vein is linked up with the Scott-Grainger idiom rather than with Negro-isms, Red Indianisms or the Debussy-Ravel idiom. (Where Debussy-Ravel is drawn upon, I suggest it is oftenest by way of Cyril Scott.)

When I played a concert with a high school band in Massillon, Ohio last spring its gifted & sympathetic conductor (George Bird) said to me "The only piece the children really like is *Victory Garden* by Harold Waters." This is a fun-making Suite (Dance of the Rhubarb, Boogie Woogie Broccoli, Carrot Capers) of the First World War wrong-note-craze (as Delius used to call it) type, only very simple & backward — really not much fun. The 2nd theme of the first movement is just Cyril Scott's Danse Negro badly remembered (see exs. 20 & 21). However, it is interesting to see what the roots are of something that *really pleases* English-speaking youth — always some Nordic (preferably with a Negro title), of course. Progress likes progress. And progressive nations, progressive composers, draw on the thoughts & art-works of other progressive nations & composers — not backward ones. So the Nordic world feeds on Nordic thought — however much they kid themselves about Negroes, Jews & other feeble members.

And then there is Arthur Fickenscher (born in Illinois of Bavarian parents) who does *not* draw his ideas & inspiration from Cyril Scott & Grainger, & who yet (with his intervals closer than the half-tone & other drastic tone-deeds) is the most original & advanced of American composers known to me, as well as being one of the most lofty, spiritual & emotional tone-wrights of all time. And then there is myself — way ahead (tho I have to say it myself) of all my time-mates, in any land, in experimentalism & go-aheadness. Other composers (Scott, Fickenscher, Schoenberg) have undertaken *some* of the experiments that lead to *Free Music*. But no one (that I know) except myself has taken the leap & done all the experiments that lead to complete musical freedom. My tone-vision of 1894 or 1895 (before I left Australia) is still half a century ahead of all the other composers. Yet my name is never mentioned in any book dealing with modern music. It is like the joke in the Swedish comic paper at the end of the last war: "This is how the British & American fighting forces look in peace-time (tiny, like specks). And this is how they look in war-time (like towering giants)." Likewise Cyril Scott & Grainger don't loom very big in books on "modern music". But the extent to which they are copied and imitated tells a more flattering story.

Percy Aldridge Grainger

Sept. 21, 1944

P.S. I musn't forget to mention my innovation of ending pieces, & sections of pieces, with a discordant (or what was then considered a discordant) chord. My most "popular" invention in this field was the ending on the chord 1, 5, 3, 6, 1, which seems to have become the normal ending in most orchestrated versions of jazz or swing music (no doubt by way of Cyril Scott, who took up this procedure from me into several of his piano pieces & other works, all of which were published several years before my originals saw the light of publication). One of the first times I used this chord was in my chorus "At Twilight", composed 1900-1909, which ends with the chord Db, Ab, F, Bb, Db. This chord ending was in the very first sketches, written in 1900. My *Hill-Song I* contains some of my earliest uses of discordant endings: The work closes with the chord Eb, Bb, Gb, Db, Gb, Bb. (This chord is also used as the close of *"Willow Willow"* but whether this preceded *Hillsong I*, or not, I cannot say. The ending on E, B, E, G, C is, however, from the 1902 material — end of 2nd verse of *Willow*.) Other discordant endings in *Hillsong I* are: Bar 115, E, B, G, B, D, G, B; Bar 383, E, B, G, C, E, B. These endings were all written before I came in contact with Debussy's music in 1902, at Dieppe. I cannot claim to have been *the first composer* to end a piece with a discordant ending because I do not know when Debussy wrote the ending F♯, C♯, A♯, D♯, G♯ to the 2nd act of "Pelleas". The opera is said to have been composed 1892-1902. But I do not know when the final chord to act 2 was conceived, but most likely before I mind-birthed any of my discordant endings. The matter is worth looking into — by some patriotic Australian; for it would be a bright feather in Australia's cap to have produced the first composer to use a discordant ending.

But as far as I know the following discordant endings were all invented by me & must be placed to Australia's credit: (I do not mention late examples — written after the appearance of Schoenberg's atonalism — such as most of those in the *Lincolnshire Posy*. I mention only such ones as I am fairly sure were the first examples of their kind, beginning around 1898 or 1899).

The unnumbered musical examples which follow were used by Grainger to illustrate the final paragraphs of the preceding essay. The numbered examples beginning on p. 279 are specifically referred to in the text beginning on p. 271.

At Twilight for chorus, 1900.

Rustic Dance (formerly called *English Dance*) for small orchestra, July 1899.

Dedication (Kipling Setting), 1901.

The Love Song of Har Dyal (Kipling Setting), September 1901.

Hill-Song I for 21 woodwinds, 1901-1902.

bar 383

Hill-Song I for 21 woodwinds, 1901-1902.

The Twa Corbies for voice & 7 strings, 1903.

Died for Love for voice & 3 winds, 1907.

Shallow Brown for voice & chamber music, 1910.

"Lord Melbourne" (from *Lincolnshire Posy*) for band, sketched in Norway 1911-1912.

Ex. 1. Grainger: "The Beaches of Lukannon" (1898).

Ex. 2. English folksong: "The Rainbow," sung by George R. Orton (1906).

And   the   ver-y   sec-ond   broad -f side _____ our

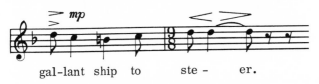

Till   we   had   scarce   a   man   on   board—

gal-lant   ship   to   ste -   er.

Ex. 3. Excerpt from English folksong: "Lord Melbourne," sung by George Wray (1906).

My—   Kings   and   brid - den-cis   like -

wise;   I   nev-er   fad-deld   in   an-y - thing—

but   one   great   vic - to - y.

Ex. 4. Grainger: *The Inuit* (1902) for a cappella chorus, 1912.

Ex. 5. Grainger: *Soldier, Soldier* (1907) for chorus, 1925.

Ex. 6. Grainger: *At Twilight* (1900-1909) for chorus, 1913.

Ex. 7. Grainger: *The Bride's Tragedy* (1908-1913) for chorus & orchestra, 1914.

Ex. 8. Grainger: "Lord Melbourne" (from *Lincolnshire Posy*) for band, sketches about 1912.

Ex. 9. Gershwin: *Rhapsody in Blue,* 1924.

Ex. 10. Gershwin: *Piano Concerto* (1927?).

(Grainger)   (1924)

Ex. 11. Grainger: *Willow, Willow* (1902-1911) for voice, guitar, 4 strings, 1912.

Ex. 12. Grainger: *Molly on the Shore* (cello part).

pizz.

Ex. 13. Morton Gould: *Pavane.*

Ex. 14. Morton Gould: *Pavane.*

Ex. 15. Grainger: *Scotch Strathspey and Reel* (measure 129).

(pizz.)

Ex. 16. Cyril Scott: *The Jocund Dance*, 1918.

Ex. 17. Morton Gould: *Pavane*.

Ex. 18. Grainger: *Mock Morris* (1907).

Ex. 19. Morton Gould: "Gavotte" from *American Concertette* (1943).

Ex. 20. Cyril Scott: *Danse Nègre*, 1908.

Ex. 21. Harold Waters: 2nd theme of "Danse of the Rhubard" from *Victory Garden* (2nd theme), 1943.

Will

Know all men by these presents that I, *George Percy Grainger,* professionally known as *Percy Grainger,* residing at number 7 Cromwell Place, White Plains, Westchester County, New York, which I hereby declare to be my domicile, do hereby make, publish and declare this to be my Last Will and Testament.

FIRST: I hereby revoke any and all Wills heretofore by me at any time made.

SECOND: I direct my executor to pay all my just debts, including the expenses of my last illness, funeral expenses and all estate, transfer or inheritance taxes imposed or assessed by the Federal or State government upon or with respect to property passing under this, my Will, and any property passing outside of my Will which is required to be included in my taxable estate to the end that no portion thereof shall be apportioned to or collected from any legatee, devisee or other recipient of property constituting part of my taxable estate.

THIRD: I request that there be no public or religious funeral, funeral service or ceremony of any kind or nature. I direct that my flesh be removed from my bones and the flesh destroyed. I give and bequeath my skeleton to the *University of Melbourne,* Carlton N. 3, Victoria, Australia, for preservation and possible display in the Grainger Museum.

FOURTH: I request my beloved wife, *Ella Viola Strom-Grainger,* in her absolute and uncontrolled discretion and at the expense of my estate to cause my drawings, paintings, musical and literary manuscripts, letters to and from me, particularly those to and from my mother, my said wife, Cyril Scott, Roger Quilter, Herman Sandby, Frederick Delius and H. Balfour Gardiner, to be copied by means of photography or some other suitable process under her supervision and to give said copies to the *Library of Congress,* Washington D.C., or some other suitable library of repository.

FIFTH: If my said wife shall predecease me, or shall die before the copies of said drawing, paintings, musical and literary manuscripts and letters have been made and given to the said Library of Congress, or some other suitable library or repository as hereinabove requested, then in either of such events, I give and bequeath to *Burnett Cross* of Hartsdale, New York, the sum of two thousand ($2,000) dollars upon condition that he complete the copying of said drawings, paintings, musical and literary manuscripts and letters and deliver the said copies to the Library of Congress, or some other suitable Library of repository, the cost of copying and transportation to constitute a charge against my estate. Should said Burnett Cross also predecease me, or refuse or fail to complete such copying and delivery, I do then give and bequeath to my niece, *Elsa Bristow*, the sum of two thousand ($2,000) dollars upon condition that she agree to comply with the same request. If all the above named persons fail, refuse or neglect to comply with this request, or if at the time of my decease, all the copying has been accomplished and the copies delivered to the Library of Congress, or other repository, then the bequests above specified shall be null and void and the said sum of two thousand ($2,000) dollars shall become part of my residuary estate.

SIXTH: After said drawings, paintings, musical and literary manuscripts and letters have been copied, as hereinbefore provided, I give and bequeath the originals of said drawings, paintings, musical and literary manuscripts and letters and the photographic negatives thereof, if any, to the *University of Melbourne*, Carlton N. 3, Victoria, Australia, upon condition that they be preserved and displayed in the Grainger Museum in said University. If the University of Melbourne fails, refuses or neglects, for any reason whatsoever, to accept such drawings, paintings, musical and literary manuscripts and letters and the photographic negatives thereof, if any, for the above mentioned purposes within one (1) year from the time they are tendered by my executor hereinafter named, then this bequest to it shall be null and void and said property shall fall into and become part of, my residuary estate.

SEVENTH: All the rest, residue and remainder of my property and estate, real and personal, of whatsoever character and wheresoever situated, of which I shall die seized and possessed or to which I may be entitled at the time of my decease, including every lapsed legacy and devise and any and every part of my estate that shall not be otherwise effectively disposed of herein, I give, devise and bequeath to my said wife, *Ella Viola Strom-Grainger.*

EIGHTH: In the event my said wife predecease me, I give, devise and bequeath the remainder of my said estate to the *University of Melbourne,* absolutely and unconditionally, but request the said University of Melbourne to use said property for the following purposes: That the University of Melbourne shall retain and keep the amount of this legacy as a separate and distinct fund, to be known as the "Grainger Museum Fund"; to invest and re-invest the same, and use, appropriate and apply the income derived therefrom toward and for the establishment, operation, equipment, furnishing, maintenance and upkeep of the Grainger Museum now established, or hereinafter to be established in said University.

NINTH: If any beneficiary shall die in a common disaster with me, I direct that for all purposes of this my Last Will and Testament, such beneficiary shall be considered to be predeceased me.

TENTH: I nominate and appoint my said wife, *Ella Viola Strom-Grainger,* to be executrix of this my Last Will and Testament; if my said wife shall predecease me, or shall fail to qualify, or shall resign or otherwise cease to act as executrix before the completion of this administration of my estate, then I name the following as alternate executors, it being understood that they not act jointly, but are selected by me in the order in which named, to fill any vacancy caused by the failure to act or discontinuance of any prior named executor in said list, said alternate executors so named being as follows:

> First: Elsa Bristow
> Second: Burnett Cross
> Third: The Chase Manhattan Bank of the City of
> New York.

I do further give to my executrix, or such alternate executor as shall qualify, full power of sale of any and all real property of which I may die seized and possessed and direct that no bond or security be required of any of them in this or any other jurisdiction for the faithful performance of their duties.

In witness whereof, I have hereunto set my hand and seal this 29th day of September, 1959.

George Percy Grainger   L.S.

Witnesses:

Marie L. Clark

James Holden

Stephen Holden, Jr.

On this 29th day of September, 1959, *George Percy Grainger,* the above named Testator, in our presence subscribed and sealed the foregoing instrument, consisting of four typewritten pages, and at the time of such subscription, published and declared the same to be his Last Will and Testament, and thereupon we, at such time, and at the request of the above named Testator, and in his presence and in the presence of each other, signed our names thereto as attesting witnesses, this attestation clause having first been read aloud to us.

Marie L. Clark	residing at	9 Greenridge Ave.
		White Plains, N.Y.
James Holden	residing at	Joanjovo Lane
		Pleasantville, N.Y.
Stephen Holden, Jr.	residing at	31 Garretson Rd.
		White Plains, N.Y.

*My free music is very different to the new kinds
of music from France and Germany that I have
heard and liked very much. Mine is an EXTENSION
of existing (normal) music, not a repudiation of it.*

Percy A. Grainger

First actual FREE MUSIC: short sample tone-wrought [composed] Melbourne (Centenary Hall) Jan 8, 1935, for Lecture 12 ("The Goal of Musical Progress") of Percy Grainger's 12 Broadcast Lectures "Commonsense about music" (A.B.C.) & forthplayed [performed] at that lecture on Jan 10, 1935 (rehearsed Jan 8-9-10).

In Free Music all the musical elements will be wholly free: the intervals will be free of all scales or fixed intervals of any kind; the rhythms will be quite free of same-beatishness in the various parts (the beats — if any — happening otherwisely in each part); the many-voiced texture quite free of harmonic thought. In the below sample no out-of-tune (intervals closer than the ½ tone) are used (as will be in Free Music, of course) to help speed in rehearsal. For the same reason the rhythms bear a closer relation to the barring (which is purely arbitrary — the melodic lines carry no beat-feeling. The bars & beats are simple like a yardstick by which the irregular duration-lengths of the tones may be gauged & readily read) than they will in fully-fledged Free Music.

Percy Grainger.

SCORE   FREE MUSIC, for string quartet.

FAST N.B. All notes, in all parts, slowly gliding — no definite intervals except the very long ones.

All notes in cello highly slid (glissando)

FREE MUSIC ideas, Cedar City, Utah, Sunday
(Oct. 31, 1943

① "Curve-tune backgrounded by roll-tone-line" (in 2 voices (both to be
sung by me) Roll-tone-line ~~~~ given
lower than curve-tune. Curve-tune keeps (in the main?) above
roll-tone-line & is slow, mournful, with very gradual
tone-height-changes. Should it sometimes veer off into
short colorature tone-sprays, like Spanish gypsy &
Northern Indian (music of the Orient) singing? First =
must sing the roll-tone-line into one disc [gramm. phone
record]. I try out many times, singing my curve-tune
on top of this sound-disc, till I get just the wording
to it. Then, into a new tone-disc, I sing my curve-tune —
the tone disc also taking up the roll-tone-tune from
the 1st tone-disc. In order to be able to note down the
outcome exactly (on paper) I must first add a ticker
(with roll on 1st of every 4 ticks, to the 1st recl [1st] tone disc.
(will it be needful to put all this on a 3rd tone disc?) Then I
note down the pitch at every tick & thus get my tone-height
bearings for my down-write-ment [notation].

② "Feelingful tone-lines with upwellment-&-plunk
background". 3 Theremins (or 3 voices, or 3 strings)
playing "upwellment", followed by "plunk" on sliding-tone
kettledrum, marimba-malleted low piano string, (bass drum?),
low tones (3 ½ tones next to each other? in wooden & xno bad
marimbas): upwellment   plunk
~~~~   again-sounded over & over, like a
soft   soft fabric   flowerpattern on Far-Eastern

Upon this a-the-highish voices sing tense, mournful manyvoicedness,
& maybe a trumpet plays an off-tone call like: 𝄞 ♩♩♩
Each time this is sounded the tone-tips must be obeyed. (sometimes, as
in birdcalls) the last highest note (high d.#) can be left out. Sometimes
the mournful "feelingful tone-lines" should run in 4ths (?).
In contrast to the end-some [final] tone disc would be used, a printed copy on hand. Feb 1, 1943

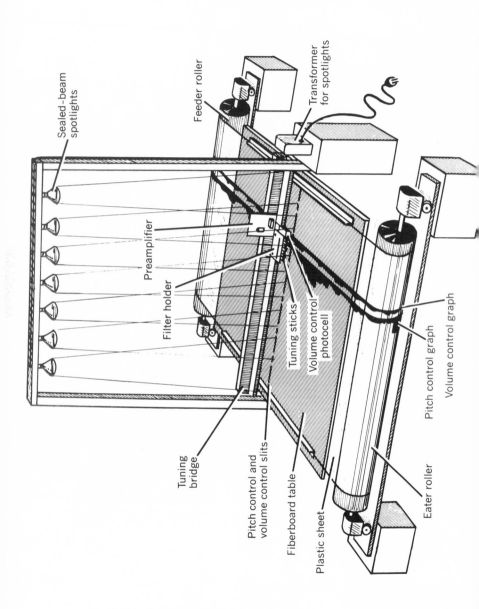

Grainger's Free Music Machine

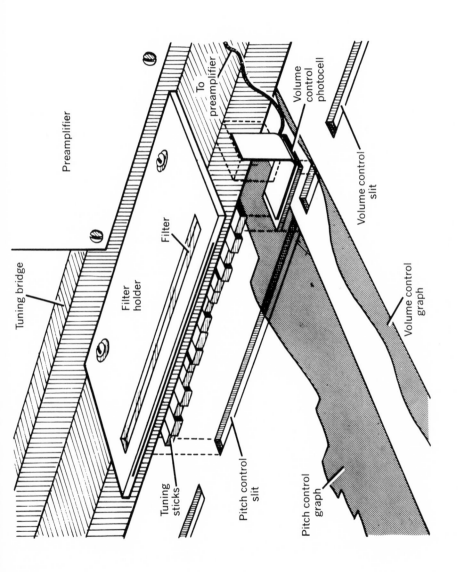

Close-up of Filter and Tuning Sticks

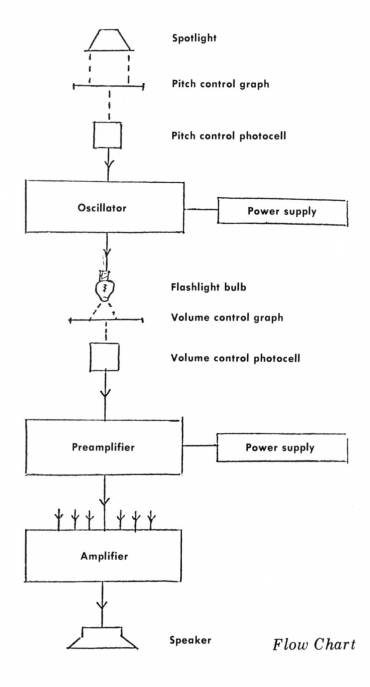

Spotlight

Pitch control graph

Pitch control photocell

Oscillator

Power supply

Flashlight bulb

Volume control graph

Volume control photocell

Preamplifier

Power supply

Amplifier

Speaker

Flow Chart

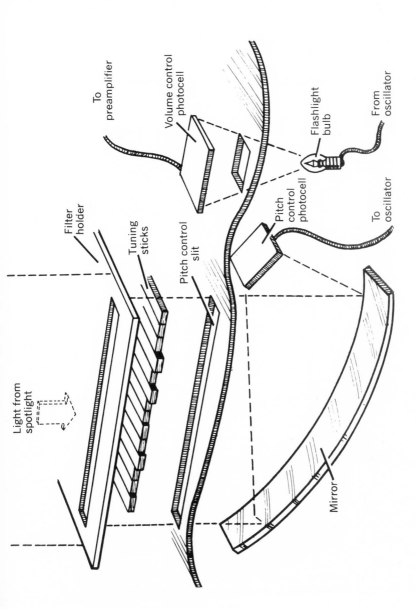

To preamplifier

Volume control photocell

Flashlight bulb

From oscillator

To oscillator

Pitch control photocell

Filter holder

Tuning sticks

Pitch control slit

Light from spotlight

Mirror

Close-up of Pitch and
Volume Controls

Bibliography

Books and Articles

Aldrich, Richard. *Concert Life in New York 1902-1923.* New York: G.P. Putnam's Sons, 1941.

The Argus (Melbourne), October 10, 1894.

Armstrong, Sir Thomas. "The Frankfurt Group," *Proceedings of the Musical Association,* LXXXV (1959), pp. 1-16.

Armstrong, William. "Percy Aldridge Grainger," *The Musician,* XX/8 (August, 1915), pp. 495-96.

Austin, William W. *Music in the 20th Century.* New York: W.W. Norton & Co., 1966.

Bauer, Harold. *Harold Bauer, His Book.* New York: W.W. Norton & Co., 1948.

Bauer, Marion and Peyser, Ethel. *How Music Grew.* 3rd ed. New York: G.P. Putnam's Sons, 1927.

Bauer, Marion. *Twentieth Century Music.* Rev. ed. New York: G.P. Putnam's Sons, 1947.

Beckles, Gordon. "Percy Grainger," *Leader Magazine* (December 11, 1948), pp. 22-23.

Beecham, Sir Thomas. *Frederick Delius.* London: Hutchinson & Co., 1959.

Bellows, H.A. "Percy Grainger and His 'In a Nutshell Suite'," *The Bellman* (March 17, 1917), p. 299.

Bowen, Richard. "The Musical Rebel," *Music and Musicians,* III/11 (July, 1955), p. 9.

Broder, Nathan. "Grainger, Percy Aldridge," *Die Musik in Geschichte und Gegenwart,* V (1956), Cols. 673-675.

Brower, Harriette Moore. *Piano Mastery.* 2nd series. New York: F.A. Stokes, 1917.

Buchannan, C.L. "Play Boy Grows Up," *The Independent* (July 28, 1917), p. 132.

Burch, Gladys. *Famous Pianists for Boys and Girls.* New York: A.S. Barnes & Co., 1943.

Catalogue of Compositions of Percy Grainger. New York: G. Schirmer, 1920.

Chappell, William. *Old English Popular Music,* rev. H. Ellis Wooldridge. London: Chappell & Co., 1893. I, p. 153.

Clough, Francis F and Cuming, G.J. *The World's Encyclopedia of Recorded Music.* London: Sidgwick & Jackson, 1952.

Colles, H.C. and Parker, D.C. "Grainger, Percy," *Grove's Dictionary of Music and Musicians*. 5th ed. 10 vols. Ed. by Eric Blom (New York: St. Martin's Press, 1954-61), III, pp. 744-45.

Cooke, James Francis. *Great Men and Famous Musicians on the Art of Music.* Philadelphia: Theodore Presser, 1925.

Covell, Roger. *Australia's Music.* Melbourne: Sun Books, 1967.

Cross Burnett. "Grainger's Free Music Machine," *Recorded Sound,* Vols. 45-46 (January-April, 1972). pp. 17-20.

Cowell, Sidney. "Obituary of Percy Grainger," *International Folk Music Council,* XIV (1962), pp. 147-48.

Damrosch, Walter. *My Musical Life.* New York: Charles Scribner's Sons, 1926.

Dent, Edward J. "Busoni, Ferruccio," *Grove's Dictionary of Music and Musicians.* 5th ed. New York: St. Martin's Press, 1954-61. I, pp. 1041-43.

_____. *Ferruccio Busoni.* London: Oxford University Press, 1933.

_____. "Moderne: Engländer," *Handbuch der Musikgeschichte.* 2 vols. Ed. by Guido Adler. Berlin: Max Hesses, 1930.

Dolmetsch, Mable. *Personal Recollections of Arnold Dolmetsch.* New York: Macmillan Co., 1958.

Dorum, Ivar C. "Grainger's 'Free Music'," *Studies in Music,* University of Western Australia Press, No. 2 (1969), pp. 86-97.

Elwes, Lady Winifred and Richard Elwes. *Gervase Elwes.* London: Grayson & Grayson, 1935.

Ewen, David. *American Composers.* New York: H.W. Wilson Co., 1949.

_____. *Composers of Today.* New York: H.W. Wilson Co., 1934.

_____. *The Light Classics in Music.* New York: Arco Publishing Co., 1961.

_____. *Living Musicians.* New York: H.W. Wilson Co., 1940.

Fairchild, Leslie. "New Ideas on Study and Practice," *The Etude,* XLIII/12 (December, 1925), pp. 845-46.

Fellowes, Myles. "Reaching Your Goal at the Keyboard," *The Etude,* LIX/2 (February, 1941), pp. 79-80, 134.

Fenby, Eric. *Delius as I Knew Him.* London: G. Bell & Sons, 1937.

Finck, Henry Theophilus. *Grieg and His Music.* London: John Lane, 1909.

_____. "A Musical Genius from Australia," *The Nation,* C/2590 (February 18, 1915), p. 206.

_____. *My Adventures in the Golden Age of Music.* New York: Funk & Wagnalls, 1926.

_____. *Richard Strauss, The Man and His Works,* with an Appreciation by Percy Grainger. Boston: Little, Brown and Co., 1917.

Forsyth, Cecil. *Orchestration.* New York: Macmillan & Co., 1914.

Fowler, James MacKinnon. *False Foundations of British History*. Melbourne: Whitcombe & Tombs, 1943.

Fred, Herbert W. "Percy Grainger's Music for Wind Band," *Journal of Band Research*, I/1 (Autumn, 1964), pp. 10-16.

"Free-Minded Percy Grainger," *The Australian Musical News*, XXIV/7 (February 1, 1934), p. 14.

"Gallery of Musical Celebrities," *The Etude*, XLVII/7 (July, 1929), pp. 511-12.

Goldman, Richard Franko. *The Band's Music*. New York: Pitman Publishing Corp., 1938.

_____. *The Concert Band*. New York: Rinehart & Co., Inc., 1946.

_____. "Percy Grainger's 'Free Music'," *Juilliard Review*, II (Fall, 1955), pp. 37-47.

_____. *The Wind Band*. Boston: Allyn & Bacon, Inc., 1961.

Gomez, Victor de. "Impressions of Percy Grainger," *Pacific Coast Musical Review*, XXX/12 (June 17, 1916), p. 1.

Goossens, Eugene. *Overture and Beginners*. London: Methuen & Co., 1951.

Gottschalk, Louis Moreau. *Notes of a Pianist*. Ed. by Jeanne Behrend. New York: Alfred A. Knopf, 1966.

"Grainger Appointed Head of Music Department at New York University," *Musical America*, LII/4 (February 25, 1932), p. 31.

"Grainger's Gift Stirs Denmark," *The Musical Leader*, LVII/11 September 12, 1929), p. 14.

Grainger, Ella. "Portrait Tiles," *Country Life* (March, 1931), p. 50.

Grainger, Percy A. "About Delius," *Frederick Delius* by Peter Warlock (Philip Heseltine), reprint with additions, annotations, and comments by Hubert Foss. New York: Oxford University Press, 1952.

_____. "Arnold Dolmetsch: Musical Confucius," *The Musical Quarterly*, XIX (April, 1933), pp. 187-98.

_____. "Can Music be Debunked?," *The Australian Musical News*, XXIV/7 (February 1, 1934), pp. 14a-14d.

_____. "Collecting with the Phonograph," *Journal of the Folk-Song Society*, III/12 (1908-09), pp. 147-242.

_____. "Culturizing Possibilities of the Instrumentally Supplemented A Cappella Choir," *The Musical Quarterly*, XXVII (1942), pp. 160-64.

_____. "Cyril Scott und seine Musik," *Rheinische Musik und Theater Zeitung*, XIV/3 (January, 1913), pp. 38-41.

_____. "Die Erganzung der Schlagwerkgruppe im Orchester," *Pult und Tachtstock*, III/1 (January, 1926), pp. 5-9.

_____. "Foreword," *The Band's Music* by Richard Franko Goldman. New York: Pitman Publishing Corp., 1938.

_____. "Foreword," *Concerto for Piano, Opus 16* by Edvard Grieg. New York: G. Schirmer, 1920.

————. "Foreword," *Five-Part Fantasy No. 1* by John Jenkins. New York: G. Schirmer, 1944.

————. "Foreword," *Psalms, Opus 74* by Edvard Grieg. New York: C.F. Peters, 1949.

————. "Foreword," *Six-Part Fantasy and Air, No. 1* by William Lawes. New York: G. Schirmer, 1944.

————. "Das Genie Delius," *Musikblätter des Anbruch,* V (January, 1923), pp. 23-24.

———— "Glimpses of Genius," *The Etude,* XXXIX/10 (October, 1921), pp. 631-32.

———— "Grieg — Nationalist and Cosmopolitan," *The Etude,* LXI/6 (June, 1943), pp. 386, 416-18.

———— "Grieg's 'Norwegian Bridal Procession,' A Master Lesson," *The Etude,* XXXVIII/11 (November, 1920), pp. 741-42.

————. *Guide to Virtuosity.* New York: G. Schirmer, Inc., 1905.

———— "The Impress of Personality in Unwritten Music," *The Musical Quarterly,* I (1915), pp. 416-35.

————. "Impressions of Art in Europe — Article 1 — Finland," *The Musical Courier,* XCVIII/22 (June 1, 1929), p. 8.

————. "Impressions of Art in Europe — Article 2 — Sweden and Norway," *The Musical Courier* (July 6, 1929), p. 8.

————. "Impressions of Art in Europe — Article 3 — Delius Reaps His Harvest," *The Musical Courier,* XCIX/13 (September 28, 1929), pp. 8, 31.

———— "Impressions of Art in Europe — Article 4 — Music in England," *The Musical Courier,* XCIX/17 (October 26, 1929), pp. 10, 12.

————. "Jazz," *Musikblätter des Anbruch,* VII/4 (April 1925), pp. 210-12.

————. "Jazz and the Music of the Future," *Great Men and Famous Musicians.* Ed. by James Francis Cooke. Philadelphia: Theodore Presser, 1925.

————. *Music: A Commonsense View of All Types.* Melbourne: Australian Broadcasting Commission, 1934.

————. "The Music of Cyril Scott," *The Music Student,* V/2 (October, 1912), pp. 31-33.

————. "Never Has Popular Music Been as Classical as Jazz," *The Metronome,* XLII/13 (July 1, 1926), p. 10.

————. "Percy Grainger: On Music Heard in England," *The Australian Musical News* (June, 1949), pp. 32-34.

————. "The Personality of Frederick Delius," *The Australian Musical News,* XXIV/12 (July 1, 1934), pp. 10-15.

————. *Rose Grainger and of 3 short accounts of her life by herself, in her own hand-writing.* Reproduced [privately] for her kin and friends by her adoring son, Percy Grainger, n.d.

————. "The Saxophone's Business in the Band," *The Instrumentalist,* IV (September-October, 1949), pp. 6-7.

_____. "The Specialist and the All-Round Man," *A Birthday Offering to [Carl Engle]*. Ed. by Gustave Reese. New York: G. Schirmer, 1943.

_____. "What Effect is Jazz Likely to Have Upon the Music of the Future," *The Etude*, XLII/9 (September, 1924), pp. 593-94.

_____. "You Can't Win Without High Ideals," *The Musician* (November, 1923), pp. 11-12.

Grier, Christopher. "Next Week in the Music Programme," *The Listener* (June 9, 1966).

Hart, Ernest. "A Musical Revolutionary," *The Musical Monitor*, VII/9 (May, 1918), pp. 413, 415.

Hee-Leng Tan, Margaret. "The Free Music of Percy Grainger," *Recorded Sound*, Vols. 45-46 (January-April, 1972), pp. 21-38.

History of the Philharmonic Society of London: 1813-1925. Compiled by Myles Birket Foster. London: John Lane, The Bodley Head, 1912.

The History of Music in Sound, No 7. Ed. by Dom Anselm Hughes. London: Oxford University Press, 1953.

Howard, John Tasker. *Our American Music*. 3rd ed. New York: Thomas Y. Crowell Co., 1946.

_____. *Our Contemporary Composers*. New York: Thomas Y. Crowell Co., 1941.

Howes, Frank. "Percy Grainger," *Recorded Sound*, I/3 (Summer, 1961), pp. 96-98.

Hughes, Charles W. "Percy Grainger, Cosmopolitan Composer," *The Musical Quarterly*, XXIII (1937), pp. 127-36.

Hughes, Eric. "The Recorded Works of Percy Grainger," *Recorded Sound*, No. 45-46 (January-April, 1972), pp. 38-43.

Hughes, Robert. "Grainger, Percy," *Music Lover's Encyclopedia*. Rev. and ed. by Deems Taylor and Russell Kerr. Garden City, New York: Garden City Books, 1954.

Hull, A. Eaglefield. *Cyril Scott*. 2nd ed. London: Kegan Paul, Trench, Trubner, & Co., 1919.

Hutcheson, Ernest. *The Literature of the Piano*. 3rd ed. New York: Alfred A. Knopf, 1964.

Josephson, David S. "Percy Grainger: *Country Gardens* and Other Curses," *Current Musicology*, No. 15 (1973), pp. 56-63.

Kammerer, Rafael. "Golden Age of Pianists Preserved on Old Records," *Musical America*, LXXVII/3 (February, 1957), p. 122.

_____. "Percy Grainger Dies at 78," *Musical America*, LXXXI (April, 1961), pp. 69-70.

Kaufman, Helen L. and E.B. Hansl. *Artists in Music of Today*. New York: Grosset & Dunlap, 1933.

Kennedy, Douglas. *England's Dances*. London: G. Bell & Sons, 1949.

Kennedy, John B. "Anybody Can Play the Piano," *Collier's* (September 24, 1927), pp. 24, 34.

Kinscella, H.G. "Fun That Lies in Making Music." *The Musician* (May, 1932), p. 7.

Lahee, Henry C. *Annals of Music in America.* Boston: Marshall Jones Co., 1922.

Lane, Jeanne. "San Francisco Writer Interviews Grainger," *The Musical Leader,* XXXII/25 (December 21, 1916), p. 674.

Lawrence, A.F.R. "Records of Percy Grainger as an Interpreter," *Recorded Sound,* No. 45-46 (January-April, 1972), pp. 43-48.

Lawrence, Harold. "About Music," *Audio,* XLII (June, 1958), p. 44.

Lee, Ernest Markham. *Grieg.* London: G. Bell & Sons, 1908.

Leibowitz, René and Maguire, Jan. *Thinking for Orchestra.* New York: G. Schirmer, 1960.

The London Musical Courier. November 2, 1901.

Lowe, George. "The Music of Percy Grainger," *The Monthly Musical Record,* XLVIII/567 (March, 1918), pp. 56-57.

_____. "Percy Grainger — The Musician of the Hour: An American Appreciation," *The Monthly Musical Record* (January 1, 1918), pp. 9-10.

Mason, Daniel Gregory. *Music in My Time.* New York: The Macmillan Co., 1938.

"Melbourne: His Music Museum," *Music and Musicians,* IV (December, 1955), p. 31.

Monrad-Johansen, David. *Edvard Grieg.* Trans. by Madge Robertson. New York: Tudor Publishing Co., 1938.

Moses, Julian Morton. *Collectors' Guide to American Recordings.* New York: American Record Collectors' Exchange, 1949.

Mount, Charles Merrill. *John Singer Sargent, A Biography.* New York: W.W. Norton & Co., 1955.

Murphy, Agnes G. *Melba: A Biography.* New York: Doubleday, Page & Co., 1909.

"Musical Genius in War," *Literary Digest* (July 21, 1917), pp. 26-27.

"Musical Viking," *Literary Digest* (September 2, 1916), pp. 558-59.

Nettl, Bruno. *Theory and Method in Ethnomusicology.* New York: The Free Press of Glencoe, 1964.

Newmarch, Rosa. "Melgunov, Julius Nikolayevich," *Grove's Dictionary of Music and Musicians.* 5th ed. 10 vols. Ed. by Eric Blom (New York: St. Martin's Press, 1954-61), V, p. 663.

The New York Times. 1915-1961.

Odegaard, Edfield Arthur. "Symphony Band, The Medium and The Music." Unpublished Ph.D. dissertation, University of Iowa, 1955.

Olsen, Sparre. *Percy Grainger.* Trans. by Bent Vanberg. Oslo: Norske Samlaget, 1963.

Orchard, W. Arundel. *Music in Australia.* Melbourne: Georgian House, 1952.

Orga, Ates. "Percy Grainger 1882-1961," *Music and Musicians* (March, 1970), pp. 28-36.

Otis, Philo Adams. *The Chicago Symphony Orchestra*. Chicago: Clayton F. Summy Co., 1924.

Palmer, Christopher. "Delius and Percy Grainger," *Music and Letters*, LII/4 (October, 1971), pp. 418-425.

Parker, D.C. "The Art of Percy Grainger," *The Monthly Musical Record*, XLV/537 (1915), pp. 152-53.

————. "Colonial Song," *The Musical Standard*, IX/227 (1917), p. 297.

————. *P.A. Grainger — A Study*. New York: G. Schirmer, 1918.

————. "Percy Grainger: A Personal Note," *Musical Opinion*, LIV/643 (April, 1931), p. 597.

Pears, Peter. "Percy Grainger," *Recorded Sound*, No. 45-46 (January-April, 1972), pp. 11-15.

"Percy Grainger," *Canon*, IV (November, 1950), pp. 179-84.

"Percy Grainger," *The Monthly Musical Record*, XLII/493 (January 1, 1912), p. 7.

"Percy Grainger," *Rheinische Musik und Theater Leitung*, X/12 (März, 1911), pp. 149-50.

"Percy Grainger Interested in New Electronic Music Box," *Musicana*, XXVI/1 (February, 1952), p. 8.

"Percy Grainger," *Outlook* (April 7, 1915), p. 799.

"Percy Grainger Speaks of the Value of the Organ as a Background Instrument," *Diapason* (February 1, 1953), p. 10.

"Percy Grainger Startles the Musical World with a Masterpiece," *Current Opinion* (August, 1917), p. 96.

"Percy Grainger — the Musician of the Hour," *The Monthly Musical Record*, XLVIII/565 (January 1, 1918), pp. 9-10.

Peyser, Ethel. *The House that Music Built — Carnegie Hall*. New York: Robert M. McBride & Co., 1936.

Prieberg, Fred K. "Percy Grainger," *Lexikon der Neuen Musik*. München: Karl Alber Frieburg, 1958.

Reid, Charles. *Thomas Beecham: An Independent Biography*. London: Victor Gollancz Ltd., 1961.

St. John, Christopher. *Ethel Smyth*. New York: Longmans, Green & Co., 1959.

Sawyer, Antonia. *Songs at Twilight*. New York: The Devin-Adair Co., 1939.

Schickel, Richard. *The World of Carnegie Hall*. New York: Julian Messner, 1960.

Scholes, Percy A. *The Oxford Companion to Music*. 9th ed. London: Oxford University Press, 1955.

Schonberg, Harold C. *The Great Pianists*. New York: Simon and Schuster, 1963.

Scott, Cyril. "Grainger, Percy Aldridge," *Cobbett's Cyclopedia of Chamber Music*. 2nd ed. 3 vols. London: Oxford University Press, 1965. I, p. 486.

_____. *Percy Grainger, A Course in Contemporary Musical Biography.* New York: G. Schirmer, 1919.

_____. "Percy Grainger: der Mensch und sein Schaffen," *Musikblätter der Anbruch,* IV/7-8 (April, 1922), pp. 106-08.

_____. "Percy Grainger: The Man and The Musician," *Musical Times,* XCVIII (July, 1957), pp. 368-69.

_____. "Percy Grainger, The Music and The Man," *The Musical Quarterly,* II (1916), pp. 425-33.

_____. *The Philosophy of Modernism.* London: Kegan Paul, Trench, Trubner, & Co., 1917.

Seven Lincolnshire Folk Songs. Collected by Percy Grainger. Ed. by Patrick O'Shaughnessy. Arr. by Phyllis Tate. London: Oxford University Press, 1966.

Sherman, John K. *Music and Maestros.* Minneapolis: University of Minnesota Press, 1952.

Slattery, Thomas C. "The Life and Work of Percy Grainger," *The Instrumentalist,* XXII/4 (November, 1967), pp. 42-43; XXII/5 (December, 1967), pp. 47-49; XXII/6 (January, 1968), pp. 36-38.

_____. "Two Hill Songs: An Analytical Study," *Journal of Band Research* (Fall, 1971).

_____. "The Wind Music of Percy A. Grainger," Ph.D. dissertation, University of Iowa, Iowa City, Iowa, 1967.

Smith, Joan Pemberton, "Review of *Percy Grainger* by Sparre Olsen," *Recorded Sound,* No. 14 (April, 1964), p. 230.

Stevens, Halsey. *Béla Bartók, The Life and Music.* 2nd ed. London: Oxford University Press, 1964.

Stonehill, Gerald. "Piano Rolls played by Percy Grainger," *Recorded Sound,* No. 45-46 (January-April, 1972), p. 49.

"A Talk with Grainger," *The Musical Courier,* CI/24 (December 13, 1930), pp. 7, 18.

Taylor, Robert Lewis. *The Running Pianist.* Garden City, New York: Doubleday, 1950.

_____. "A Matter of Kicking Out At Space," *The New Yorker,* (January 31, 1948), pp. 29-37.

_____. "The Running Pianist," *The New Yorker* (February 7, 1948), pp. 32-39.

_____. "Top Notes Glassy," *The New Yorker* (February 14, 1948), pp. 32-43.

Thesiger, Ernest. *Practically True.* London: W. Heinemann, Ltd., 1927.

The Times. (London), 1900-1915.

"Tribute to the Music of the American Negro," *Current Opinion* (August, 1915), pp. 100-01.

Van Buren, R. "Musician: Percy Grainger, U.S.A.," *Everybody's Magazine* (November, 1917), p. 44.

Warlock, Peter (Philip Heseltine). *Frederick Delius.* Reprinted with additions, annotations, and comments by Hubert Foss. New York: Oxford University Press, 1952.

Watanabe, Ruth. "The Percy Grainger Manuscripts," *The University of Rochester Library Bulletin,* IXX/2 (Winter, 1964), pp. 21-26.

Waters, Edward N. "Music," *The Library of Congress Quarterly Journal of Current Acquisitions,* XX/1 (December, 1962), pp. 35-37.

Wells-Harrison, W. "Some Notable British Music," *The Musical Standard,* VIII/193 (1916), pp. 190-191.

Whelbourn, Hubert. *Standard Book of Celebrated Musicians Past and Present.* New York: Garden City Publishing Co., 1937.

Willetts, Pamela J. "The Percy Grainger Collection," *The British Museum Quarterly,* XXVII/3-4 (Winter, 1963-64), pp. 65-73.

Young, Percy. *Elgar, O.M.* London: Collins, 1955.

Unpublished Materials

Falconer, Winifred. "The Life and Works of John H. Grainger, Architect and Civil Engineer." 2 page typescript located in the Library of Congress, n.d.

Grainger, Percy A. "The Aldridge-Grainger-Ström Saga." 233 page typescript located in the Library of Congress, dated 1934.

_____. "Bird's-Eye View of the Together Life of Rose Grainger and Percy Grainger." 18 page typescript located in the Library of Congress, dated 1947.

_____. "English Speaking Leadership in Tone-Art." 13 page typescript located in the Library of Congress, dated Oct. 21, 1943.

_____ "English Speaking Music and the War Effort." 2 page typescript located in the Library of Congress, dated 1943.

_____. "The Life of My Mother and Her Son." 75 page typescript located in the Library of Congress, dated 1922-30.

_____ "P.A. Grainger: English Pianist & Harold Bauer." Unpublished typescript sketch for article, dated February 19, 1945, Jacksonville, Florida.

_____. "Remarks on Hill Song No. 1." 5 page typescript located at White Plains, dated September 1949.

_____. "My Wretched Tone-Life." Autograph sketches located in the Grainger Museum, Melbourne, Australia, n.d.

Guemple, Mary Jolliff. "Percy Grainger's Contributions to the Musical World." Unpublished Masters Thesis, Baylor University, Waco, Texas, 1959.

Scott, Cyril. "Percy Grainger and the Frankfort Group." Unpublished typescript dated October, 1936. Copy located in the Library of Congress.

Other Sources

Interview with Mr. Burnett Cross. Hartsdale, New York, September 2, 1965.

Interview with Mr. Richard Franko Goldman. Katonah, New York, August 29, 1966.

Interviews with Mrs. Percy Grainger. White Plains, New York, August 28-September 1, 1966 and later.

Interviews with Mr. Stewart Manville. White Plains, New York, August 30-September 3, 1965 and August 28-September 1, 1966 and later.

Interview with Dr. Harold Spivacke, Chief, Music Division, Library of Congress. Washington, D.C., August 28, 1965.

Interview with Mr. Edward N. Waters, Assistant Chief, Music Division, Library of Congress. Washington, D.C., August 27, 1965.

Letter to the author from Mr. Burnett Cross, 170 East Hartsdale Avenue, Hartsdale, New York, dated July 17, 1965.

Letters to the author from Richard Franko Goldman, 17 West 60th St., New York 23, New York, dated July 7, 1965 and December 22, 1965.

Letters to the author from Mrs. Ella Grainger, 7 Cromwell Place, White Plains, New York, dated June 17, 1965; July 15, 1965; and December 30, 1965.

Letters (624) to Karen Holton, Copenhagen, Denmark, from Percy A. Grainger, London, England, dated 1905 to 1939, inclusive. Located in the Library of Congress, Washington, D.C.

Letters (20) to Percy A. Grainger, London, England, from the family of Margot Harrison, London, England, dated July, 1913. Located in the Library of Congress, Washington, D.C.

Letters to the author from Dom Anselm Hughes, O.S.B., Nashdom Abbey, Burnham, Bucks, England, dated June 17, 1965 and March 12, 1966.

Letter to the author from Professor George Laughlin, University of Melbourne, Melbourne, Australia, dated December 10, 1965.

Letter to the author from D.C. Parker, 7 Ainslie Place, Edinburgh 3, Scotland, dated January 5, 1966.

Letters to the author from Cyril Scott, 53 Pashley Road, Eastbourne, England, dated August 5, 1965 and November 11, 1965.

Letters to the author from R.W. Trumble, Acting Music Supervisor, Australia Broadcasting Commission, Melbourne, Australia, dated December 22, 1965 and January 5, 1966.